James Dean
Rebel with a Cause

James Dean in a signature troubled teen pose from
East of Eden *(1955)*.

INDIANA BIOGRAPHY SERIES

James Dean
Rebel with a Cause

WES D. GEHRING

GENERAL EDITORS
RAY E. BOOMHOWER, KATHLEEN M. BREEN, AND PAULA J. CORPUZ

INDIANA HISTORICAL SOCIETY PRESS

INDIANAPOLIS 2005

This book is a publication of the

Indiana Historical Society Press

450 West Ohio Street

Indianapolis, Indiana 46202-3269 USA

www.indianahistory.org

Telephone orders 1-800-447-1830

Fax orders 317-234-0562

Order online @ shop.indianahistory.org

Library of Congress Cataloging-in-Publication Data

Gehring, Wes D.

James Dean : rebel with a cause / Wes D. Gehring.

p. cm. — (Indiana biography series)

Filmography:

Includes bibliographical references.

ISBN 0-87195-181-9 (hard : alk. paper)

1. Dean, James, 1931–1955. 2. Motion picture actors and actresses—
United States—Biography. I. Title. II. Series.

PN2287.D33G35 2005

791.4302'8'092—dc22

[B]   2005041440

Printed in Canada

To Sarah and Emily—Like James Dean,
Indiana Born and Raised, and His Greatest *Fans*

The JD Factor

In the mindless enthusiasm
Of the Eisenhower era,
Teens were bobbing bottles
On a sea of indecision.

James Dean's embodiment
Of a poetry of anxiety
Gave a blood transfusion
To the disenfranchised young.

When the metaphorical car
Wreck that is life became
A James Dean reality,
Youth mourned itself.

Would James Dean have
Remained riveting in ruin,
As did Marlon Brando,
Is anyone's guess . . . but

The paradox of profiles
Is that private persons
Become overly public personae . . .
Such was Dean's dilemma.

Where does the spirit
Of a live action J. D. Salinger
Character go in death . . .
Somewhere "East of *Eden*?"

—Wes D. Gehring

TABLE OF CONTENTS

Conrad Lane

I WELL REMEMBER A HOT AFTERNOON IN MAY OF 1957 when I first became aware of the James Dean phenomenon. I was seated at my desk in an office building in Sacramento, California, attempting to take care of some business before leaving on a trip to visit my home state of Indiana. In mid-afternoon I looked up into the faces of seven or eight young women from our stenography pool who had gathered around my desk. One of them asked if it was true that I would soon be visiting in Indiana, and I replied in the affirmative. "Where in Indiana?" they queried. Knowing that they would never have heard of my hometown of Elwood, I told them that I would be visiting about forty miles north of Indianapolis. The next question was, "Is that near Fairmount?" I answered, "Yes, about 20 miles or so." And with that their eyes widened considerably and the truth began to be revealed to me.

"Do you plan to visit in Fairmount?" was next asked, and I replied in the negative. "But could you please do it for us," they said pleadingly. I told them that I could probably spare the time, but I wasn't at all sure what they wanted me to do for them in Fairmount. They then, ever so cautiously, reminded me that James Dean had been buried there and that a memorial had been erected. And would I please bring them a souvenir from Fairmount— anything at all. A clod of dirt, a clump of grass—something from his grave or the grounds surrounding the memorial.

The request struck me as being somewhat bizarre, but I replied that I would "see about it," all the while in deep puzzlement. I was aware that there were those rabid fans that clung to the hope that Dean had not been killed in that accident, and that his mangled body and disfigured face were to be found in some private sanitarium in California. One of the letters I read implored, "Please come back to us, Jimmy. We don't care how you look. We love you."

I was aware of the deep love of movie fans for Rudolph Valentino, who had died at an early age, but I had never encountered anything like this growing cult devoted to James Dean. Being somewhat of a student of motion picture history, I have since followed the growth of the Dean phenomenon with considerable interest and astonishment. I remember how very surprised I was when on assignment in northern England in 1975, tuning in the

BBC one evening to see Fairmount, Indiana, and James Dean being given the full treatment. Adulation of Dean is truly worldwide.

Since 1957 I have seen and read much about the short and provocative life of my fellow Hoosier. The first, and for many reasons my favorite, was the simple and straightforward memoir of Dean's friend William Bast, *James Dean*, which was published in 1956. Since then, the plethora of books on Dean has grown increasingly murky and manipulative with the authors' personal agendas sometimes too apparent.

Wes Gehring has gone a long way toward restoring Dean's basic humanity. One gets a vivid portrait of a generously talented young man growing to maturity amidst love and approval in a midwestern version of *Our Town*. The angst endured by Dean is neither minimized nor overemphasized. He was a relatively normal boy growing up in a relatively normal American environment, subject to all the fears and follies of so many in his age group, something he communicated brilliantly to audiences in his three feature films.

Gehring also presents the manipulative side of Dean and explores the manner in which Dean so cleverly posed as the angst-ridden adolescent and played it to the hilt (not unlike Marlon Brando's lifelong performance as the rebel-outsider). Like his hero, Brando, it seems that much of Dean's moodiness was carefully planned. Labeling Dean a "poseur" may sound pejorative, but his behavior is not at all uncommon in human society.

Through Gehring we learn that Dean, despite the loss of his beloved mother at age nine and his father's subsequent rejection of him, was not the tormented youth often depicted. He was, especially during those formative Fairmount years, relatively normal and happy. In this book, for example, one learns about Dean's delightful sense of humor. He had an exceptional talent for mimicry that had his listeners in stitches. Jim Backus, who played the father in *Rebel Without a Cause*, thought that Dean's real ambition was to become a nightclub comic.

It is always a pleasure to read any of Wes Gehring's works because one knows that he strives very hard to get at the truth of the matter. I believe that he has written a book that is one of the most eminently readable and solidly factual accounts of the extraordinary legend that is James Dean.

Conrad Lane is a Ball State University emeriti professor who remains active as a film essayist and an Elderhostel movie history instructor. He also formerly hosted the PBS film review program, Now Showing, *on WIPB-TV in Muncie, Indiana.*

"I don't have to explain anything to anybody."
—JAMES DEAN'S *EAST OF EDEN* (1955) CHARACTER

LIKE THIS JAMES DEAN COMMENT FROM *EAST OF EDEN*, the real-life attitude of the actor could be prickly, too. As an early Dean critic noted, "He has been cussed, discussed, loved and hated."[1] But Dean's bravado and humor (sadly neglected on the screen), tends to win over even the most reluctant biographer. Still, in writing this text, I was reminded of a line from director Nicholas Ray's *In a Lonely Place* (1950). Ray, of course, later directed Dean in his signature film, *Rebel Without a Cause* (1955). This director's oeuvre was one of mavericks, misfits, and the misunderstood. *In a Lonely Place* was no exception; it starred Humphrey Bogart as an antiheroic screenwriter. His mercurial personality made him his own worst enemy, with the character's best friend observing, "You've got to take him all—the good and the bad." This became my mantra on the book in hand.

Coupled with this philosophy is a biographer's predilection for new angles of vision neglected in previous Dean literature. First, for too long the actor has been totally confused with the troubled teenager he played in the movies. The real Dean was never that aimless, tortured screen soul. He was a hardworking performer with an agenda for success. James was aware, however, of the public's tendency to blur the line between a star's screen persona and the real person. Consequently, this biography will explore how Dean consciously *posed* as the angst-ridden youngster. Indeed, it was easily his greatest and most sustained acting job. The book's second angle of vision, which is really an extension of point one, is that his Indiana upbringing by a beloved aunt and uncle (Ortense and Marcus Winslow) was a vital and continual source of strength for his later artistry. In contrast, there are countless Dean biographies that treat Indiana as nothing more than a meaningless way station on the road to recognition. Worse yet, some texts suggest his Hoosier heritage was largely spent just crying on his mother's grave. This is a romantic homage to his *screen persona*. Like most romantic homages, it is patently false.

Rare is the Dean profile that includes such idyllic heartland memories as that of his childhood friend Jerry Payne: "I can remember the two of us taking walks down the road—kicking stones, talking baseball, and throwing rocks at crows."[2] As his adored cousin and surrogate brother, Marcus Winslow Jr., told me, "I'm sure he missed his mother. But if he had a lot of grief over it, he certainly never expressed it. Mom and Dad [the Winslows] went out of their way for him."[3] And as one pre-legend Dean article observed, "beneath the mask of non-conformity that he presents to the public he is really an 'aw shucks, thank you ma'am' boy of the soil, with roots plunged deep into the conservative earth of Indiana."[4]

One way to chronicle this lesser-known Dean is to document it with stories, such as the one from his young baseball buddy. Examples such as these are peppered throughout the book. However, another way to showcase this anything-but-morose-boy/man is to record what a real-life comic he was among friends and family, such as his always crowd-pleasing imitation of Marlon Brando doing Charlie Chaplin. Frequently, Dean would then reverse the process, mimicking Chaplin doing Brando. This biography goes out of its way to log the laughter of which few Dean fans are aware. This humor moved *Rebel* costar Natalie Wood to remark, "more than anything else, Jimmy loved to laugh and make other people feel good too by doing and saying things that would make them laugh."[5]

Regardless, the comic irony of this, or any author's preface, is that while they open a book, prefaces are the last thing written for the texts; that is, though one plunges into the task of writing a book with a preconceived plan, the creative process has a tendency, thankfully, to throw periodically insightful riffs one's way. But this always scrambles the game plan of even the most organized author. Thus, the preface becomes a tidying-up detail, affixing order to all those random epiphanies that occur during the course of creating a book. Plus, it is a last chance to throw in a final scrap of pertinent information that has somehow been neglected.

The real catalyst for this book was a late-night movie viewing of *East of Eden* with my dad when I was twelve or thirteen. Even then I was especially moved by the scene in which Dean's screen father, played by Raymond Massey, turns down his son's birthday gift of investment-earned cash. The look of excruciating pain on James' boy/man face remains seared onto my mind—still one of the most memorable movie moments of my life. But the sequence was made all the more notable to me by the fact that unlike Massey, I had the most compassionate of fathers. When I later researched *Eden* for this book, my admiration for the scene was enhanced even further. It turns out the young actor improvised the poignant hugging of Massey that so pointedly punctuates his pain. Moreover, when one factors in *Eden* director Elia Kazan's lush use of CinemaScope and WarnerColor, it is easy to see how eminent critic Pauline Kael affectionately chided the beauty of my favorite Dean film: "A boy's agonies should not be dwelt on so lovingly: being misunderstood may easily become the new and glamorous lyricism."[6]

Every biography presents special challenges. The greatest demand for this book was the sheer volume of Dean literature available. With the possible exception of preparing a biography of Charlie Chaplin (Dean's favorite comedian), I have never had to wade through so much material. I am reminded of a related anecdote by another remarkable Hoosier, Yankee pitcher Don Larsen. His perfect game in the 1956 World Series paralleled the opening of Dean's film *Giant*. About his sudden fame, Larsen observed, "Before yesterday, no one knew I was alive. . . . Today, everyone is telling me they went to school with me."[7] That's the way it was with Dean, except in his case everyone wrote an article, too!

All in all, had James Dean lived, I think he might have modestly deflected his cutting-edge screen "rebel" status by saying, "Rebels have been an integral part of American culture since the country's inception. It's just another way of saying the 'good guys versus the bad guys.' " However, given James' wry sense of humor, he might very well have added, "But just who are the good guys?"

This study was enhanced by the New York Public Library's Performing Arts Library at Lincoln Center; the Margaret Herrick Library of the Academy of Motion Picture Arts and Sciences in Beverly Hills, California; the main branch of the New York Public Library at Fifth Avenue and Forty-second Street; the Fairmount Public Library in Fairmount, Indiana; the Fairmount Historical

Society; and the James Dean Gallery Library in Gas City, Indiana.

Numerous people helped make this project possible, starting with Marcus Winslow Jr., who granted me an extensive interview. My department chair at Ball State University, Nancy Carlson, assisted by facilitating university financial help. David Loehr, whose James Dean Gallery contains the world's largest collection of Dean memorabilia, opened his establishment's library to me. And Linda Magers, the director of the Fairmount Public Library, has gone the proverbial extra mile for me several times.

Ball State emeriti professor and film historian Conrad Lane was a sometimes sounding board for the manuscript, as well as writing the foreword. As usual, Janet Warner logged time as my copy editor. The computer preparation of the manuscript was done by Jean Thurman. Ball State emeriti professor and former dean of the College of Communications, Information, and Media Earl L. Conn provided both advice and James Dean stills from the actor's high school years. And a special thank you is in order for Ray E. Boomhower, Indiana Historical Society Press managing editor. I am forever grateful to his support of my writing, from the pages of *Traces*, which he edits, to my earlier biography of Carole Lombard. An accomplished historian himself, Ray is a wonderful catalyst for any biographer with a life to tell.

For me, as for most writers, the craft ultimately comes down to the love and support of family. Their "safety net" makes me feel like an airborne fiddler in a Marc Chagall painting—capable of anything! More specifically, this rooting section keys upon my parents and my daughters, Sarah and Emily. Thank you one and all.

PROLOGUE

―――

*"Grown-ups never understand anything by themselves,
and it is tiresome for children to be always
and forever explaining things to them."*[1]

—FROM ANTOINE DE SAINT EXUPÉRY'S FANTASY, *THE LITTLE PRINCE*,

JAMES DEAN'S FAVORITE BOOK.

THE FRIDAY MORNING OF SEPTEMBER 30, 1955, BEGAN early for budding film star James Dean. The twenty-four-year-old actor, who had thrown himself into three successive film productions, *East of Eden* (1955), *Rebel Without a Cause* (1955, though not yet released), and *Giant* (to open the following year, 1956), was now just as enthusiastically embracing his first break from filmmaking in more than sixteen months. The multitalented Dean's latest passion was racing sports cars, though this fascination with speed dated from his Hoosier childhood. Indiana, then and now, is a state most synonymous with the Indianapolis 500. And no one was ever a bigger fan than Dean. Indeed, one of his goals his freshman year of college was to someday race in the 500. Moreover, as a teenager growing up on a farm just outside of Fairmount, his favorite means of transportation was a motorcycle—a speeding motorcycle. Naturally, when James later graduated to sports cars, he continued his habit of helter-skelter haste. When passengers complained, the actor said, "I've got to go places in a hurry. There just isn't time."[2]

While Dean had done some professional racing early in his brief Hollywood career, he had been banned from participating in the sport by *Giant* director George Stevens for the duration of the lengthy, expensive shoot. Thus, once Dean's scenes on the film were completed, he was raging to race again. By this time, the young man had become positively poetic about the subject of speed: "It's the only time I feel whole."[3] Consistent with this fervor, Dean had gone "Hollywood" with his first pricey purchase—a silver Porsche 550 Spyder. This model was already making a name for itself on racetracks in both Europe and America. Dean paid for the car with a check for approximately $3,000 and by trading in his white Porsche 356 Speedster.

The high monetary amount paid by Dean for the Spyder was unlike the normal frugality exercised by the actor, whose tightness rivaled the comic cheapness of one of America's then most popular comedians, Jack Benny. Dean seldom picked up a check and usually avoided any ostentatious displays. Consequently, this atypical financial behavior further underlined the hold racing had on him. James so related to this symbol of speed that he had his own provocative nickname, "Little Bastard," painted in red on the Porsche's tail.

Metaphorically, of course, speed defined Dean's acting, too. As one biographer noted, "There was about
Dean a sense of urgency, a desire to get to the top of the
acting profession as rapidly as possible. He didn't want to
be bothered with such details as technique."[4] This was the
reason he had dropped out of the University of California
at Los Angeles and had minimized his involvement with
Lee Strasberg's Actors Studio, which had been cofounded
by *East of Eden* director Elia Kazan. Coupled with this
"urgency" was a proclivity to take chances, both as an
actor and as a racer. Dean's tendency to constantly push
the proverbial envelope was entertainingly exciting and
dangerous. And it was a key reason why many people saw
him as a "Little Bastard."

On the highlighted last day of September in 1955,
Dean was driving to a Sunday race in Salinas, California,
located three hundred miles north of Los Angeles. This
was familiar territory for the actor, since it was the hometown of novelist John Steinbeck and the setting for much
of his book, *East of Eden*, with some of the screen adaptation actually being shot there. After the race, Dean
planned on a short vacation in San Francisco. Leaving his
small Sherman Oaks rental cabin in the San Fernando
Valley before eight in the morning, Dean drove his late-
model Ford station wagon to Competition Motors, where
the actor had purchased the Porsche. A pivotal part of
his Salinas racing entourage, master mechanic Rolf

Wütherich, was already there doing some final fine-tuning on the sports car. The eternally impatient Dean attempted to help, but as was the case when he was a boy at the local motorcycle shop in his native Fairmount, the mechanic waved him into the waiting room.

Wütherich was James' preferred mechanic at Competition, with the sales agreement for the Porsche contingent on Wütherich crewing for the actor in his forthcoming races. Emblematic of Dean's circle of friends, the mechanic was yet another colorful character. Gifted with movie star good looks to rival even those of Dean, Wütherich's past included a stint as a teenaged German fighter pilot in the final days of World War II, when the Third Reich's armed forces were largely composed of boys and senior citizens.

The two men were soon joined at Competition Motors by the other two members of the Salinas contingent, Bill Hickman and Sanford Roth. Hickman was a stunt man and sometime character actor in his mid-thirties. Dean had met him during the production of director Samuel Fuller's Korean War film, *Fixed Bayonets* (1951), in which both actors had bit parts. Their friendship was cemented when they discovered a mutual fascination with fast cars. Hickman's greatest claim to fame would be his later work as a stunt driver in the celebrated chase sequence in *The French Connection* (1971). At that time, however, Dean knew Hickman best for his work as Clark Gable's

COLLECTION OF WES D. GEHRING

*Clark Gable (right) as an Indianapolis 500 racer
in* To Please a Lady *(1950).*

mechanic in the Indianapolis 500 racing film *To Please a
Lady* (1950). (With a portion of *Lady* being filmed on
location at the Indianapolis track, this had been a major
media event in Indiana. And naturally, Gable's devil-may-
care character took racing chances in the picture.)

As Hickman was a car crony, Roth was a photography
friend to Dean. In the transplanted Hoosier's myriad of

interests, photography ranked second to only acting and racing, and maybe bullfighting. Moreover, despite Dean's alleged angst over the phoniness of fame, he flirted with hypocrisy in his obsession to have his every mood and movement photographed. Roth was then working on a Dean photo layout for *Collier's* magazine. But the actor also liked the idea of having him document the racing trip, showing off another side of his life. James had met the photographer during the making of *Giant*, when Roth had been hired by Warner Brothers to shoot publicity stills. Although Roth's later notability is directly attributed to his association with Dean, he was no stranger, even then, to the famous. Prior to his work with this young movie star, Roth had done photo essays of such eminent subjects as Pablo Picasso, Albert Einstein, Marc Chagall, and Jean Cocteau. Dean enjoyed being included in such heady company. Plus, it enabled Dean to not only pick Roth's brain on the subject of photography (the actor had an inclination for choosing friends and associates based upon what he might learn from them), he could also quiz Roth about his celebrated subjects.

While the actor had many friends and contacts, remaining on a friendly basis with him could sometimes be an iffy proposition. He was what might be called a "user," forever scrambling to feed a gargantuan appetite for knowledge and success. His need to constantly find new mentors probably dated from his mother's attempt to immerse her child in the arts, from dance lessons to art classes. Coupled to this hungry mind, however, was a fragile psyche, dating back to his mother <u>Mildred's</u> early death in 1940, when Dean was only nine years old. These combined to saddle the actor with a mercurial personality. He might be the most brilliant of companions, from entertaining his friends with an inspired impersonation of Marlon Brando to performing various comic dialects. But this could quickly turn to sullen rudeness, or late-night calls and visits, when being alone was more than Dean could handle.

Later that last September morning in 1955, the actor's father, Winton Dean, and a visiting uncle, Charles Nolan, stopped at Competition Motors. James' relationship with his father had long been strained, starting with the death of the boy's mother. At that time the young widower had sent his child back to Indiana, where James would be raised by Winton's sister and brother-in-law, Ortense and Marcus Winslow. Consistent with this lack of father-son rapport, Winton had turned down his son's invitation to attend the Salinas race. Winton and Charles, however, had come to the dealership to see the young man off.

As anxious as the actor was about starting this mini-adventure, the foursome of Dean, Wütherich, Hickman, and Roth did not leave the Los Angeles area until about two o'clock in the afternoon. They had been delayed by

Wütherich going home to get cleaned up, Dean giving his uncle a test ride (Winton refused a similar offer), and a late breakfast at a local restaurant. The four men would caravan to the race in two cars. Sadly, Dean had already made a *fatal* decision that morning—he would drive the Porsche to the race, with his mechanic riding shotgun. The original travel plan had all four men riding together in the actor's station wagon, with the sports car in tow on a trailer. But Dean believed he needed more time behind the wheel of the new Porsche, which he had purchased just two weeks before. The hectic schedule of being *James Dean* had not afforded him enough driving time. Plus, his surrogate parents, the Winslows, had been visiting from Indiana. Wütherich seconded Dean's change in plans, given that it would also be beneficial to have more miles on the car before the race, not to mention a final monitoring of the powerful but sensitive Porsche Spyder engine. Of course, the new travel arrangement was fueled by the fact that Friday was a beautiful summer-like day. Had the weather been bad, the topless Porsche would have been banished to the trailer. Thus, the movie star's acting buddy Hickman and photographer Roth followed the streaking sports car in the more pedestrian Ford.

Historically, Dean literature suggests the Hoosier-born actor had a death wish. Certainly, he had a fascination with the macabre, from a well-publicized *Life* magazine photo in a coffin, to a friendship with the sexy television horror movie hostess known as Vampira, who might have stepped out of a Charles Addams cartoon. The star also gravitated toward deadly sports, from automobile racing to bullfighting. Indeed, as a New York actor Dean enjoyed doubling as a matador when he jaywalked in busy midtown, using his coat like a cape on speeding taxis. But be this as it may, Dean savored being outrageous. It was no coincidence that many of rock and roll's soon-to-be pioneers, starting with Elvis Presley, emulated the provocative poser known as the original "rebel." Moreover, there was a bravado about Dean the person that might simply be equated with the aura of invincibility associated with youth. In fact, the actor was said to have once admonished someone who had attempted to drag race with him and was nearly injured, "You can't do the things I'm doing. I can flirt with death and come through—you can't."[5] Dean's uncle and surrogate father, Marcus Winslow, had a definite opinion on the subject of Dean's alleged death wish, calling it "a bunch of crap."[6]

Certainly Dean's immediate plans for the future necessitated, if not living forever, at least sticking around for a reasonably lengthy lifetime. He had just signed a long-term contract with Warner Brothers. He also was set to portray boxer Rocky Graziano in the film *Somebody Up There Likes Me*, which was to be followed by a loose biography of Billy the Kid titled *The Left-Handed Gun*. Both pictures were ultimately made (in 1956 and 1958

Bent cigarette notwithstanding, the Dean bravado is apparent here on the set of Rebel Without a Cause *(1955).*

respectively) with Paul Newman finding fame as the title character of each production. (In television's New York-based live production beginnings, Dean and Newman had often competed for the same parts.) The Hoosier-born actor also planned to form his own production unit, in collaboration with his *Rebel* director, Nicholas Ray. Dean's immediate 1955 plans, after competing in several races, were to return to his favorite city, New York, and star in several television specials, including a series of Shakespeare plays. The ambitious actor also believed television would be the perfect medium in which to work on his long-term goal of becoming a director. Both Ray and Kazan had encouraged these aspirations by way of their collaborative filmmaking styles. Consequently, instead of someone with a death wish, Dean might be called a *Rebel WITH a Cause*.

The only addendum to death is that the actor feared any long-lingering illness, such as the cancer that ultimately killed his mother. Death by inches was just not Dean's style. This also helps explain why he was so drawn to both bullfighting and Ernest Hemingway's artistically concise take on the subject in *Death in the Afternoon* (1932): "The only place where you could see life and death, i.e., violent death now that the wars were over, was in the bull ring."[7] While the actor had no plans to "check out" early, he also believed, as did Hemingway, that a life without dangerous ritual was not worth living. Ironically, this flies in the face of Dean's new type of screen antihero, a vulnerable cross between the rebellious Marlon Brando persona and the psychologically troubled Montgomery Clift, both of whom Dean idolized. A final footnote on death and Dean must acknowledge his curiosity factor, with the actor noting, "if you're afraid to die, there's no room in your life to make discoveries."[8]

The fact that the real Dean was more provocatively adventuresome than his screen persona merits a brief consideration of the evolving American hero in the early 1950s. For the young actor, as for much of the world at this time, Hemingway set the standard. This was never more true than with his work *The Old Man and the Sea* (1952), where baseball legend Joe DiMaggio represents a microcosm of America that fortifies the novel's title character, who states, "I must have confidence and I must be worthy of the great DiMaggio who does all things perfectly even with the pain of the bone spur in his heel."[9] But while DiMaggio today remains an enduring figure of what Hemingway once described as "grace under pressure," early 1950s pop culture had another "J. D." factor in addition to DiMaggio through which to filter hero (or more precisely, antihero) worship.

J. D. Salinger wrote his watershed work *The Catcher in the Rye* in 1951. This tour de force chronicle of the comic alienation of young Holden Caulfield could be called a blueprint for the Dean screen persona that would follow. Had Salinger sold the novel's rights to Hollywood, James playing Holden would have been inspired casting. Both Dean and Caulfield have now come to symbolize the estranged youth of post–World War II affluence, fighting the inherent phoniness of a society lost in consumer decadence. Whether one's preferred iconic "J. D." factor is James Dean, J. D. Salinger, or Joe DiMaggio, there is little debate that the antiheroic configuration has now been in ascendancy for some time.

This transition was driven, in part, by another strain of early 1950s American history, the dark chapter known as the McCarthy Era, with the hunt for supposed communists in government by the House Un-American Activities Committee and U.S. Senator Joseph McCarthy. Suddenly the long-heralded inherent wisdom of the populist people seemed easily hoodwinked by demigods such as McCarthy. American pop culture responded with the derailing of a host of traditional folk heroes, from the clay feet of the Ruthian Roy Hobbs (a character "as American as a figure in a Norman Rockwell magazine cover"[10]) in Bernard Malamud's classic baseball novel *The Natural* (1952), to the corrupted homespun rustic Lonesome Rhodes (Andy Griffith) of director Kazan's *A Face in the Crowd* (1957). McCarthyism as a factor in the emergence of Dean will be further addressed later in the text, especially as it pertains to the actor's creative involvement with Kazan, a "friendly" HUAC witness.

As Dean and company sped toward Salinas that last day in September 1955, it is unlikely, however, that anyone was thinking of McCarthyism. With the Senate's censure of the controversial politician late the proceeding year, he probably seemed like ancient history. Moreover, when the young actor got close to a competition he tended to obsess about said event. The situation was further intensified this time because it was both a new car and a new racing category—the Porsche Spyder's more powerful engine put Dean among the premier drivers. Indeed, enough novelty was involved that the actor's mechanic simply wanted him to be competitive, learn the ropes, and *not* push for a win. For someone with a warrior mentality such as Dean, however, this was not the kind of racing advice he wanted to hear. Tragically, the actor decided to apply his go-for-broke philosophy to the sports car even *before* the race. Years after the accident, Wütherich confessed that the studio had paid him to say that Dean had been going the speed limit at the time of the accident. "I'd tried to tell Jimmy since we left Hollywood . . . that he couldn't run such a new machine in that manner—like a monkey beating on something without considering what he might break," Wütherich remembered. "Jimmy would say one way to win was to go for broke. . . . [He] drove like a crazy person. I said, 'Ease up.' He wouldn't hear me because he was out of view of anyone he supposed was watching to make sure he didn't get into trouble. 'Ease up!' I told him."[11]

At approximately 3:30 that afternoon, both Dean and Wütherich in the Porsche and Hickman and Roth in the trailing Ford were stopped for speeding. Dean became upset by the ticket, given that his home studio had recently pressured him into making a National Safety Council driving commercial with actor Gig Young. But he was polite to the patrolman, who did not recognize either the name or the face of the young star. The officer was, however, interested in the Porsche, and they talked briefly about the sports car.

On the road again, Dean soon returned to his speeding ways. In his defense, the pre-interstate route from Los Angeles to Salinas, first on Highway 99 and then on Highway 466, represented a lengthy day of driving, even at normal speeds. Of course, if one looks at a 1955 road map of California, Dean hardly picked the most direct route to Salinas. Had he gone the long way to log more time behind the wheel of his new sports car? Regardless, in the roughly two hours remaining in Dean's life, his racing foursome would make one more brief stop, at a place called Blackwell's Corner, where Highway 466 met Route 33. The actor had recognized a fellow driver's sports car at this combination gas and food store. The racer in question was Lance Reventlow, the son of Woolworth heiress Barbara Hutton. As Dean drank a Coke, he showed Reventlow his speeding ticket and complained, "I just done a road safety film. Some fucking journalist is going to love to pick that up."[12] Paradoxically, he then bragged that he had just had the Porsche up to 130 miles per hour.[13]

Though this might have been an exaggeration, something the actor was famous for (a tall tale trait he traced to his grandfather), later calculations by authorities

suggest Dean must have been driving at a highly dangerous speed. To clock the distance between where he was
stopped for speeding and the fatal accident site, Dean
would have needed to average roughly 75 miles per hour,
even without the Blackwell's Corner pit stop. Factor in
this bull-session break, and "he must have been hitting 90
to 100 most of the time."[14] Moreover, several Dean biographers have documented a near head-on collision shortly
before the accident, when the actor's risky pass on the
two-way highway forced an oncoming vehicle off the
road.[15]

The irony of the fatal crash, just minutes later, was
that Dean was not at fault. As the Porsche flew down
Highway 466, a college student in a 1950 Ford
approached the highway's Y-turn intersection with Route
41. The young man about to accidentally change
Hollywood history had a name that might have graced a
filmland adaptation of *Tobacco Road*—Don Turnupseed,
a navy veteran. As Turnupseed started to turn left from
Highway 46 onto Route 41, he paused, as if he had finally
seen the Porsche. Sadly, this was not the case.

Several circumstances aggravated the situation. With
the late afternoon's setting sun, Dean's small, silver,
extremely low-to-the ground sports car was all but invis-
ible. Thus, Turnupseed proceeded to turn directly into
the path of the Porsche. And because the Ford's stutter-
effect stop at the intersection had fooled both Dean and

Wütherich, the actor made no attempt to brake until it was all but meaningless. Plus, his high rate of speed gave the young movie star no insurance space to avoid the accident.

The resulting crash was more of a one-way demolition derby. The tank-like Ford was not badly damaged; Turnupseed walked away from the accident. In contrast, the Porsche was crushed like a soda can. The lightweight aluminum sports car, sans bumper and with a rear engine, offered no protection for its riders. (After recently examining a facsimile of the shiny, toy-like vehicle two words kept going through this writer's mind—"death trap."[16]) In a twisted tribute to the Porsche's "flying" speed, the car had become airborne, performing several horrific cartwheels. Wütherich was thrown from the vehicle and suffered multiple injuries, including a serious skull fracture that would necessitate several surgeries in the months to come. Dean essentially died on impact from a broken neck; his body was pinned in the Porsche by a steering wheel that had caved in both his chest and forehead. Wütherich later claimed he believed that the actor had briefly survived the crash, since he had heard the release of air coming from James. This was undoubtedly, however, some macabre body function that had nothing to do with life. Dean was dead.

As with most tragedies, paradoxes abound. The last words of this now screen immortal were poignantly desperate: "He's gotta see us."[17] The flat northern California farmland that was the backdrop for Dean's final drive was also surprisingly similar to the level countryside of his beloved north-central Indiana, a fact the actor even noted that final September day of 1955.[18] (Consistent with this thinking, in 1959 Alfred Hitchcock would shoot the crop- dusting Indiana portion of *North by Northwest* near this same area of California.) When the trailing Hickman and Roth eventually caught up to the accident, Roth's concluding photo shoot with Dean documented the actor's grisly death. The twisted wreck was, as film director Francois Truffaut poignantly described it, "a silent ruin, one wheel spinning slower and slower like a raffle wheel."[19] After a lengthy rehabilitation, Wütherich fully recovered, only to die in a 1981 automobile accident. But the greatest irony of Dean's death was that while his brief life had ended, the legend was about to begin.

1

The Early Years

"In all of our souls there are empty spaces that we want to fill, and apparently in the American soul there is a vacuum at a point that Dean will fill."[1]

ENTERTAINER/AUTHOR STEVE ALLEN

AS AN ACTOR JAMES DEAN LIKED TO SURPRISE HIS COSTARS and his audiences with the unexpected. He came by the trait naturally, since he was an exercise in the unexpected even before he was born. The future iconic star was an unplanned baby, causing his parents to marry only six months before his February 8, 1931, birth. The fact that the father, Winton Dean, was the one dragging his feet on the union is a fitting foundation to the lifetime of indifference he showed his son. In marked contrast to Winton, the boy's mother, Mildred Wilson Dean, was the most nurturing of parents. Her activities would range from enrolling a pre-school "Deanie" in dance lessons to offering him a smorgasbord of culture at home, such as reading to him nonstop and playing acting-orientated games of improvisation. It was almost as if Mildred knew she would die young and had to pack as much creative love as possible into the youngster's first nine years. Moreover, as if to leave a permanent reminder of the arts after she was gone, the child's middle name was that of her favorite poet, Byron.[2]

In James Dean's first starring film role, and the one most favored by revisionist critics, as John Steinbeck's Cal Trask in *East of Eden* (1955), his character is fascinated by the soil. Appropriately, Dean spent the greater part of his youth on the Indiana farm of his surrogate parents (Winton's sister and brother-in-law, Ortense and Marcus Winslow). Not surprisingly, the *Eden* film would be the Winslows' favorite, also. But Dean took a roundabout path to his aunt and uncle's farm.

He was born at the first home of his parents, the poetic-sounding Green Gables Apartments in Marion, Indiana. This was a typically midwestern small town, seventy-odd miles north of Indianapolis. Though these were the proverbial hard times of the Great Depression, Winton had a good government job as a dental technician at Marion's veterans' hospital. Mildred had worked in a drugstore, but James quickly became her new career. During the boy's first five years, the family lived in a series of dwellings in both Marion and nearby Fairmount, Winton's hometown. For a time they lived in a cottage on Ortense and Marcus's farm, just outside Fairmount.

In 1936 Winton was given the opportunity to transfer to a veterans' hospital in Santa Monica, California.[3] This was the same year that Charlie Chaplin, James Dean's favorite comedian, released his celebrated *Modern Times*.

COLLECTION OF WES D. GEHRING

Charlie Chaplin during the assembly line sequence of his inspired
Modern Times *(1936).*

For an entertainment-starved Mildred, movieland southern California represented a kind of "modern times" to her. After all, this was the free spirit that her rather staid and colorless husband called his "little bohemian," who would, at the drop of a hat, take a bus to Indianapolis to see *anything* related to the arts.[4]

Like the mother of an earlier Hoosier-born Hollywood star, Carole Lombard, Mildred transferred her own unrealized dream of being a star to her child.[5] Consequently, she continued to nurture his every artistic tendency, from violin lessons to encouraging his near obsession with drawing. Music and art remained special passions for the rest of his short life. In fact, during his poverty-stricken early New York acting days, when he could not afford to buy someone a gift, Dean would draw him or her a picture.

Be this as it may, the mentoring Mildred had a tendency to prepare tutorials with Indiana ties. For example, she loved reading aloud to "Deanie" from the works of beloved Hoosier poet James Whitcomb Riley, whose populist verse celebrated the everyday life of the common man. Though his fame has since faded, early in the twentieth century Riley was considered one of America's premier poets. Mildred also enjoyed sharing Indiana tall tales with her son, such as stories about Johnny Appleseed. Coincidently, young Dean forever afterwards would have a "creative" take on the truth. The young mother's greatest original talent was the ability to mimic the mannerisms of people, famous or otherwise. She would regale James with a litany of impersonations, just as he would later do among his friends. His "impersonations were so larcenous that when friends and fellow actors saw him doing *them*, they sometimes felt oddly violated. As one friend said of him, 'There goes my personality!' "[6]

James Dean (left) with his Rebel *screen parents Ann Doran and Jim Backus (pointing).*

COLLECTION OF WES D. GEHRING

A tantalizing snippet of Dean's mimicry skills are preserved late in his signature film, *Rebel Without a Cause* (1955). The scene in question is at the empty mansion, when the three neglected teenagers played by Dean, Natalie Wood, and Sal Mineo form their own surrogate family. Just as they go to explore the estate's drained pools, Dean improvises a brief verbal impersonation of the cartoon character Mr. Magoo. The line James delivers as

Magoo is the darkly comic, "Drown them like puppies." As random as mimicking Magoo sounds, it was not inconsistent for a 1950s teenager to impersonate a then-popular cartoon figure. Of course, the in-joke bonus here is that the real voice of Mr. Magoo was provided by actor Jim Backus, who plays Dean's father in *Rebel*. This was not a random humor homage, either. The young actor actually went to Backus for tips on impersonating Mr. Magoo!

In a perversely comic manner, perhaps Dean's fascination with Mr. Magoo and other cartoon characters may have contributed to his real-life sense of cocky invincibility, since cartoon figures are bulletproof—inhabitants of a realm without consequences, in a permanent present tense. But while an impersonating Dean on film is rare, stories of his mimicking abound. One such example occurred on the set of *Rebel*, when Dean and supporting player Nick Adams entertained the cast and crew with their take on Marlon Brando and film director Elia Kazan, who had directed Dean in *East of Eden*. Adams played Brando and Dean "essayed" Kazan. This demonstrated the Indiana-born actor's versatility, since he was famous among friends for his complex impersonations of Brando, such as Brando mimicking Charlie Chaplin, or Chaplin doing Brando. The "team" of Dean and Adams was such a hit during the production of *Rebel* that they flirted with putting an act together. In a 1955 Warner Brothers press release, Dean said: "I shall be busy for the

COLLECTION OF WES D. GEHRING

*Charlie Chaplin (left) and Orson Welles during the 1940s, when
Chaplin's private life began to overshadow his art.*

rest of 1955, and Nick will be doing film work for the next
six months. Come 1956, however, I wouldn't be surprised
to find myself with Adams doing a two-a-night nightclub
routine—or acting in a comedy by William Shakespeare."[7]

Backus left the *Rebel* production convinced that his
young friend's "real ambition" was to be a nightclub
comic. And as he pondered the subject in his autobiography, Backus was certain the mimicking James would have
"killed" [comically entertained] his audience.[8] With

Dean's death in 1955, a 1956 teaming with Adams will always remain conjecture. But it seems undeniable that the transplanted Hoosier felt compelled to try some sort of comedy soon. In the aforementioned press release, the actor added that he would soon have been in three consecutive "emotional dramatic roles. I think no actor should tie himself to one particular brand of acting."[9] Who knows, maybe he would have even worked with his comedy favorite, Chaplin. After all, Dean's acting idol, Brando, to whom he was often compared, later teamed with Chaplin on *A Countess from Hong Kong* (1967). Beyond the comedy, the always controversial Dean was probably also attracted to Chaplin's forever provocative private life. Nonetheless, in a closing footnote to mimicry, Dean and Adams would have a final, bizarre impersonation collaboration *after* James' death. Although Dean had completed his scenes on *Giant* (1956) *before* his fatal car crash, technical problems on his character's drunken banquet speech necessitated that it be "looped" (rerecorded by the actor as he watched the projected picture). Since that was impossible, Adams now became the voice of his friend for that one scene.

Sadly, while Mildred Dean's artistic attention to her son, be it mimicry or music, undoubtedly contributed to his later film greatness, the boy's unusually early dance and violin lessons made him an odd duck in elementary school, subject to frequent teasing. Classmates also mocked his poet-inspired middle name. Add to this the fact that the boy was both small for his age and did not take criticism well (perhaps due to all that unconditional praise from his mother), and the youngster had few new friends while in California. Even worse, James' father seemed to echo the bias of the child's fellow students. He believed his son was "girlish" and spent entirely too much time with his mother.[10] But the inability of both "Deanie" and Mildred to find West Coast friends actually drove them closer together. This link was further heightened by the slow unraveling of Winton and Mildred's marriage. The two found they had less and less in common with each passing day.

Ironically, like a bad movie melodrama, just as Mildred's California dream was dying (1939), she was diagnosed with ovarian cancer. The disease was so advanced there was little doctors could do. Winton later confessed: "How do you tell an eight-year-old boy his mother's going to die? I tried, but I just couldn't make it. Jim and I—we'd never had that closeness. And my Jim is a tough boy to understand."[11]

Of course, communication in that era was often an underrated phenomenon. For example, Winton thought it best to not tell his wife that her condition was terminal. Given that this was 1939, one is immediately reminded that baseball legend Lou Gehrig was diagnosed with the still-incurable amyotrophic lateral sclerosis (ALS) that

COLLECTION OF WES D. GEHRING

Lou Gehrig (left) and Babe Ruth at Yankee Stadium, July 4, 1939, the day of Gehrig's "luckiest man on the face of the earth" farewell speech.

same year, and his spouse also claimed he was never told.[12] Such statements, however, insult the intelligence of both Dean's mother and Gehrig, as well as ignoring contradictory period evidence. For example, one pioneering biography (1942) of the Yankee slugger credits him with stoically observing of some cheering children, "They're wishing me luck . . . and I'm dying."[13] Though Mildred's recognition of her true situation was less dramatic, it was no less real. An Indiana friend who frequently visited the bedridden Mildred later recalled, "One day she told me to go to the dresser drawers and get her rings and try them on. Then she said, 'When I'm done with those rings, they're yours.'"[14]

Beyond the tragedy of a mother dying at twenty-nine was the fearful confusion that began to haunt her son: "his immediate reaction to her illness . . . [was] resentment and even anger. Grief and incomprehension came later as he watched her beauty, energy, and resilience fade away."[15] Mildred's legacy of love was threatened by the boy's sense of abandonment. Only nine at the time of her lingering death, the child somehow felt her dying was a rejection of him. Through no conscious fault of "Deanie," this must have made Mildred's terminal illness even more excruciating. The woman who, among other things, had had her son put wishes under his pillow, which she would then try to make happen the next day, was now facing his angry confusion for leaving him.

The one minor miracle that might have come out of this tragedy was bringing the father and son closer together. But it did not happen. Indeed, things became worse, possibly exacerbated by Winton finally telling the boy that his mother was near death. The only saving grace during Mildred's final weeks was that Winton had asked his mother, Emma Dean, to come out from Indiana in order to help them through this difficult time.

If the death of Dean's mother on July 14, 1940, was not the deciding event in an actor's life later synonymous, on-screen and off, with alienation, then a decision immediately following that death was paramount. "Deanie" was about to be sent back to Indiana to be reared by his aunt and uncle, Ortense and Marcus Winslow. Overnight, Winton had voluntarily made his son an orphan. The history of damning Dean's dad had begun. Since the actor's two greatest roles, in *Eden* and *Rebel*, both revolve around troubled father-son relationships, the aftereffect of Winton's abandonment never goes away. Whether one is reading a biography of Dean or studying scholarly criticism of his films, Winton's decision has become the central piece in the jigsaw puzzle that is the actor's heavily scrutinized life.

Personally, as a man who largely defines himself through being a father, part of me can never understand how Winton could send a child away, particularly at that time. I am a student of Sidney Poitier's spiritual autobiography *The Measure of a Man* (2000), which defines its title as the way a man provides for his children. But I am also cognizant of a democratic observation by the celebrated humanist filmmaker Jean Renoir: "Everyone has their reasons."[16] My goal here is to both open a wider window onto the process, and to begin to defuse the suggestion that the actor's ensuing Indiana childhood was a study in angst.

A pivotal point has been lost concerning the young-ster's return to the Midwest: his mother's disappointment

about California had gone beyond disillusionment, even
before her illness. Simply put, she felt it was not the best
place to raise her son. In 1938 she had told a friend visiting from Fairmont, "I don't want Jimmy to grow up out
here. I've even been thinking about going back home to
Indiana. Everything's so artificial here. I want my Jimmy
to grow up where things are real and simple."[17] Thus,
while sending the boy back to Indiana matches the popular Winton profile of indifference, it also could be interpreted as an attempt to honor his dying wife's wish. It
would also help explain why the boy's aunt and uncle
would come forth so quickly to offer a home for him.
(Interestingly enough, Dean the budding film star later
echoed his mother's comments on the Los Angeles area's
artificiality.)

The family's ongoing defense of Winton's action has
consistently hinged on his precarious financial situation.
Mildred's hospital expenses had put him in debt, forcing
him even to sell his car. Add to this projected child-care
costs while he would be at work, and things seemed over-
whelming. There was also a general expectation that with
Adolph Hitler initiating a European war the preceding
year, it was only a matter of time before President
Franklin D. Roosevelt started the first peacetime draft in
American history. If Winton were drafted, James would
be coming back to Indiana anyway. So why not address
the potential problem while Emma Dean was already in

California? (Consistent with this thinking, a peacetime draft was established just two months after Mildred's death, though it would be a year and a half before Winton was called up.)

Dean had also been a sickly child, and his family believed that an Indiana farm was a much healthier place to grow up than in greater Los Angeles. Indeed, this was the key explanation Dean himself gave for the move in a later interview with Hollywood columnist Hedda Hopper: "I was anemic, so I went back to the farm."[18] Moreover, this variation of Jeffersonian democracy (celebrating the rural or small-town setting) was not simply predicated on health reasons. Like James' mother, the family believed the heartland was simply a better place to be a boy. (Midwestern mindsets often stay constant. A generation after Dean, my urban parents encouraged summers on my grandparents' farm because it seemed a "better place.")

These are all reasonable points, and no doubt they played a part in the decision. But reading between the lines, the deciding factor was likely the desperate situation Winton's mother found in California. Between a non-speaking child bordering on shock, to a never-enthusiastic parent stretched beyond his coping skills, Emma Dean initiated what amounted to a mercy mission—take the boy back to Indiana. Although Emma never criticized her son's lack of parenting skills, she had always believed

Ortense and Marcus were exemplary along those lines, noting they were "wise and gentle and have a great gift for loving. Theirs is like a Quaker home should be. You never hear a harsh word. Best of all, they are happy as well as good—and that's what Jimmy needed most after the shock of losing his mother."[19]

Whatever the final catalyst, selfish or otherwise, that had Winton sending James to his sister and brother-in-law's Hoosier farm, it was ultimately a very good decision. The actor would later movingly validate this action in a conversation with actress Liz Sheridan, best known today as comedian Jerry Seinfeld's television mom in the long running sitcom *Seinfeld*. In the early 1950s, both Sheridan and Dean were struggling New York performers who also happened to be in love. Dean later confessed to her: "When my mother died, I felt like I'd been thrown off a cliff—like I was all alone in empty space, not falling, just hanging there. When my dad sent me to live with my aunt and uncle, it was kind of like a release. They are really nice folks. They've always been good to me, and I liked growing up on the farm. I want them to meet you someday. You'd really like them, and I know they'd love you."[20]

Of course, this is in no way an attempt to minimize the initial shock for the boy of essentially losing both parents simultaneously. However, as Dean biographer Donald Spoto agrees, the central sin of the father was that Winton "did not at least go to Indiana with Jimmy, there to discuss the matter [of relocating], in his presence" with Ortense and Marcus Winslow.[21] Again, the excuse is financial—train tickets for his mother and son and transportation costs for his wife's body. The thinness of this explanation borders on the criminal. But hypothetically, another component to this sad equation was probably humiliation. Forget the lack of rapport between father and son or that the move for "Deanie" made sense. To sign off on a son, whatever the circumstances, has to be embarrassing.

For Emma and her grandson, the train trip back to Indiana went beyond a sad, drawn-out journey. During each stop, when the boy saw the loading and unloading of luggage, he would dash from his seat to the baggage car, making sure that his mother's coffin was still there. Despite the trip's nightmare quality, the child would eventually ask the train's conductor for something he could keep to remember this last journey with his mother. Thanks to an assist from a porter, young Dean received a cup and saucer that bore the train's monogram, *Challenger*. Fate could not have provided a more fitting name for the train.

Mildred would be buried in her hometown of Marion less than a week after her death. For a time, the boy would keep a funeral wreath ribbon under his pillow at night. Besides providing a comfort, like his *Challenger* cup and saucer, the ribbon also probably reminded him of the wishes his mother had encouraged him to place under his pillow. Much has been made through the years, however, about a lingering abandonment bitterness he felt toward his mother. For example, a *Look* magazine article, published a year after Dean's death, cited the following: "'My mother died on me when I was nine years old,' he cried some years later in a Hollywood tantrum. 'What does she expect me to do? Do it all by myself?'"[22]

Variations of this quote have surfaced in countless Dean publications in the intervening decades. But the optimum word here is *Look*'s descriptive term "tantrum." These might have been the initial feelings of the young Deanie. Yet, coming from an adult Dean, one can best chronicle this as another example of the actor's later proclivity for angst-ridden posing. Remember, he rose to fame playing a series of troubled youths, first on television and then in the movies. His approach to acting also embraced the then-cutting-edge Method style, in which the performer attempts to "live" each part, supposedly feeling life exactly as the character, and most provocatively, often staying in character off camera. As Dean stated: "An actor should thoroughly understand the character he is portraying and there is no better way than trying to be that person in the hours away from the camera. I developed a program of understanding Jett [his Giant character] and of doing the things he'd be likely to do."[23]

Granted, the actor might have revisited his childhood turmoil to better play a later troubled youth. But that should not be interpreted to mean his whole short life was one of turmoil. His artificial angst in real life is best revealed in an incident recalled by acting friend Karen Sharpe, who knew Dean before he was famous. "He told me, 'If anyone comes in here [a café], you'll see me change. Just play along with me,'" Sharpe recalled. "And someone did come in that he knew. He did act strangely—brooding, incoherent, and staring into his coffee, not looking up. Later I came to understand that his notorious 'strangeness' was just an act. But he played that part so long, maybe he became the act."[24]

In sifting through a mountain of Dean material, this was a common take on Dean's "strangeness" among his pre-fame friends. James' biographers have been slower to embrace this truth, given that it is not nearly as romantic as the idea of the troubled artist. Still, recognition is occurring here, too. For example, biographer William Russo observed, "Dean suffered personal torment, according to reports. In point of fact, he more often bedeviled others."[25]

A more knowing slant on what his mother's death ultimately meant to this child comes from his later best friend and sometime roommate William Bast, who wrote the first book-length profile of the actor, *James Dean: A Biography* (1956). It remains the seminal text on the actor. Bast's suggested "reading" of his close friend was that once the boy got beyond the pain of his beloved mother's death, he built upon the high expectations she had established for him. Mildred's mantra for him was nothing short of monumental. Theirs was simply an "uncompleted mission." According to Bast, "All through the years to manhood, he [Dean] had kept and preserved, buried deep within his soul, the obligation to a mother who had left him . . . [with this goal]. Was his burning desire to succeed, his need to excel, sparked by the subconscious memory of that mysterious obligation? Perhaps."[26]

This "uncompleted mission" would be greatly assisted by the most nurturing of substitute parents, Aunt Ortense and Uncle Marcus, "who Jimmy would soon start to call Mom and Dad."[27]

2

Back Home in Indiana

"Studying cows, pigs and chickens can help an actor develop his character. There are a lot of things I learned from animals. One was that they couldn't hiss or boo me. I also became close to nature and am now able to appreciate the beauty with which this world is endowed."[1]

JAMES DEAN

LIKE THOSE ANIMALS THAT "COULDN'T HISS OR BOO" HIM, Indiana became a safe haven for James Dean, first as a grieving youngster and later as a struggling actor. But before examining the various ramifications of this Hoosier haven, the Fairmount farm of his Aunt Ortense, Uncle Marcus, and their daughter Joan (five years older than "Deanie") came to represent two additional keys to Dean's success. First, as suggested by Robert Altman and George W. George's documentary, *The James Dean Story* (1957), the farm also symbolized "a place to replenish himself."[2] This recharging was especially important in Dean's early New York acting years as he scrambled to find stage and television work. For example, in October 1952, he hitchhiked home with two close friends, William Bast and Liz "Dizzy" Sheridan. Bast later wrote of the visit in the groundbreaking first biography of the actor: "After all the years of seeing Jimmy alone and without a family, it was a wonderful thing to watch him touch again the gentle roots of his early years. He was back in his element again, and he loved it."[3]

Second, beyond replenishing Dean, his hometown served as a confidence booster. Despite the axiom doubling as the title of Thomas Wolfe's 1940 novel, *You Can't Go Home Again* (the same year the boy returned to Indiana), Dean became a hero in Fairmount long before the rest of the world knew him as an antihero. For example, in the aforementioned 1952 return to Indiana, Dean's high school drama instructor, Adeline Nall, arranged for the trio of friends to team teach her class. Not only were they a big hit with the students, the three young New Yorkers found they enjoyed sharing their passions. Dancer/actress Sheridan later entertainingly described their exit from campus: "Afterwards we were delighted with ourselves, like professors striding across Harvard Yard. 'I thought your lecture quite good, today, Mr. Bast.' 'Why, thank you, James. Yours too was quite excellent.' 'Hey! What about me?' I whined. 'Oh, I'm [Dean] sorry, Professor Sheridan, but I'm afraid I drifted off during yours. I'm sure it was quite adequate.'"[4]

Before Fairmount helped to replenish and boost Dean, it served as a haven for a little boy who had lost his mother. His surrogate parents were an incredibly caring Quaker couple. They were also older and more experienced at parenting than Winton Dean, the boy's biological father and Ortense's brother. In fact, the couple had always wanted a son. But Ortense and Marcus's compassion is best demonstrated by their response to Dean's immediate fondness for the master bedroom with its bird's-eye maple furniture—they traded bedrooms with him. Like the youngster's biological mother, Ortense encouraged the boy's every creative whim. But maybe more important, given Dean's lack of previous male nurturing, was how Marcus responded to the young boy's growing interest in sports. Dean's paternal grandmother, Emma Dean, later recalled one of his classmates saying: "Ma Dean, I always envied Jimmy. My Dad never took time to play with me, but Marcus was forever out there shooting baskets with Jimmy or passing a football or taking him hunting or showing him how to do stunts."[5]

The athletic additions to the farm ranged from basketball hoops in the barn to Christmas lights around the family pond in winter in order to play night hockey. In addition to providing the youngster with some valuable attention, Marcus's team sports boosts also helped the friendless-in-California child suddenly become popular.

Indeed, the family's barn soon became an area hoop Mecca. Dean's friend Rex Couch later remembered: "Every Sunday, there were anywhere from ten to thirty-five guys playing there. At an early age, Jimmy was playing with guys much older than he was."[6] Cornering the county hoop activity was no mean task given that Indiana,

41

then and now, is synonymous with high school basketball. (The state is still home to four of the five largest high school basketball arenas in the nation.) Dean would go on to letter in this sport, as well as baseball and track (Marcus also constructed him a pole-vaulting pit to practice in).Yet appropriately for Hoosierland, basketball would be Dean's best sport. He was an undersized (five foot, eight inches tall) but tenacious guard with a deadly long-range, two-handed set shot. How tenacious? Marcus later observed: "He smashed fifteen pair of eyeglasses in tryin' to be an athlete. Breakin' em as fast as I could get 'em."[7] Of course, the addendum to the breakage was that it did not always occur in the heat of athletic battle. Anticipating by many years the fiery intensity of Indiana University's legendary coach Bob Knight, Dean had a tendency to throw his glasses when questionable foul calls went against him.

While we will return to some specifics of Dean's high school basketball career in the next chapter, two pivotal aspects of the sport would have an ongoing impact on the actor. First, the competitiveness of Hoosier hoops evolved into a personal philosophy. Bast, best known today as a successful television writer, recalled, "He [Dean] had confided to me that he looked at life as though it were simply a sporting event, like basketball. It was a game to be played and won at all costs."[8] Second, Dean's athleticism, best showcased in roundball, became a corollary to his acting style. To illustrate, James' college friend, author Larry Swindell, said that Dean's *East of Eden* director Elia Kazan "told me he was first attracted by Dean's wonderful use of a very athletic body and that body-acting is a natural faculty that can't be taught."[9] As an Indiana footnote to Kazan, another Hoosier, Paul Osborn, was the catalyst for the director choosing Dean for Eden. In a later interview, Kazan observed: "Paul Osborn had seen him in a play [*The Immoralist*, 1954] and told me I ought to take a look at this kid. . . . So I met with Dean. I talked to him about ten minutes and called Paul up and said, 'This kid is it.'"[10] (The Evansville-born Osborn received a 1955 Academy Award nomination for his adaptation of *Eden*, while Dean would be up for a statuette in the Best Actor category.)

The Oscars might seem to be a long way from an Indiana farm, but young Dean enjoyed talking to Ortense and Marcus about someday being in the movies. Though both thought this would be an unlikely development, the couple never discouraged the dream. Indeed, they might be said to have indirectly fed the boy's interest, since Ortense later remembered, "We used to go to the movies, a lot." Dean's aspiration might have been further fueled by the fact that a major Hollywood star of the period, Carole Lombard, had been born in nearby Fort Wayne, Indiana, and was married to perennial box-office superstar Clark Gable. The couple stood as the film capital's reigning first

The famous 1939 photo that often accompanied the announcement of Carole Lombard and Clark Gable's marriage.

family. With Lombard's tragic death in a 1942 plane crash after returning to Indianapolis for the nation's first bond rally of World War II, she assumed iconic status in Indiana.[11]

When the boy was not planning his film career or playing sports, he was more than busy being a farm kid. Throughout Dean's life people never ceased to comment on his insatiable curiosity. This was especially evident on the farm, from his fascination with animals to a burning desire to learn how to drive a tractor. Not surprisingly, he mastered the task before his tenth birthday. Farm children, with their accompanying chores, learn about responsibilities earlier than most youngsters. This was yet another way that the Hoosier haven could help James feel better about himself. While he would never see himself as a farmer, with the arts always winning out over manual labor, there was an honest sincerity about this midwestern life that he always respected.

This rural connection was brought home to me by a Dean anecdote from Dick Dunlap, who directed the actor's first small-screen leading role as an ex-convict searching for his missing wife in an episode of NBC's dramatic anthology *Kraft Television Theatre* (1947–58). This Dean/Dunlap collaboration, titled "A Long Time Till Dawn," was broadcast in November 1953 after an intense week of rehearsals. Initially the actor was not responding to direction, but then Dunlap introduced "Dean to his [own] father, an Iowa farmer visiting New York, and the two avidly discussed the care and feeding of hogs. Once James realized he and Dunlap were both farm boys, he became fully compliant."[12] One could further argue, as a corollary to Kazan's analogy between acting and sports, that Dean also saw this physicality in his art, but more as an extension of his rural past. For example, he told reporter Howard Thompson, "My father [Uncle Marcus] was a farmer . . . [and] he did have this remarkable adeptness with his hands. Whatever [acting] abilities I may have, crystallized there [for me in a comparable physicality] in high school, when I was trying to prove something to myself—that I could do it, I suppose."[13]

Acting during Dean's Indiana childhood, however, took the direction of most boys in the 1940s—playing cowboys. The Western was *the* entertainment genre of the period, with approximately one of every four Hollywood films having a sagebrush storyline. Moreover, since this was the heyday of B-Westerns and Saturday matinees, it could be argued that children's programming was geared even more toward cowboy country. Radio, the sole source of home entertainment for most Americans in the 1940s, had its fair share of Westerns, too. They included such favorites as *The Lone Ranger*, *The Roy Rogers Program*, *Death Valley Days*, and *The Sheriff*. (Ortense and Marcus did not purchase a television until 1952, the first year Dean started to regularly appear on the small screen.)

46

James Dean as a contemporary cowboy in Giant *(1956).*

Some time prior to his mother's 1940 death, James had become interested in the legendary outlaw Billy the Kid. As he became a student of this dime novel example of an antihero, several factors probably fueled this fascination. First, there was simply a plethora of B-Westerns dealing with the outlaw. Between 1938 and 1949 (the year Dean graduated from high school), there were twenty-six such matinee movies, starting with the Roy Rogers picture *Billy the Kid Returns* (1938).[14] In fact, most of these films were produced for a popular Billy the Kid B-Western series that ran from 1940 to 1943. Initially, the films starred Bob Steele, but Buster Crabbe assumed the title role in late 1941. Due to this high visibility, Metro-Goldwyn-Mayer would make the 1941 A-Western *Billy the Kid*, with major star Robert Taylor. This popular success was a big-budget, romanticized, Technicolor production.

Second, Dean's interest in this Western outlaw is also tied to his beloved mother, beginning with the odd coincidence that both individuals shared the same death day (July 14). One is also tempted to assume that the boy would have been attracted to a legendary fact that was emphasized in 1930s cinema: "Billy shot his first victim because of an insult to his mother."[15] Third, most period pictures emphasized the cowboy's misunderstood nature, surely a selling point for the young James. Fourth, one could add an Indiana factor. Billy the Kid spent several of his formative years, in the 1860s, living in and around Indianapolis.[16] Then, flash forward to an unusual B-Western fact: an inordinately large number of cowboy stars during Dean's Hoosier youth were also from Indiana—Buck Jones (Vincennes), brothers Ken and Kermit Maynard (Vevay), Allan "Rocky" Lane (Mishawaka), and "Tex" Terry (Terre Haute). Strangely enough, Terry's wife later briefly acted as an unofficial agent for Dean at the California beginnings of his career.

Regardless, the fundamental appeal of Billy the Kid, or the B-Western in general (whether one is eight or eighty), is that the genre represents an American fairy tale. For the better part of an hour, the disillusionment of modern life's compromises can be shelved in favor of old-fashioned action. In psychologist Frederick Elkin's study of why B-Westerns once so appealed to children, he especially keys in upon the frustrations inherent to youth: "The child, of necessity, cannot freely express his impulses. . . . This being the case, it is psychologically satisfying for the child to have outlets for the blocked energies and impulses, and one outlet is the expression of aggression. Such aggression appears in the Western. . . . In this way, the Western relieves a child's tensions."[17] Given the early disappointments of Dean's life, which precipitated his move to Indiana, the youngster would seem to qualify as a poster child for Elkin's study.

Dean so embraced the cowboy milieu that it colored many of the actions of his too-brief adulthood. For example, one of his first Hollywood purchases after he signed with Warner Brothers was a horse. The actor's mount was a thoroughbred palomino he named after a pop-culture cowboy, the Cisco Kid. (The horse was boarded at a Santa Barbara stable.) Dean had enjoyed riding since his Hoosier childhood. Indeed, riding was synonymous with

Ortense and Marcus's farm; a neighborhood boy loaned the family a pony when James first came back to Indiana.[18] Even before his Hollywood success, when he was struggling to find West Coast film work, the actor had a friend tutoring him in riding and roping: "Jimmy felt that the skills would increase his chances of being hired for Western films."[19] Plus, part of the later attraction to joining the cast of *Giant* (1956) was to star in a contemporary Western shot on location in Texas. And the unrealized project at the time of Dean's death that he had most looked forward to doing was a biography film of Billy the Kid. The picture was eventually made as *The Left-Handed Gun* (1958, with Paul Newman in the title role). The importance that Dean had placed on orchestrating every nuance of this film biography is demonstrated by his desire to also direct the movie. Consequently, it should come as no surprise that as a little boy not only did he passionately play cowboys, but he also enjoyed acting out Western skits for Ortense, Marcus, and Joan. The youngster would often couple these family living room cowboy routines with his patented gift for mimicry. At this point he focused on imitating his family. According to Ortense, her "son" had an amazing skill along these lines: "If Grandpa Dean set with his legs crossed, Jimmy crossed his. If Grandpa stretched his legs out, Jimmy did, too. It was more than just mocking Grandpa's gestures. Jimmy seemed able to be another person. . . . His gift for make-believe had us helpless with laughter one moment and gripped the next moment by a sudden change of mood."[20]

The boy's playfulness was probably further stoked by the 1944 birth of Ortense and Marcus's son, Marcus Jr., when Dean was thirteen. Close family friend and neighbor Evelyn Washburn Nielsen remembered, "In spite of the difference in their ages, Jim and Markie, as he was called, grew remarkably close. Jim had a great fondness for children."[21] As Dean's mother had mentored him, James counseled Markie. Even when Dean was an aspiring New York actor, Markie would send him his drawings, and the young actor affectionately critiqued them. One such Dean letter seemed to very much reflect the Quaker upbringing he had received from Ortense and Marcus. During the Korean War Markie sent his "brother" some battle drawings. A grown Marcus Jr. later paraphrased Dean's words: "It's easy to draw pictures of soldiers and people shooting guns. . . . But he said I shouldn't draw these things because they aren't good to draw. He told me that I live in a land that God has blessed with trees and rivers and the ocean and all the animals. . . . He said these are the things to draw and all I have to do is look around to see."[22]

Even when Dean later became a bit jaded by success, he always made time for the children of friends. This was probably a legacy of both Markie and the actor's favorite book, *The Little Prince*, which gently preached that adults need the guidance of children.[23]

Despite the haven young Dean found in Fairmount, he could still have his moody days. He once told Ortense he talked to the trees. Upon probing by his aunt, the boy confessed he was really talking to his deceased mother. Still, the love and distractions on the farm were limitless. Moreover, the boy loved to play the huckster, too. He might impersonate the tragic orphan for added attention, or just act out in general, to see what would happen. Dean later encapsuled this tendency for a teacher with the axiom, "It's better to be noticed than ignored."[24] Interestingly enough, fifty-plus years later this credo would seem to have inspired the most memorable line in the entertaining 1989 dark comedy *Heathers*: "The extreme always seems to make an impression."[25] Fittingly, it is uttered by a talented young actor, Christian Slater, then being heralded as the next James Dean. (In the picture Slater's character is referred to as "J. D.") While Slater's career did not live up to the billing (Slater was actually more of a young Jack Nicholson), no one else has, either. Regardless, Dean the actor would often use provocative real-life behavior as sort of a performance exercise, to learn from how people might respond to a given stimuli.

One could argue, however, that Dean's occasional moodiness or bouts of obstinacy as a youngster were neither angst nor acting, but rather an outgrowth of being spoiled by Ortense and Marcus. No gifts from the couple were more appreciated by Dean than those with wheels. An early, much cherished bicycle got his attention, but nothing matched the motorcycle he received at fifteen. And "Deanie," who now went by the moniker of "Deaner," began his love affair with speed, but this was a relative term at the time. As his cousin and frequent passenger Marcus later told me: "The bike probably did not go over fifty, though everyone commented on how noisy it was, like a bumblebee."[26] Years later, Dean's friend and *Eden* costar, Julie Harris, described the actor as a Huckleberry Finn type. But her charming embellishment of that designation, in the documentary *James Dean and Me* (1995), is just as applicable to the teenage Hoosier: "I always looked at Jimmy like he was Huck Finn. He always had a scam going somewhere or an adventure he was looking for. He was full of excitement. And he wanted people to get riled up. He enjoyed that."[27]

The James Dean as Huck Finn analogy works on two additional levels. First, going beyond Ernest Hemingway's famous pronouncement that "all modern American literature comes from one book by Mark Twain called Huckleberry Finn," the novel is essentially about an antihero doubling as the conscience of the country.[28] More to the point, Finn is generally acknowledged to be the spiritual blueprint for Holden Caulfield in *Catcher in the Rye* (1951), the phony-buster who anticipated the appeal of Dean's characters in *Eden* and *Rebel Without a*

Dean and Julie Harris in East of Eden *(1955).*

Cause (1955). Second, like the fictional Huck, Dean also had an absentee father. The difference, however, was that Finn had an affectionate but dictatorial surrogate mother, Widow Douglas, while Dean's aunt and uncle were loving facilitators.

For a child such as James, forever interested in learning and/or trying new things, life can often be reduced to a series of mentors. After Ortense and Marcus, a pivotal early guru for Dean was his drama instructor, Adeline Nall. She would also be his high school teacher in Spanish and speech, with him triumphing in the latter subject but nearly failing the former. However, her association with the youngster predated his high school years. Both had come to Fairmount at the same time (1940); the boy's first teacher (India Nose) was a close friend of Nall. Thus, besides hearing about the boy from Nose, Nall remembered seeing Dean, as an attentive elementary student, attending each semester's play dress rehearsals at the high school. When his aunt encouraged his thespian tendencies in middle school, by way of a Woman's Christian Temperance Union reading, Nall helped coach Dean.

Besides her nurturing nature, Nall was similar to Ortense and Marcus in a key way—she was flexibly casual in her teaching. Nall never played the martinet. In fact, "Her supervisors thought she didn't enforce enough discipline in her classroom . . . but her students and their parents adored her."[29] Throughout Dean's career, from high school to Hollywood, he did his best work when the actor-director relationship was collaborative, instead of dictatorial. Thus, it was very difficult for him to work on *Giant*, with an old-fashioned, by-the-book George Stevens behind the camera. Of course, the tension on that film was further acerbated by the fact that the actor had just come from two consecutive independent film-like productions, where the directors (Elia Kazan on *Eden* and Nicholas Ray on *Rebel*) constantly considered Dean's input.

Even in collaborative situations, however, Dean could be a handful. Indeed, Ortense had involved him in that watershed temperance union reading because the boy was prone to irrational moments of anger. She decided that his "passion should be used to better effect, and she brought Jimmy along with her [to temperance meetings], where he would participate in their drama competition and even deliver impassioned diatribes against the evils of drinking."[30] This was also the catalyst for his early creative writing, since he would often author his own provocative material—what he called "gory odes."[31] There is also a direct link between these over-the-top "gory odes" and the greatest joint venture between Dean and drama instructor Nall: a state championship in oratory. In the spring of his senior year (1949), Dean entered the Indiana National Forensic League competition. With Nall as his coach, Dean performed "The Madman," a story within Charles Dickens's *Pickwick Papers*. Originally titled "A Madman's Manuscript," the tale reads more like Edgar Allan Poe. The opening, which Dean enjoyed prefacing with a shocking scream, is as follows: "Yes!—a madman's [manuscript]! How that word would have struck to my heart, many years ago! How it would have roused the terror that used to come upon me sometimes; sending the blood hissing and tingling through my veins, 'til the cold dew of fear stood in large drops upon my skin, and my knees knocked together with fright! I like it now though. It's a fine name."[32]

Dean's bravado performance seems to have bordered upon what is now called scenery-chewing excess, as his raving delivery was coupled with a twisted body language that culminated in his physical collapse on the stage. The future Method actor was seemingly already flirting with that approach. His selection of the piece might have been influenced by a comic national news story involving "A Madman's Manuscript." In the late 1930s this excerpt from the *Pickwick Papers* "achieved fresh notoriety when an American bride applied for annulment of her marriage because her husband had forced her to read it on her honeymoon. 'It'll frizzle anybody's hair,' said her lawyer."[33]

Nall's main challenge in prepping Dean for the presentation of this "frizzle" factor was to make sure he was understood, no matter how outrageous his performance. She was less successful in getting him to either dress up for the competition or to shorten the piece, which ran over the ten-minute limit. Dean's argument against a dress code was imbued with a certain comic logic, "How the heck can I go crazy in a suit and tie? It wouldn't work."[34] The question of length later came back to haunt him. But at the state competition Dean's madman was a triumph, or as he later described it, "I came on stage screaming and tearing at my clothes. [I] Really woke those old judges up."[35] (Nall later suggested that Dean had embellished the extravagance of his opening, which was "foreign" to her training.[36]) Regardless, his grueling victory, which necessitated being a madman in three rounds over two days, qualified him for the nationals, to be held in Longmont, Colorado. In a small town such as Fairmount (approximately three thousand people), this significant accomplishment was an even bigger front-page story.[37] This level of hometown support for the chronically insecure youngster is rarely ever factored into the Dean story.

Winning a first in dramatic speaking was an especially sweet victory for James, whose intensity during an earlier high school run-through of the monologue had gotten him in trouble. A fellow student and class-clown type, David Fox, had attempted to disrupt Dean's performance. Upset by these comic antics, and maybe fueled by some budding Method "madness" related to his Dickens performance piece, Dean started a fight with his critic. This is not good behavior, especially when one's high school mascots are the Fairmount Quakers! The result was a two-day suspension from school and what was worse—being kept out of a high school basketball game against Sweetser. Consequently, to come back and win the state title was gratifying, and given Dean's devilish nature, probably justified his artistic temperament.

Consistent with the Hoosier haven theme of this chapter, the forthcoming trip to nationals generated more front-page coverage, with the most affectionate of headlines, "Good Luck At Longmont—Jim."[38] In a large metropolitan setting his accomplishment would have been buried somewhere in a back-section, school-news part of the newspaper. The *Fairmount News* front-page focus was not just the work of a sympathetic local editor. It was generated by a populist scene reminiscent of Gary Cooper's rousing small-town send-off in director Frank Capra's *Mr. Deeds Goes to Town* (1936). Dean was given the most memorable of good luck adieus. Organized by his high school principal, Mr. DuBois, these hometown festivities included everything from cheerleaders to the school's marching band. While the actor's later screen persona was a study in angst, on this day (April 27, 1949) the private Dean was a populist, too. He told an unnamed local reporter that he would "do his best to show his appreciation to Fairmount citizens, by speaking well."[39] One should add, moreover, that Dean's own poetic definition of acting was pure populism, "behavior of and for other people."[40]

The compassionate show of support for James' Colorado trip reduced him to happy tears. When he and Nall then left by train from nearby Marion, it was in sharp contrast to the grief-stricken child who had arrived at that same depot just nine years before. At that time, accompanying the coffin of his mother back to Indiana, he felt totally abandoned. Now he was leaving with the cheers of a whole community behind him. Paradoxically, even part of this new rail journey would backtrack the sad route he had followed in 1940. Given both contrasting travel scenarios, and his home community's open display of affection, there were probably additional tears on the train.

3

Finishing the Hoosier Heritage

"But we keep a-comin'. We're the people that live.
They can't wipe us out. They can't lick us. We'll go on forever,
Pa, 'cause we're the people."

MA JOAD'S (JANE DARWELL) CLOSE TO *THE GRAPES OF WRATH*
(1940), ONE OF JAMES DEAN'S FAVORITE FILMS.

AS HIGH SCHOOL SENIOR JAMES DEAN AND HIS DRAMA
teacher, Adeline Nall, headed west from Indiana to
Colorado for the National Forensic League competition,
she had time to reflect on their history. While she had
been providing him with acting tips since he was in middle school, Nall was most moved by a gift from Dean during his junior year. Nall's students had given her orchids
after their first class play. But multitalented Dean wanted
to put a more permanent accent on his classmates' thank
you, so he gave her his drawing of an orchid.

Though best known, even as a youngster, for his dramatic skills, Dean had more recently surprised Nall with
his comic skills. He had played both the eccentric Russian
character Boris Kolenkhov in *You Can't Take It with You*
and Frankenstein in a parody production titled *Goon with
the Wind*. Years later, when Nall reflected upon the secret
of James' success at the state level of the Forensic League

competition, performing the Charles Dickens piece, "The Madman," she focused on both his passion and his eyes: "Jimmy, as in anything he did, put in his whole heart; he had wonderful use of his eyes. I think his eyes were one of the most effective things that made an impression on the teachers [judges] at the meet."[1] One of the first-round Indiana judges, Frieda Bedwell of Terre Haute, seconded Nall's comments about his eyes, "I was deeply moved [by Dean]. I was especially impressed with the eerie expression in his eyes. They actually looked glassy and mad at times."[2]

If the Forensic League trip had been a Hollywood movie, Dean and those eyes would have won the competition, hands down. Though this was not to be the case, he finished a respectable sixth at the nationals. Unfortunately, a negative James trait surfaced when he did not make the finals, presumably because his sketch had run long. A warning about this had first surfaced during the Indiana competition, and Nall had persistently tried to shorten the sketch, but Dean kept stonewalling about any abridgement. Ironically, he blamed her for not being more forceful about cutting the piece. Dean then sulked most of the way back to Fairmount. The actor neither responded well to criticism nor accepted responsibility for defeat. These tendencies would only escalate in his more high-profile future. It was a description which would also be equally applicable to any number of Dean's later friendships and/or affiliations: "We [Nall and Dean] used to squabble when he was my student. We'd always get back together somehow. Once, he offered me a cigarette in class just to be smart. I almost popped him. He was just that kind of a maverick kid."[3] Interestingly enough, much later Nall added another possible factor as to why he did not win the national competition. James had been "goofing off" instead of rehearsing the night before his last presentation, which she felt was a "crucial lesson" that contributed to the depth of concentration Dean later became famous for.[4]

Despite the national recognition his performing skills gave him in the spring of 1949, Dean had already achieved a certain degree of Indiana sports fame earlier in the year by his exploits on the basketball court. Hoosier hoops, which have their own national noteworthiness, found a driven participant in James. Though Fairmount had lost four out of five starters from the previous year, Dean was largely responsible for two upset victories in the sectional tournament over Van Buren and Mississinewa. Then he nearly orchestrated another underdog triumph against the perennial power and aptly named Marion Giants. Indiana historian and academician Earl L. Conn later wrote: "Fairmount lost 40–34. But this was Jimmy's game. He scored fifteen points, high for both teams. His aggressiveness on defense was a thorn in the side of the Marion team all night long."[5] Marion sports writer Bob

Fairmount basketball star James Dean.

Lee credited James with getting Fairmount to the finals: "He was a pretty fair driver and, of course, was spectacular . . . with his long shots."[6]

Not surprisingly, Dean was the leading scorer for this three-game sectional tournament and frequently was singled out for his defense. For example, Mississinewa star Jack Colescott recalled, "He could knock the eyes out of the basket and he was a good defensive man. . . . [He was all about] hard work and determination."[7] Dean's teammate and close friend, Jim Fulkerson, reinforced Colescott's comments, as he later remembered: "Jimmy was a very determined young fellow. He might not have been the best player in the world, but he was determined to be good and he was. We always felt Jimmy would be tops in whatever he tried and would succeed because he was so determined to excel."[8]

Fairmount basketball coach Paul Weaver's ultimate take on James, whom he called "a clean-cut All-American type boy," was not unlike that of the boy's drama instructor, Nall: "Jimmy was a hard worker and I never felt as though I had to push him to practice. He might not always have been the most thoughtful and considerate person he could have been, but then how many boys are? I felt sometimes that he had an inferiority complex that he was covering up . . . [but] he was a pretty fair athlete."[9] Like Nall, Weaver had to be overly careful with any constructive criticism of the sensitive Dean.

Dean was also a respectable athlete in other sports. The summer before his senior year, he played third base and batted .333 for the local American Legion junior baseball team. This is an excellent average, especially given that Legion squads are essentially composed of area all-stars. And at the sectional track meet his senior year, he tied for third in the pole vault, with a then-respectable height of ten feet, three inches. But as the myth of James Dean has grown, so have his alleged athletic accomplishments, from setting a county pole-vaulting record to being an all-state player in his favorite sport, basketball. The facts do not bear this out.[10] If truth be told, he was often a relatively average athlete who occasionally pushed his slight five-foot-eight, one hundred-thirty-five-pound frame to above-average accomplishments.

Inflated high school "glory days," however, are pretty standard stuff, whether one is famous or not. A more disturbing tendency in the Dean literature is the frequency with which Indiana is called to task for somehow being a cultural wasteland. Ironically, this was partly spawned by James himself. As Dean biographer David Dalton observed, with comic insight, consummate actor "Jimmy mined and undermined his own history; the material for his star would be made out of the plasma of that past."[11] A neglected tragedy of the actor's early death, beyond the many unrealized parts (both professional and private), was that he left during that awkward, even ugly, first flush of fame.

High school baseball player Dean (front row, center).

Like his Jett Rink character in *Giant* after he struck oil, movie star Dean did not always wear his new status gracefully. For example, when a reporter later asked about his Charles Dickens performance piece from high school, James simply characterized drama coach Nall as a "frustrated actress."[12] As Dean biographer Val Holley noted, by the time of his last trip home, the actor's "new policy of forgetting his old friends carried over to Fairmount."[13]

The key point to keep in mind here is, however, that Dean kept coming home. Maybe, as Dean profiler Alice Packard has suggested, by now there were "two personalities that were Jimmy Dean. The first, the farm boy who had never grown completely away from home . . . [and the actor] outside it [life], evaluating it, trying to see how it would help him understand and portray some role that might lie ahead."[14] All this "evaluating" made for a gifted performer, but an often moody or challenging companion.

But before focusing on his post-Fairmount days, one more early Dean mentor must be addressed—Reverend James DeWeerd. Paradoxically, Dean's close relationship with DeWeerd is sometimes used as further proof of the boy's rejection of an allegedly provincial Indiana. DeWeerd was the worldliest person James had ever met. While the Wesleyan minister had grown up in the Fairmount area, he came home from World War II a hero. As an army chaplain close to the fighting in the St. Lo region of France, DeWeerd was critically wounded while rescuing several soldiers under fire.[15] For his bravery and sacrifice, he was awarded a Silver Star and a Purple Heart. After the war, DeWeerd returned to his Indiana ministry, yet found time to travel extensively as an evangelist in the United States and Mexico. He was following the path of his father, Reverend Fred DeWeerd, who had been a nationally known evangelist earlier in the century.

James DeWeerd was also a well-read, charismatic personality whose gift for public speaking made him an actor, of sorts, in Dean's eyes. While the minister's war adventures attracted hero worship from Fairmount teenagers, including Dean, the boy was further motivated by DeWeerd's interest in the arts, from poetry and classical music to the pageantry and bravery of bullfighting. Indeed, Dean became hooked on the sport after the minister showed him a home movie of an actual Mexican bullfight that he had attended. Moreover, DeWeerd further fueled Dean's fascination with racing by both taking him to an Indianapolis 500 race and encouraging James' circle of friends to make their own motorcycle dirt track near a favorite local garage owned by Marvin Carter.

It is easy to see the allure of DeWeerd. Between his World War II exploits and the bullfighting, the handsome, heavyset minister comes off as Hemingwayesque. In fact, DeWeerd even aped one of Hemingway's traits of macho bravado—a proclivity to show off his battle scars! For someone such as Dean, whose paternal grandmother said his many interests had given him the nickname "Quiz Kid," DeWeerd must have been a revelation.[16]

The minister's greatest gift to Dean, however, was some peace of mind. Between DeWeerd's religious calling and his zeal for living, the reverend had created an atmosphere in which the boy felt comfortable confessing some lingering anxieties he had about his mother's death. Like many people who have lost a loved one as a child, at times Dean somehow feared that he had been responsible. Intellectually he knew this was not true, but fear is hardly the most rational of subjects. Given DeWeerd's no-nonsense directness and his awareness of the boy's philosophical tendencies, the minister attacked Dean's anxieties with a line of reasoning more cerebral than sectarian: "I taught Jimmy to believe, as I do, that death is merely a control of mind over matter."[17]

This bit of intellectualism seems to have put the youngster in a comfort zone. In fact, just hanging out at DeWeerd's home relaxed the tightly wired Dean. For example, the minister later observed, "Jimmy was usually happiest stretched out on my library floor reading Shakespeare or other books of his choosing. He loved good music playing in the background—Tchaikovsky was his favorite."[18] Thus, DeWeerd "preached" the eternal solace of art to a boy who was introspective by nature. Dean's meditative nature brings to mind an observation by author Ann Patchett on the nature of writing: It "is a job, a talent, but it's also the place to go in your head. It is the imaginary friend you drink your tea with in the afternoon."[19]

In a better world, this would be the close of the DeWeerd chapter of Dean's life—hometown mentor helps sensitive youth to succeed. This is a special story but not a unique one, because most people have had some sort of populist sage in their youth. Indeed, there are often several, just as young Dean had Nall and DeWeerd, as well as his aunt and uncle. However, the first misuse of DeWeerd in the Dean literature is the general suggestion that one cannot be both sophisticated and from a small town. DeWeerd's worldliness somehow makes him a Fairmount "outsider." (One text simplifies the phenomenon by mistakenly making him originally a geographical "outsider," too.[20]) Sinclair Lewis's *Babbitt* and *Main Street* notwithstanding, American pop culture is just as likely to celebrate the small town/rural milieu, á la Jeffersonian democracy. In the largely Quaker community of Fairmount, education received respect, a fact enhanced by Earlham College, a Quaker institution located in Richmond, Indiana. Founded in 1847, this coeducational college has long accented the liberal in liberal arts. To illustrate the breadth of this phenomenon, Dean's surrogate father, Marcus Winslow, was a farmer with a college degree from Earlham.

A second more disturbing misuse of DeWeerd is to make him a sexual predator to Dean. One biographer, Joe Hyams, claims the minister told him that he had a sexual relationship with the boy.[21] But the story is full of holes. The best rebuttal comes from Dean biographer Val Holley, author of the most in-depth examination of the actor's life. At the time of DeWeerd's alleged confession, he was the pastor at Indianapolis's celebrated Cadle Tabernacle and a prominent speaker on national radio and local television. Holley asks why a minister would confess this to a stranger. "It strains credibility to imagine

71

that DeWeerd would jeopardize his career at its height and risk vigilante reprisals were such revelations to leak out and become public. Hyams did not substantiate the story," Holley wrote.[22]

Other research discrepancies weaken Hyams's claim. First, while he had written extensively on Dean, both before and after DeWeerd's 1972 death, he does not drop the sexual bombshell until his 1992 biography of the actor. Why does he only then, two decades after the minister's death, suddenly remember this conversation? Second, Holley also documents Hyams' sloppy DeWeerd-related research in an early *Redbook* profile of Dean.[23] Consistent with these mistakes, which are not corrected in Hyams' subsequent Dean writings, is his later less-than-credible status as a *National Enquirer* writer.[24] Not surprisingly, Dean's cousin, Marcus Winslow Jr., later expressed disappointment about Hyams' claims. But being a populist sort, Winslow magnanimously added, "I think Joe got backed in a corner by his publisher. His book needed help [something provocative]."[25]

Thankfully, most biographies of the actor have recognized the thinness of Hyams's claim and ignored it. But naturally, some Dean books, such as Paul Alexander's *Boulevard of Broken Dreams*, have attempted to capitalize on the sensationalism factor, and even embellished it with misleading statements. For example, Alexander quotes a former Fairmount High School student, several years younger than the actor: "There was something funny about James DeWeerd and homosexuality. He sounds gay to me. He was a small-town hick. . . . I have a funny feeling that he had sex with them [Dean and his classmates]."[26] Alexander made the DeWeerd home sound like sex central. Yet he neglected to note that this minister and esteemed community leader served on the school board and lived with his mother, Lelia DeWeerd, a schoolteacher.

Of course, one catalyst for the continued interest in this topic, beyond basic tawdriness, is that Dean eventually proved to have bisexual tendencies. If truth be told, he seemed to have been a heterosexual who also wanted to explore new experiences, both for his art and himself. (His breakout role in the 1954 Broadway play *The Immoralist* was that of a seductive homosexual houseboy. This part led to his star-making turn in *East of Eden*.) His later close California friend, sometime roommate, and eventual biographer William Bast described Dean's curious approach to sexuality: "Jimmy was a dabbler in life. I am positive he tried homosexual activity. But it was all part of a learning experience for him as an actor and as a human being."[27]

Beyond any "learning" slant to his bisexuality, Dean had always enjoyed going against the traditional norm. Flirting with homosexuality in the 1950s had the ability to shock. But besides being provocative, Dean believed that such shock tactics revealed basic truths.

The actor's iconoclastic tendencies, as applied to every subject under the sun, were later replicated in the short but memorable life of Dean disciple Janis Joplin. Singer Rosanne Cash's description of this rock and roll legend could be equally applied to Dean: "an unshakable commitment to her own truth, no matter how destructive, how weird or how bad. Nothing else seemed to matter."[28] In both cases, their swinging-for-the-fences philosophy led to a premature exit from life. Yet one could argue that without that intensity, they would never have otherwise been noticed. To recycle an axiom Dean's *Rebel Without a Cause* director Nicholas Ray sometimes borrowed from his earlier film, *Knock on Any Door* (1949), "Live fast, die young and have a good-looking corpse."

This link to Joplin also reminds one of Dean's broader legacies as a precursor to the counterculture 1960s. The actor's antiheroic tendencies have resulted in some commentators calling him the "first hippie."[29] Several rock stars, from the Beatles to Bob Dylan, have suggested this then-new development in music had Dean as a catalyst. For example, John Lennon once noted, "I suppose you could say that without Jimmy Dean, The Beatles would never have existed."[30] Moreover, as one biographer has suggested, just the name James Dean has become a metaphor for rock music, such as in David Essex's rock anthem, "Rock On," with the lyrics "prettiest girl I've ever seen, see her shake on the movie screen, Jimmy Dean—James Dean."[31]

While Dean's bisexual experimentation (another tendency followed by Joplin) will be addressed at greater
length later in the text, suffice it to say that it is highly
unlikely that he explored this path during his high school
years, either with DeWeerd or anyone else. Still, some
Dean biographers insist on trying to make a connection,
however ludicrous. For example, one profiler suggested
that if DeWeerd had not introduced the actor to sex, possibly James' touching of the minister's war wounds had
led to latent homosexual tendencies in the young man.[32]
Another Dean biographer has suggested that the actor
exhibited homosexual tendencies in high school by way of
simply not dating extensively.[33] Yet the fact remains that
Dean did date, despite two mitigating factors. First, there
was the basic matter of time. Dean played three sports,
joined practically every school club on the books, had
major parts in all the plays, did chores on the farm,
obsessed even then about his motorcycle (both riding it
and rebuilding the engine), and fed his fascination with
books. Second, and probably more significantly, for all of
Dean's now-celebrated androgynous beauty, he was
hardly anybody's prize as a teenager. Add to this that he
was barely five feet, eight inches tall, weighed a mere one
hundred and thirty-five pounds, and was so nearsighted
that his spectacles had lenses as thick as shot glasses. As
further evidence of this less-than-romantic presence, a
coed friend at the time affectionately kidded, "When

Jimmy peers at me through those heavy glasses, I feel like a mouse with a hoot owl in pursuit."[34]

As Dean finished his senior year of high school, he made peace with drama coach Nall over losing at the National Forensic League finals. In a *Fairmount News* front-page story, the two jointly "expressed their deep appreciation to the kind townspeople and school board members who made their trip possible."[35] Dean became even more of a local celebrity with additional perform-ances of "The Madman," including a "highly applauded" turn at a Lions Club Meeting that again landed him on page one.[36] Nall also paid further tribute to her prize stu-dent: "Certainly great credit is given to Jim for interesting Fairmount students and citizens in speech as an impor-tant part of the school program."[37]

Consistent with such praise, he was "awarded the school's top athlete medal for his last year in high school, at which time he was also given the art department medal."[38] No doubt feeling magnanimous over all this recognition, Dean even comically forgave the boy who provoked a fight with him on "The Madman" monologue. The Fairmount High School yearbook had a regular sec-tion entitled "Footsteps on the Sands of Time," in which each senior bequeathed something, often in a tongue-in-cheek nature, to an underclassman. For James, this meant leaving his "short temper to David Fox."[39] The yearbook's take on Dean, which ran under his senior

A less-than-cool Dean, the pre-Hollywood youngster.

picture, accented his entertainingly athletic nature: "Jim is our regular basketball guy, and when you're around him—time will fly."[40] Once again, this was not remotely close to the picture of a tormented youth that is so often painted about Dean's formative years in Indiana. As Marcus Winslow later observed: "Jimmy Dean was just like any other kid who grew up in this town. He played basketball, he went to Sunday meeting at Back Creek Quaker Church and he did his chores on the farm. He used to tag around after me opening gates so I wouldn't have to get off the tractor. And he loved to ride that little black [motor]cycle. . . . But Hollywood and the rest of the world refuse to believe any of that. So we've just about quit saying it."[41]

Of course, some Hollywood insiders did know the relatively normal, but less dramatic, real Dean story. For example, the actor's close friend and *Rebel* costar, Natalie Wood, later vividly recalled the actor's take on the subject: "'I had a happy childhood,' Jimmy would tell you. . . . [An Indiana farm] was a fine place to grow up, to go to school. Although Jimmy never had any aspirations for farming, the only rebelling he ever did was to skip cleaning the chicken coop once in a while."[42] Wood was also on hand to witness an example of Fairmount's continuing support of its hometown hero. During the *Rebel* production, Dean received a scroll signed by his first three thousand fans—friends and neighbors from the Fairmount area.

The actor later related to Wood, "I was just sitting and thinking how nice it was for those three thousand people to sign the scroll, to tell me they liked my acting."[43]

One cannot help thinking that the moxie Dean showed in leaving his Hoosier haven for college in California (the site of so many painful memories), and hopefully an acting career, was born of the nonstop support he had received in Fairmount. Long before Dean was famous, he was the proverbial big fish in a small town. And sometimes that makes all the difference.

4

College in California

"First Jimmy wanted to go to Earlham [College], where Marcus
[Winslow] went, but Marcus pointed out that if he wanted to act,
he'd better go to California."[1]

EMMA WOOLEN DEAN

JAMES DEAN'S EVER-SUPPORTIVE FATHER FIGURE, HIS UNCLE
Marcus, also hoped that a return to California might help
the estranged relationship between the actor and his biological father, Winton Dean. Initially, progress seemed to
have been made. Arrangements were made for the young
man to stay with his Santa Monica-based father while
attending college. Winton even provided a car for his
son's college commute.

Though Dean's initial plan was to go to the University
of California at Los Angeles, he spent his freshman year
at nearby Santa Monica City College, the local two-year
junior college. In addition to being more convenient to
his father's home, it also allowed him to establish
California residency and eventually qualify for cheaper,
minimal, in-state fees. The junior college also gave the
young man a chance to improve his grades. For all the
Fairmount love and support, Dean had not always

applied himself in high school. His favorite and most influential teacher, Adeline Nall, later remembered, "Kids of Jim's age didn't think it was too 'hep' to be good in school."[2] Dean's explanation for his poor grades was more poetic: "Why did God put all these things here for us to be interested in?"[3] Consequently, outside of art and theater, Dean's report cards often had a sprinkling of Ds.

Unfortunately, the father-son experiment, part two, did not go any better than it did during Dean's early childhood. First, Winton found acting to be neither a practical nor an appropriate profession for a young man. He encouraged his son to consider a career in coaching or law. They were not bad suggestions, given James' talent for both athletics and public speaking. The problem was in the dictatorial manner in which the advice was given. To humor his father, who was covering expenses, Dean enrolled in a pre-law program. However, in fairness to Winton, who is sometimes further vilified for seemingly pushing his son toward the alien profession of law, Dean had a certain fascination with the *theatricality* of the courtroom. In fact, "He later said that stories of Clarence Darrow and Earl Rogers, two legendary trial lawyers, had whetted his interest in criminal law."[4]

Second, Dean's attempt at a new relationship with his father was further complicated by Winton's remarriage to Ethel Case in the mid-1940s. The "nervous little woman" who became James' stepmother never connected with him, neither during an earlier visit to Indiana with Winton nor after James came to live with them.[5] Blended families are never an easy arrangement, and since the pivotal father-son relationship had never been close to begin with, ties between Dean and his stepmother were probably jinxed from the start. Moreover, for a young man who had all but deified his deceased mother, resentment toward a stepmother would have been undoubtedly difficult to suppress.

Still, one cannot help pondering how Dean's relationship with his father might have changed had he and his stepmother become friends. Throughout his abbreviated life, Dean had made a habit of generating a wayward-waif wavelength that had attracted an army of surrogate-mother figures. These included special teachers (including Adeline Nall), agents, fellow actors, countless girlfriends, and so on. What happened with Case? Had she resisted the boy's needs, or had he simply not put out any emotional distress signals? Of course, given Winton's stubborn, controlling nature (traits James shared with his father), it is entirely possible that Case simply shrank from any situation that might have displeased her husband.

Despite this return to domestic friction, Dean's SMCC experience was a good one. The school was in a transition period, about to move to a new site. But during Dean's freshman year, the college was temporarily located on the campus of Santa Monica High School.

Both institutions shared classroom and athletic facilities, though some of the college buildings had formerly been World War I barracks and were never intended to still be in use more than thirty years later. Students nicknamed the college "Splinterville."

In addition to bonding over the less-than-ideal physical setting, many SMCC freshmen, including Dean, seemed to feel less threatened by the connection with the high school. Indeed, when one reviews Dean's first-year activities, it is reminiscent of his always overbooked schedule back in Fairmount. He did announcements for the college's FM radio station, made the basketball team, joined several clubs (including a jazz group), and attached himself to any and all theatrical projects. While Dean was honoring his father's request that he take pre-law and physical education classes (á la coaching), he had not turned his back on acting. Fortuitously, he had even found another supportive theater teacher, not unlike Fairmount's Nall. The new drama instructor/mentor was Jean Owen. Fittingly, James first impressed her with a reading seemingly reminiscent of his award-winning turn as a madman under Nall's direction.[6] Owen later recalled, "He was always polite and thoughtful; his enthusiasm for everything that pertained to the theatre was boundless. . . . One day in class Jimmy read some scenes from Edgar Allan Poe's *Telltale Heart*. He was magnificent."[7] Dean's later interest in one day playing Hamlet stemmed from the tutelage of Owen, who encouraged him to become a student of the figure often considered the greatest literary character in Western civilization. But Owen's original push for Dean to work on Shakespeare was to both improve his enunciation and lose his Hoosier accent. Owen remembered, "I told him if anything would clear up fuzzy speech it would be the demanding soliloquies of Shakespeare. And so we began, on a one-on-one basis, what was to be a fascinating and revealing [Hamlet] study for both of us."[8]

By the second week, Owen was amazed at the youngster's "intensity and originality." She noted that Dean had, in "only a dozen [opening] lines . . . established a deeply disturbed young Hamlet who touched my heart. I had seen the play with every great actor in both England and America in the role, and I had never heard those lines expressed quite so well."[9] Dean's nickname, the "Hoosier Hamlet," stems from this period.

After this productive freshman year, with both improved grades and a brief romance with the college's homecoming queen, a more confident Dean felt ready to move on to UCLA. But it was not a popular idea with either his father or Owen. Winton continued his opposition to acting and withdrew his financial support. Despite Owen's belief in Dean's talent, she believed that the academic rigors of UCLA (of which she was a graduate) necessitated that he spend another preparatory year at the junior college. The stubborn Dean, however, had made up his mind. In addition to his longtime interest in attending this prestigious university, which his father had already managed to derail for a year, a further catalyst was the school's strong commitment to theater. This was something James had seen firsthand the previous summer, when his involvement with the Santa Monica Theater Guild had made him aware of both UCLA's performing arts center, Royce Hall, and the ambitious number of theatrical productions staged on campus in a given year.

One person who believed Dean was ready for the academic jump to UCLA was a junior college friend from Owen's drama class, Richard Shannon, a war veteran attending college on the GI Bill. The relationship was yet another example of Dean's ongoing need for a knowledgeable parental mentor. "After school and between classes we used to sit and talk about acting and about life in general," Shannon said. "Jimmy had a tremendous curiosity about everything. It was kind of a father-and-son relationship, with me answering the questions but proud he chose me to be the one he talked with."[10]

Of course, beyond the question of whether Dean was ready or not for UCLA was the real need to leave his father's house. Winton, Case, and Dean all "felt cramped, as Jimmy would later say, 'like cats ready to jump on another's back at any moment.'"[11] Dean was fascinated by felines, perhaps a legacy of being raised on a farm. Regardless, James believed that studying this animal would both help him relax and improve his acting. His elaborate theories about cats were diligently passed on to succeeding generations by Nall. Why belabor this point? Well, besides being an interesting down-home take on acting, it influenced another famous Fairmount High School graduate whose name is now synonymous with felines—cartoonist Jim Davis, creator of the comic strip *Garfield*. What follows is Davis's explanation, as taught to him by Nall, of Dean's captivation with this animal: "to him [Dean] cats were the most relaxed of all animals on the outside. But yet right under the surface they were all energy, all tension, all nervousness. And so he would imitate movements of cats, like blinking. Whereas we blink quickly, cats blink very slowly. And I put a little of that in Garfield."[12]

This description of a cool surface covering an interior that was "all energy, all tension, all nervousness" is equally applicable to Dean, especially when he again found himself with his father. Unlike the encouragement Dean received to verbalize his thoughts back in Fairmount, communication seemed verboten with Winton. One is reminded of a comic observation by Woody Allen, an artist, like Dean, born in the first half of the 1930s: "We didn't open-up in my family; we grew tumors."[13] Dean's take on his father was ultimately one of sad, mystified resignation: "I never understood him. I never understood what he was after, what sort of person he'd been, because he never tried to get on my side of the fence, or to try and see things the way I saw them when I was little."[14]

James' unhappiness with his father and stepmother triggered what became a defining pattern in his lifestyle—late night wandering in whatever city he found himself. The means of movement varied, from walking to traveling by car or motorcycle. In 1950, after his freshman year of college, Dean found a summer job that provided a paid exit from Winton's house, serving as a physical education instructor at a boys' military camp in nearby Glendora, California.

Ironically, while friction remained between James and his father, this summer job undoubtedly pleased Winton because it demonstrated how marketable a physical education background was. Regardless, working at a military camp, although for youngsters, brings up the subject of Dean's draft status during the volatile summer of 1950, when North Korean troops initiated a surprise invasion of South Korea. The commitment of American forces, as part of a United Nations police action, was immediate. While ceasefire negotiations began as early as summer 1951, an actual armistice was not concluded until July 1953. James chose early on not to enter the armed forces and serve in the Korean War.

A handful of Dean biographies court controversy by suggesting he received a deferment by telling his

Fairmount draft board he was a homosexual.[15] This is so much poppycock. At the time of his Indiana registration for the draft (April 1950), there was no Korean crisis and thus no reason for such a dramatic play. President Harry S Truman did not raise draft quotas until that summer. Dean's subsequent deferment once the United States became involved in the Asian conflict hardly needed an exit card attached to homosexuality. Reared as a Quaker, Dean embraced a conscientious-objector philosophy, as previously suggested in this book by way of an anti-gun letter he had written his cousin Marcus Winslow Jr. Moreover, on top of his Quaker status, Dean was so near-sighted that he was all but blind without his thick-lensed glasses. There was no way Dean could have gotten into uniform, even had he wanted to.

In fall 1950 Dean started his sophomore year at UCLA. Though he had saved much of the money from his summer job, he was soon overwhelmed financially and had to juggle part-time work with classes. Paradoxically, the young man whose films would one day be part of college curricula in cinema studies found a job as a student projectionist in classes using movies. Financially tight times also necessitated certain compromises on Dean's part, something he was never very good at. For example, to keep the lines of communication open with his father, he continued with his pre-law major, but now added a theater arts minor. More problematically, he joined a fraternity, Sigma Nu. James only lasted a semester in the fraternity, and the most diplomatic assessment, although elitist, came from fellow pledge and future novelist Jim Bellah, the son of writer James Warner Bellah: "He was too eccentric. Mind you, I found him amusing. You never knew what he was going to do next. He was a born performer; he loved to take the stage. But Sigma Nu was establishment, and Dean was not establishment. He was just undesirable."[16]

Given this snobbery, is it any wonder that the more succinct story of why Dean washed out of Sigma Nu was that he struck a fraternity member who had suggested that being a theater arts student was less than manly? For all the angst-ridden indecisiveness of his future film persona, the real Dean had moments of populist aggression. One is reminded of Gary Cooper punching out the elitist poets in Frank Capra's *Mr. Deeds Goes to Town* (1936) or Jimmy Stewart doing the same to some aristocratic reporters in Capra's *Mr. Smith Goes to Washington* (1939). And of course, Dean's fraternity fight brings to mind a similar incident during his senior year of high school. When a student had attempted to disrupt his theater competition piece, Dean had hit him, too.

Fittingly, Dean was a major fan of two-fisted Gary Cooper, Capra's stereotypical hero. The admiration was later reciprocated by Cooper, which was not the norm for establishment Hollywood of the early 1950s. When James

Gary Cooper (right) and Frank Capra on the set of
Mr. Deeds Goes to Town *(1936, with Jean Arthur).*

died, Cooper's comments were easily the most magnanimous of any Hollywood insider: "[Dean's] death caused a
loss in the movie world that our industry could ill afford.
Had he lived long enough, I feel he would have made
some incredible films. He had sensitivity and a capacity to
express emotion."[17] The encyclopedic Dean expert
Randall Riese has documented a number of parallels
between the two actors, from a shared background in art
to being less than articulate verbally. Riese was most
provocatively insightful, however, when he noted how
both Cooper and Dean "used the same technique with
women": "Director Howard Hawks once said about
Cooper, 'If I ever saw him with a good-looking girl and he
was kind of dragging his feet over the ground and being
very shy and looking down, I'd say, 'Oh-oh, the snake's
gonna strike again.' He found that the little bashful boy
approach was very successful.' Hawks could just as easily
have been talking about Dean."[18]

Dean's friend and costar from *Giant*, Oscar-winning
actress Mercedes McCambridge, entertainingly documents the actor's fascination with all things Cooper by
way of a lengthy anecdote in her autobiography.
McCambridge and Cooper were friends, and he gave her
one of his authentic Texas cowboy hats when she signed
to appear in *Giant*. This was a memorable gesture, since
at this point in American film no actor was more synonymous with the Western than Cooper, who had recently

Mercedes McCambridge in character for Giant *(1956).*

won a Best Actor Academy Award for the classic sagebrush saga *High Noon* (1952). Consequently, when one
combined Dean's admiration for both Cooper and the
cowboy genre in general, McCambridge comically chronicles how Dean lusted after Cooper's hat: "Before either

of us was officially on film in *Giant*, Jimmy tried several times to steal my Stetson hat. He knew that if he switched my hat with his hat and was photographed wearing it, *I* couldn't be photographed wearing it! [This Cooper gift] was the perfect Texas hat! I had to watch it like a hawk until after the first scene in which I wore it, making it forever identified as *my hat*! Jimmy Dean wanted that hat. Jimmy Dean didn't get it!"[19]

Though the "heady" world of Hollywood movies and Cooper hats was still several years away for UCLA sophomore Dean, it is not too early to reveal a "secret truth" about him. In David Halberstam's moving biography of Boston Red Sox teammates Ted Williams, Dom DiMaggio, Bobby Doerr, and Johnny Pesky, he suggests that lives, especially memorable lives, are driven by "secret truths." For example, with Williams, arguably baseball's greatest hitter, the "secret truth" was "he needed to be great in order to escape from that terrible home . . . [with] an alcoholic father and a religiously strident mother."[20]

If there was a "secret truth" for Dean it was his need to be great in order to fulfill the high expectations his mother had given him as a child. All the gentle nurturing he had received since that time, from surrogate parents Marcus and Ortense Winslow to supportive drama instructor Nall, had simply reinforced that need to succeed. It is only with Dean's move to UCLA that one starts to see behavioral changes noted by friends and acquaintances. His SMCC friend Larry Swindell, who later found fame as a biographer, believed that "Jim changed after . . . [leaving the junior college]. His wanting to climb [socially, artistically] became more obvious at UCLA."[21] Swindell saw this firsthand, since his transfer to UCLA paralleled James'.

Along related lines, Dean's close UCLA friend and post-fraternity roommate, William Bast, found the aspiring actor very expansive about an almost mystical (presumably mother-connected) force driving him toward greatness. "Have you ever had the feeling that it's not in your hands?" Bast quotes Dean as asking. "I mean, do you ever just know you've got something to do and you have no control over it?"[22] Moreover, James' conversations with Bast were preoccupied with rather profound dissertations on the subject of art and immortality: "I think there's only one true form of greatness for a man. If a man can bridge the gap between life and death . . . then maybe he was a great man. To have your work remembered in history, to leave something in this world that will last for centuries—that's greatness."[23]

This may hardly be a typical sophomore monologue. Yet that age is frequently peppered with deep pronouncements and a healthy dose of bravado. What makes Dean's comments sobering is that he achieved his own definition of greatness so early.

Be that as it may, the young man's first high-profile action at UCLA proved less than promising. Surprisingly, the transplanted Hoosier had won the prominent part of Malcolm, the oldest son of King Duncan, in the university's prestigious production of *Macbeth*. But despite his proclivity for *Hamlet*, the general reaction to Dean's Malcolm was negative. To illustrate, the normally sympathetic Bast likened the performance to "an agonizing dental extraction."[24] The UCLA newsletter *Spotlight* said Dean's Malcolm "failed to show any growth, and would have made him a hollow king."[25] Unlike his later tantrum tendencies when panned, however, Dean worked hard on improving his work in succeeding performances.

The best thing to come out of the *Macbeth* production was Dean's friendship with Bast, who was dating another student in the cast. Since Dean was then seeing her best friend, the two couples started double dating. Moreover, Bast and Dean quickly found they had much in common, from their joint theater arts status to being transplanted midwesterners. (Bast was from Wisconsin.) Both were also beginning actors, though Bast soon focused on writing. As so often happened with Dean, part of his interest in Bast was as yet another mentor. In Bast's later biography of his friend, however, he entertainingly postulates how this was a positive for each of them: "Fortunately, Jimmy was aware of his need for growth. He turned to me for assistance. Being inherently lazy, I

---

was happy to let him prod me on. It was good for me to get off my dead mental haunches. Jimmy became a stimulus and kept the mental ball rolling for both of us."[26] From this reciprocal relationship came the first, and in many ways still definitive, biography of Dean.

Paradoxically, while Dean and Bast were evolving this unique friendship, one of Dean's fraternity connections gave him his first acting breakthrough. Jim Bellah had an agent who needed several young people for a Pepsi-Cola commercial. Ultimately, three dozen budding actors turned up at the merry-go-round at Los Angeles's Griffith Park, the site of the two-minute commercial. Dean not only made the cut, the director decided to key in on the young actor, both at Griffith Park and in some studio interiors shot the following day.

For this first professional work Dean received a grand total of $65 and a box lunch. More importantly, the commercial earned him a union card and the attention of agent Isabel Draesemer. Though she is sometimes mistakenly credited with discovering Dean at the UCLA production of *Macbeth*, it was the soft drink spot that got her attention.[27] Beyond this, the commercial proved to be strangely prophetic. Griffith Park was the site of the pivotal planetarium scenes in Dean's later signature film, *Rebel Without a Cause*. Moreover, two of his fellow Pepsi performers in this December 1950 shoot, Nick Adams and Beverly Long, also performed in *Rebel*. Indeed, Long

Dean at the planetarium in Rebel Without a Cause *(1955).*

later comically chronicled the simplicity of the commercial, noting, "We were all supposed to be drinking Pepsi-
Cola, going round and round on the merry-go-round,
having a wonderful time. And then they [the producers]
had a jukebox set up [in the studio], and we were dancing
and being silly."[28]

Silly or not, this soda spot "hastened the end of his
[Dean's] connections with the Theatre Arts department at
UCLA."[29] Since the panning of his *Macbeth* performance,
James' college acting opportunities seemed to have dried
up. Consistent with his maverick tendencies, nothing
pleased him more than launching an acting career by way
of circumventing the system. Unfortunately, this is also
the time from which one can begin to date his inclination
to be "insufferably immature."[30] Though not quite yet the

angst-ridden poseur, the predisposition to follow this self-centered path is obvious. In Dean's defense, possibly the failure of his second-chance attempt to reconnect with his father may have contributed to his proclivity for being difficult. Or maybe he simply missed the security-blanket normalcy of his Indiana home. But as the meager time he had left to live (five years) progressed, his ever more rigorously narrow perspective on acting contributed to his often antisocial behavior. For example, early in his career he had this to say about acting: "The stage is like a religion: you dedicate yourself to it and suddenly you find that you don't have time to see friends and it's hard for them to understand. You don't see anybody. You're all alone with your imagination and that's all you have. You're an actor."[31]

Ironically, Dean's most influential acting instructor was 180 degrees from the reclusive loner just described. Humorist character actor James Whitmore would have a profound impact on Dean. The fact that Whitmore's acting "classes" were outside of the UCLA system was yet another signal to the young man that his college days were over.

5

The Opportunist

"There's always someone in one's life who stimulates you to the point of trying to find the right direction. For myself, that man was James Whitmore, the movie actor."[1]

JAMES DEAN

UNLIKE JAMES DEAN'S ALL-TOO-SHORT ACTING BLIP ON THE radar screen, his Los Angeles performing guru, James Whitmore, has played the actor, and played it well, for sixty-plus years. Ten years Dean's senior and educated at Yale, Whitmore was yet another World War II veteran who mentored the young man. At the time of his friendship with the transplanted Hoosier, Whitmore was most famous for both his Broadway debut in *Command Decision* (1947, as a tough but comic sergeant) and an Oscar-nominated Best Supporting Actor performance in *Battleground* (1949). Fittingly for the former U.S. Marine, both of these popular films were about World War II. His later roles would range from another Oscar-nominated performance as President Harry Truman in *Give 'em Hell, Harry!* (1975) to a poignant role as an aging librarian in the cult classic *The Shawshank Redemption* (1994). Of special significance for Dean was

COLLECTION OF WES D. GEHRING

*James Whitmore in his Oscar-nominated role
from* Battleground *(1949).*

the fact that Whitmore had been a student at New York's
Actors Studio, where he had been taught by Method pioneers Lee Strasberg and Elia Kazan. Thus, the soon-to-be
college dropout Dean suddenly had a link, via Whitmore,

to what was then the top of the acting food chain. And, of course, Kazan would eventually give him a shot at stardom by casting him in *East of Eden*.

These acting classes with Whitmore were made possible by Dean's roommate and future biographer Bill Bast, who had met Whitmore on several occasions and was aware of how much the young star missed the intellectual atmosphere of New York and especially the Actors Studio. Couple this with the fact that Bast and Dean and most of their fellow UCLA theater arts students were dissatisfied with the academic acting classes then available, and Bast suddenly had a solution for all their problems. He would ask Whitmore to teach an acting class. Though Bast was initially slow to make the request for fear of being turned down, Whitmore jumped on the idea. Unlike the overly analytical and professorial Strasberg, Whitmore was a more casually nurturing sort who preferred to be seen as a guide rather than a teacher. Moreover, his approach to the craft mixed working-class values with an athleticism that appealed to the young Dean, who, until recently, had been a midwestern farm boy who defined himself through sports: "You work until you're ready to drop, and then go on and work some more. By the time you're ready to call yourself an actor, you'll . . . feel good, like you feel after a workout, when you ache all over and you're aware of every inflated muscle . . . but it'll hurt good."[2]

As noted earlier, and consistent with Whitmore's sports-related take on acting, when Kazan first witnessed a Broadway performance by Dean, he praised the young man's technique in athletic terms. Perhaps Dean's sports-obsessed youth, when he sometimes fantasized about being a professional athlete, may not have been so far from Hollywood after all. Interestingly, one of his most entertaining part-time jobs during the struggling actor part of his career directly hinged upon his athletic ability. After following Whitmore's advice about going to New York to find himself as an actor, Dean helped make ends meet by being a stunt tester on a popular television game show called *Beat the Clock*. The long-running (1950–58) CBS program involved studio audience contestants attempting various stunts with a time limit of sixty seconds or less. What made the series a hit "were the stunts themselves, which were full of whipped cream, custard pies, and exploding balloons, always frantic yet always ingenious."[3] The show's producers maintained a "stunt factory" where unemployed actors such as Dean made sure the stunts could be done. Television producer Franklin Heller, who got Dean the job, remembered the young man as "the best-coordinated human being I ever knew! There was no trick or stunt he couldn't accomplish with the greatest of ease; we had balancing stunts and all that jazz—nothing he couldn't do. He had absolute unerring control over his body."[4] Ironically, Dean lost the job because he was too athletic! Many of the stunts, which he made appear easy, were all but impossible for the average person. Still, Heller's comments about James' "absolute unerring control over his body" are consistent with the athletic-orientated assessments of Dean's acting.

One might ask, with his physical gifts, why Dean did not continue toward a sports career, instead of acting. Actress Liz Sheridan, a close friend and love interest of Dean, would later address that fact in her insightful book, *Dizzy & Jimmy: My Life with James Dean*. Just after telling Sheridan, "I could have been a professional [athlete]," Dean explained what had drawn him to acting: "I knew right away, deep down in my soul, that I wanted to be an actor—well, actually, I realized I *was* an actor, and that by being an actor I could be anyone, a scientist, a lawyer, or a musician. I could be Mozart or Bach. I could be a general, a king, or even the president."[5] As portrait artist Simmie Knox recently observed, "I think we are all born with a program in place. Many people ignore it or don't pay attention to it, but some people are lucky enough to access it."[6] Dean had the added blessing of "accessing" his special "program" amazingly early. Dean's acting revelation also gives added credence to this book's position that he was a poseur—"I realized I *was* an actor"—someone playing parts years *before* he had a thespian resumé.

Much of Whitmore's mentoring mission for Dean, Bast, and their fellow UCLA aspiring actors was merely theater basics, with the former marine continuing to use sports metaphors. Thus, his "exercises" to work the "muscles [imagination] of acting" involved fundamental tasks such as peeling an illusionary piece of fruit.[7] But as significant as these seemingly simplistic exercises were (they helped to keep the hyperactive Dean with the "program"), of greater importance was Whitmore's ability to push the young people to a level of concentration they had never imagined possible. For example, Dean and Bast were once asked to improvise a sketch in which Bill played a jeweler and James a thief trying to get back a stolen watch. Bast's assignment was to delay Dean's retrieval attempts long enough for the authorities to get there. The boys' initial try was less than successful. When Whitmore asked the duo to try again, but in the most supportive manner, without the harsh dissections that later alienated Dean from Lee Strasberg, they responded with a tour-de-force performance. In fact, they so lost themselves in the improvisation that they nearly came to blows. Whitmore and several students had to separate them. This was an epiphany for Dean. As Bast recalled, "for the first time in his [James'] life, he realized that to understand was not sufficient; to be able to apply what you understood was the immediate goal . . . for the first time acting made sense."[8]

The Method performance push to the next level, where one literally becomes the character, was not without its psychological toll. After the jewelry store improvisation, Dean was reduced to a state of nervous exhaustion, followed by depression. Like a New Age Dr. Jekyll after the exhilaration of becoming Mr. Hyde, Dean found the return to normalcy a supreme letdown. Sadly, this would become part of the price of Dean's art, for his post-performance emptiness would become normal for the actor. Though this was an extreme response to his craft, it was not unprecedented. Consider what Dean contemporary Peter Sellers told a journalist during the production of *Dr. Strangelove* (1964): "When a role is finished, I experience a sudden loss of identity. It's a funny thing, but when I'm doing a role I kind of feel it's the role doing the role. When someone says, 'You were great as so-and-so,' I feel they should be telling so-and-so and not me."[9] Obviously, such an identity transference would play havoc with any emotional equilibrium, and it helps to explain Dean's often volatile nature, especially during a production.

The artistic window Whitmore opened for Dean came at an opportune time, as the young actor's first dramatic television production began shooting just a week after the initial Whitmore workshop. This small-screen play, *Hill Number One*, was a sixty-minute installment of the syndicated religious program *Family Theatre*. This particular episode drew an analogy between the crucifixion of Christ and a group of American soldiers struggling to retake a hill during the Korean War. It was broadcast on Easter Sunday, 1951. Dean had a small but memorable part as John the Apostle. A number of name actors appeared in the production, including Raymond Burr as the Apostle Peter and Roddy McDowall as an American GI. While Dean's audition for the youngest of Christ's disciples had come through a contact from his Pepsi commercial, he was effective in the part. His director, Arthur Pierson, was later full of praise, though he hinted at James' tendency to *play* the rebel in real life, even before the fame: "He gave a fine, simple, straightforward performance. A year later [1952] he was in New York learning to be a mumbling [Method] rebel."[10]

Hill Number One produced a Los Angeles fan club for Dean. A local high school, Immaculate Heart, created the "James Dean Appreciation Society." They invited their hero to the society's first meeting, and "Bill Bast, who went along, noticed that Jimmy loved every minute of it, as what twenty-year-old aspiring star would not?"[11] But this apparent fast track to success suddenly hit a wall. *Hill Number One* did not generate the ensuing parts for Dean everyone expected, and Bast was still trying to balance UCLA classes with a part-time job as an usher at CBS. Worse yet, Dean fell victim to increased periods of depression. He returned to the late-night wanderings that had begun after his attempted reconciliation with his father had failed. James also spent increased time in his room working on surrealist drawings of a Salvador Dali

nature. Dean's fascination with hallucinatory eyes is reminiscent of Dali's general description of his work—"hand-
painted dream photographs."[12] (Fittingly, Dali's work
often featured eyes that had multiple meanings.)

Dean did find time, however, for romance. In early
1951 he was seeing Kay Mock. But he then became more
serious about Beverly Wills, the high-school-aged daughter
of Joan Davis, best known today for her NBC television
show *I Married Joan* (1952–55). The seventeen-year-old
Wills was then a regular radio cast member of CBS's *Junior
Miss* and later joined her mother on *I Married Joan* for that
series' final two seasons. Davis was not pleased with her
daughter's choice of boyfriend, in large part because of
Dean's moodiness.

There are countless explanations for James' increased
depression at this time, from added anxiety over the esca-
lation of the Korean War to still coping with the childhood loss of his mother. But a more logical explanation
was that for the first time in his life he was operating without a proverbial safety net. His Fairmount family-support
system was half a continent away, and there was no more
front-page newspaper coverage of his every speaking and
athletic accomplishment. The attempted reconciliation
with his biological father had failed. He had dropped out
of UCLA to focus on real-world acting, but the real world
had failed to take notice. Moreover, unlike a then-popular Winston Churchill axiom that "success is going from

failure to failure without loss of enthusiasm," Dean seemed to almost savor the setbacks.[13] His posing as the angst-ridden artist was already a work in progress.

Of course, part of the young man's moodiness around Beverly might have been driven by hunger. Dean and Bast's overpriced apartment left them little money for groceries. They were stretching their food dollar by concocting strange new dishes, including a casserole composed of breakfast cereal and mayonnaise! Consequently, Dean and Wills had numerous picnics (courtesy of her mother's pantry) and he frequently came to dinner at the Davis estate, with Wills arranging for his favorite meal— pot roast—to be served.

While obviously taken with Wills, Dean was also desperately attracted to his girlfriend's entertainment-world lifestyle. This was brought home to him firsthand at Beverly's parties, when he found himself among the young elite of Hollywood. Just how taken Dean was with entering this world was demonstrated by a pivotal but very provocative contact he made while he was dating Wills. The person in question was Rogers Brackett, the influential radio director of CBS's *Alias Jane Doe*. Brackett was also affiliated with the important advertising agency of Foote, Cone and Belding. Fifteen years older than Dean, this well-connected sophisticate met the actor in the CBS parking lot, where Dean was moonlighting as an attendant.

The young man quickly shared his struggling actor story, and once again Dean had an older mentor to look out for him. In fact, the resulting makeover was so extensive that it has been compared to literature's classic transformation in *Pygmalion*, the basis for *My Fair Lady*. But as one Dean author has wryly observed, Brackett was not simply teaching the young man about "the rain in Spain."[14] While Brackett seems to have had a genuine affection, if not love, for the actor, Dean appears to have entered this relationship simply as a way to advance his career. He became a kept man. Granted, there is nothing inherently new about this. Indeed, Marilyn Monroe, the single Hollywood star to rival the amazing ongoing iconic impact of Dean, was playing the same sexual card to success at roughly the same time.

James' liaison with Brackett also represented the young actor's first unquestioned exploration of bisexuality. As one biographer has boldly noted, "If the goal is to understand a subject's character, sexual life is too interesting to ignore."[15] Consistent with this, from childhood on Dean enjoyed doing the most provocative acts to elicit a shocked response from people. Initially the effect was justification enough. Later on he seemed to sanctify the action as an actor's learning tool—gathering possible reactions for future roles. Whatever the added motive, if any, few things would be more controversial in the conservative 1950s than bisexual behavior. Though nontraditional sexual mores thankfully no longer raise eyebrows, sleeping to success is still hardly a résumé item. But as one of biography's oldest axioms suggests, "There are two reasons why a man does anything. There's a good reason and there's the real reason."[16] The biographer's task is to track down the real reason. While some forthcoming facts will document the real reason for a relationship with Brackett (Dean tended to be a user), it is equally true that the actor probably saw shock effect as a "good reason." More than one text notes Dean's pleasure at how surprised his friends were about his personal life.[17]

In James' favor, however, there are some possible mitigating factors. First, Dean had a long history of attaching himself to older mentoring figures, albeit without the sexual component. Second, Dean and roommate Bast had a temporary falling out, and James' friend had vacated the apartment. (Ironically, part of their differences involved a joint relationship with a young lady.) Regardless, since Dean and Bast took turns being a bastion of support for each other, one might argue Dean became involved with Brackett at a particularly vulnerable time. Third, one could play the naïve rustic card—that a fresh-off-the-farm James had found himself in the proverbial Hollywood Babylon, and Brackett was considered a world-class charmer.

Any of these items, or other factors such as Dean's predisposition for shock, might have played a part in his decision. After all, the genre of biography is all about assessing various "angles of vision."[18] In fact, sometimes a biographer is so swamped by variables that he or she simply presents a smorgasbord of choices for the reader. This was certainly the case with Gretchen Rubin's engaging *Forty Ways to Look at Winston Churchill*[19] These things being said, however, one still has to deal with a particularly damning (in the sense of a manipulative agenda by Dean) conversation the actor had with his early agent, Isabel Draesemer: "Jimmy came to me and asked whether marrying Beverly Wills [whom he was then dating] or moving in with Rogers Brackett would be better for his career."[20] One should add here that the sexual liaison with Brackett is a given in the Dean literature, unlike the unsubstantiated claims about the Reverend James DeWeerd that were addressed earlier in this book. As John Howlett's biography of Dean states, "Of all Dean's supposed or claimed homosexual relationships, this friendship with Rogers Brackett is the most documented and the most authentic."[21]

The opportunist aspect of the actor's arrangement with Brackett was later underlined by the fact that Dean dropped him once he could no longer be of any assistance to him. Moreover, when Dean was later in a position to help Brackett, when the director had hit a rough spot in his career, the former protégé did nothing. This so disturbed a mutual friend, composer Alec Wilder, that he had the moxie to draft an apology letter to Brackett that he then had Dean copy in his own hand and send. But if there are still any questions regarding the actor's original ties with Brackett, a less-than-contrite Dean told Wilder, "I didn't know it was the whore who paid, I thought it was the other way around."[22]

So what did Dean get from his liaison with Brackett? First, it seems to have been an ongoing tutorial. Brackett gave the always intellectually curious Dean books to read and discuss and took him to an assortment of cultural events. These activities ranged from stage productions to regular attendance at the Silent Movie Theatre in Los Angeles. Brackett complemented much of the previous mentoring Dean had received. For example, while Reverend DeWeerd had planted in Dean a seed of interest in bullfighting, Brackett actually took Dean to Mexico to see the sport firsthand. Plus, these special activities were made all the more memorable by Brackett's countless contacts. Thus, in Mexico, James met bullfighting aficionado Budd Boetticher, later most famous for a celebrated series of Randolph Scott Westerns he directed. Boetticher presented to Dean an actual bloodstained matador cape that immediately became the young man's most prized possession. This item's status never changed for the rest of his life. In the roughly four remaining years left for Dean, the cape would always find a prominent space on the walls of the numerous apartments he occu-

James Dean (center) and Rebel *father Jim Backus,
with screen mother Ann Doran looking on.*

COLLECTION OF WES D. GEHRING

pied. Moreover, he would periodically play at being a
matador, using the cape both on friends willing to double
as bulls or the unsuspecting passing motorist—an activity
he frequently engaged in while later living in New York.

The Boetticher encounter was typical of the impressive circles to which Brackett had access. To illustrate,
here is part of a shared observation Dean had with Bast
that both demonstrates the fast-company phenomenon
and the actor's almost little-boy enthusiasm for this "every

day is Christmas" world he found himself in: "Finished [reading] *Moulin Rouge* last night. The end [great]! You've got to read it. It's the novel about [artist Toulouse] Lautrec's life. Rogers flipped over it, too. So we picked up the phone and called [Pierre] La Mure, the guy who wrote it."[23]

Like the ongoing *Hamlet* tutoring Dean had received from his Santa Monica City College drama instructor, he also received encouragement from Brackett to work on Shakespeare's most acclaimed play. Consequently, it is no wonder that in later years Dean aspired to play Hamlet, a character widely considered to be the most significant in the history of Western civilization. Indeed, this frequent schooling in *Hamlet* might have influenced what would become Dean's screen persona. Hamlet's ongoing relevancy to the often overwhelmed modern audience is couched in his indecisiveness, which is timelier with each chaotically passing year. Along similar lines, the Dean of *East of Eden* and *Rebel Without a Cause* is also the most uncertain of figures, as these characters, too, attempt to resolve situations that have fathers at their centers. In fact, one might also look to the morose, brooding Hamlet as a possible catalyst for Dean's decision to play at being the angst-ridden artist, at least when the public was watching.

Besides Brackett's finishing-school impact upon James, the once-struggling actor was now getting parts, too. Dean appeared on several CBS radio programs, including

Brackett's *Alias Jane Doe*. More impressively, Brackett saw to it that Dean had bit parts in three high-profile pictures. The first was *Fixed Bayonets* (1951), a Korean War film directed by Brackett's friend, Sam Fuller, in which a band of American soldiers find themselves cut off during a Chinese offensive. Though a B movie, Fuller's oeuvre has now reached cult status, so Dean's debut is in a significant film, though his one line of dialogue was later cut.

James' second small part was in the Dean Martin and Jerry Lewis comedy *Sailor Beware* (1952). Unfortunately, this picture seldom receives more than a passing reference, if that, in Dean literature. Yet the movie was a huge commercial smash, one of the top five box-office hits of 1952.[24] More people saw *Sailor Beware* that year than such now-renowned 1952 productions as *High Noon* and *Singin' in the Rain*. The film is widely considered to be Martin and Lewis's best, and 1952 also found the team ranked number one at the box office among all Hollywood stars.[25] Though Dean only has one line, "That guy's a professional!," he is also much better showcased in *Sailor Beware* than in *Fixed Bayonets*. Not only is he onscreen for several minutes, playing a corner man for Lewis' boxing opponent, but his appearance helps usher in the movie's two most amusing scenes, a punch-drunk parody dialogue between Martin and Lewis, followed by Lewis's tour-de-silly fight sequence. James very much enjoyed the experience, especially because of the wild-man

*Dean Martin and Jerry Lewis clowning on the set
of* Sailor Beware *(1952).*

antics of Martin and Lewis on the set. And since the young Hoosier's favorite anecdotes were invariably of a comic nature, he later shared the following story about *Sailor Beware* with girlfriend Sheridan: "I did a tiny part in a Dean Martin-Jerry Lewis movie. Those two guys are really crazy—at breakfast on the set one morning, they ran around pouring pancake syrup over everyone's head, cast and crew and everyone. It held up production for hours. I thought it was hilarious. The director was mad as hell, but they didn't seem to care. Someone told me they're always doing stuff like that."[26] His experience on the film also made Dean realize that Hollywood revolved around the whims of the star, a lesson he took too much to heart later on. Brackett's contact person on the picture was Lewis, who later took complete credit for casting James.[27]

The third movie in Dean's bit part trilogy was the period comedy *Has Anyone Seen My Gal?* (1952), which starred Piper Laurie, Charles Coburn, and Rock Hudson. Though not in the same class as *Sailor Beware*, the movie was a popular success and featured Dean's first foreground dialogue. He entertainingly orders an ice cream dish from Coburn, who is doubling as a soda jerk. James' vocabulary is in the hip lingo of a 1920s teenager: "Hey, Gramps, I'll have a choc malt, heavy on the choc, plenty of milk, four spoons of malt, two scoops of vanilla ice cream, one mixed with the rest and one floating." The major footnote to this film is that four years later, bit player Dean would be costarring with the romantic lead of *Has Anyone Seen My Gal?*—Rock Hudson.

After the early rush of appearing on the big screen, Dean began to feel he was stuck in a small part dead end. Brackett, like Whitmore, encouraged Dean to think about going to New York, with its hotbed of activity for both stage and live television work. (In the early 1950s, the small-screen industry was still largely based in New York.) But the ultimate catalyst for Dean going east was Brackett's advertising work relocating him to Chicago, with an eventual transfer planned for New York.

When one loses a carte blanche situation, it is easier to accept new challenges. Still, Dean's route to New York took him through Chicago for a brief stay with Brackett. And with Indiana's close proximity to Chicago, Dean squeezed in side trips to both his hometown of Fairmount (staying with his surrogate parents, Marcus and Ortense Winslow) and Indianapolis (visiting Reverend DeWeerd at his new church). After a week in the Midwest, with everyone generously contributing to his New York war chest, Dean was off to the bright lights of Broadway. Despite a healthy bankroll and several letters of introduction, Dean was once again about to enter the sizeable ranks of the struggling actor.

6

Struggling New York Actor

"It's a fertile, wonderful, generous city, if you can accept its violence. It offers so many things to do. I go to dancing school, take percussion lessons, acting lessons, attend concerts, operas."[1]

JAMES DEAN

JAMES DEAN HAD FLIRTED WITH GOING TO NEW YORK EVEN before both James Whitmore and Rogers Brackett had encouraged him to make an actor's pilgrimage to the cultural capital of America. In April 1949 Dean, a high school senior, was at a national speech competition in Colorado. Befriending the student representative from New York, he made tongue-in-cheek reservations with the young man for sometime in the near future.

While there is no record of Dean ever reconnecting with this student, he did finally make it to New York in September 1951. Both Whitmore and Brackett had given Dean several letters of introduction, but the young actor's first important contact in the city was composer Alec Wilder, an old friend of Brackett's. Wilder lived at the celebrated Algonquin Hotel, famous for the literary wits who dined there regularly in the 1920s. Billed as both the "Vicious Circle" and the "Algonquin Round Table," the membership included such literary and comedy figures as Robert Benchley, Dorothy Parker, Alexander Woollcott, George S. Kaufman, Ring Lardner, Charles MacArthur, Edna Ferber, and an occasional Marx Brother.[2] (Dean's later movie *Giant*, 1956, would be based on Ferber's 1952 novel of the same name.)

Wilder helped Dean settle in at the more modestly priced Iroquois Hotel, which was close to the Algonquin. (Both hotels are on Manhattan's West Forty-fourth Street.) But James spent more time at the Algonquin. He and Wilder sometimes just watched people in the lobby, with Dean entertaining with his gift for mimicry. The composer later said of James, "Until [*See the Jaguar*, Dean's Broadway debut], he was a pleasant companion, a cheerful, noisy kid."[3] (Wilder wrote the incidental score for *See the Jaguar*.)

Though the actor quickly grew to love New York, he was initially rather intimidated by the city. Thus, when left to his own devices, Dean seldom strayed beyond the nearby movie theaters of Times Square. Between his fascination with film and the security of the cinema darkness, he would sometimes see as many as three or four films a day. Of course, if he was particularly moved by a certain performance, as was the case with Montgomery Clift in *A Place in the Sun* (1951), he might economize by sitting through repeated screenings of the same picture all day and into the evening. (One is reminded of novelist

Michael Chabon's description of the ultimate film fan in *Wonder Boys*, who "climbed into a movie as into a time machine or a bottle of whiskey and set the dial for 'never come back.'"[4]) Dean's fascination with Clift was only topped by the influence of Marlon Brando, with James having also logged multiple viewings of *The Men* (1950, Brando's film debut) the previous year.

An often neglected footnote to *A Place in the Sun*, however, is the fact that the director, George Stevens, directed Dean's last picture, *Giant*. While their clash of styles, old Hollywood versus the new Method, is all that gets remembered today, Dean had earlier been full of nothing but praise for Stevens—praise born of *A Place in the Sun*. (Clift's costar in the movie, Elizabeth Taylor, also later resurfaced in *Giant*, becoming a close friend to Dean.) Regardless, with all these movie screenings, James' New York nest egg was soon seriously depleted. To economize, Dean moved to the YMCA on West Sixty-third Street, close to what is now Lincoln Center. But whenever the actor got a few dollars ahead, he would return to the Iroquois Hotel, which often doubled as his address over the next three years. Even when he was not there, Dean frequently used the hotel as his New York mailing address.

During James' initial YMCA stay, he met a young dancer/singer named Liz Sheridan, whose later credits would include the zany neighbor on television's *Alf* and

Jerry Seinfeld's mother on the acclaimed series *Seinfeld*. The daughter of Frank Sheridan, the classical pianist and recording artist, Sheridan met Dean when she was living at New York's Rehearsal Club, a dorm-like residence for girls attempting to enter show business. Affectionately known as "Dizzy" to her friends, she would soon be much more than that to Dean. They became inseparable soul mates and ultimately lovers, living together briefly and considering marriage. In her funny and poignant joint biography of their New York time together, one has the ultimate evidence that Dean was not the angst-ridden, tortured soul he later liked to pose as. Even when his periodic depression is documented by Dizzy, it puts one in mind of normal frustration. For example, Dean is quoted as saying: "If I *live* long enough. I want it [acting success] now. Jesus, I'm ready. I can feel it. Dammit, I come home to you every night empty-handed. I got no job! I got no money! I'm going through all this bullshit so I can prance around a stage. It's insane!"[5]

Sounding like a frustrated husband trying to pull his weight in a relationship, this is a more palatable pain for the average fan to follow. But this is precisely why such *normal* disappointment is seldom chronicled in Dean's life—it's boring! People enjoy the stereotype of the troubled tragic artist. It both satisfies our sense of triumphant resiliency and maybe provides an out as to why most of us do not attain fame—we have not been tested by the calamity. Dean figured this romantic dynamic out early, possibly fueled by the fact that it would reinforce the troubled teen persona he established on numerous live television dramas, before the polished cinema versions of *East of Eden*, *Rebel Without a Cause*, and *Giant*.

This was undoubtedly a calculated pose. After all, as his relationship with Brackett had clearly demonstrated, James could be quite the opportunist. One could argue, however, that Dean fell into this troubled pose along both intuitive lines and as a touch of his own film-fan tendencies. As has been demonstrated, the young man was obsessed with Clift and Brando. In many ways the Dean screen persona is an amalgamation of the then image of both Clift and Brando—the vulnerability of Clift mixed with the rebelliousness of Brando. Or, as Dean later crassly described the combination, "In this hand I'm holding Marlon Brando saying, 'Fuck you!' and in the other, I'm holding Montgomery Clift saying, 'Please forgive me.'"[6] But long before Dean was concerning himself with a persona, he was simply attempting to emulate the big-screen mystique of these stars in his personal life. Brando addresses this copycat phenomenon in his autobiography, documenting more than one meeting between the two actors: "He [Dean] was nervous when we met and made it clear that he was not only mimicking my acting [Method] but also what he believed was my lifestyle. He said he was learning to play the conga drums and had taken up motorcycling [both synonymous with Brando], and he obviously wanted my approval of his work."[7]

Later at a party, Brando even called Dean to task for repeating a bit of rudeness from one of Brando's films, where a jacket is taken off, rolled into a ball, and thrown on the floor. Ultimately, he advised the young actor, "Jimmy, you have to be who you are, not who I am. You mustn't try to copy me. Emulate the best aspects of yourself."[8]

While the commonsense contacts with the likes of a Brando came later, Sheridan's comparable comic rationality no doubt helped contribute to the relative normalcy of Dean through much of his time in New York. But if she failed with comic common sense, sarcasm was also an option. For example, Dean once claimed to feel suicidal, so Sheridan played along and opened a window.[9] Dean suddenly found he had been mistaken. Years after directing Dean in *East of Eden*, Elia Kazan commented that he believed the appeal of Dean's character in the movie, as well as the actor himself, was best described as, "Pity me, I'm too sensitive for the world. Everyone's wrong except me." But Kazan's practical comeback, which is consistent with Sheridan's, was forget the "'I'm neurotic because this happened to me.' They should shake this off and go on to solve the problem."[10] Or, put more bluntly, Dean might have adopted something like the later life mantra of Jim Knipfel's recent darkly comic memoir, *Slackjaw*: "Deal with It"![11] Knipfel's contemporary classic text goes on to describe a poignant but fleeting swing set memory from childhood. He then observes, "Even in the worst of lives . . . there are moments, bright and lucid moments, which for some reason that is never clear at the time, remain with us forever."[12] While Dean would later have one believe his short existence had been the "worst of lives," Sheridan's memoir is peppered with so many "bright and lucid moments," both of their time together and memories of his Indiana past, that there should be a moratorium placed upon any and all terms having to do with angst in future publications about James.

While Sheridan references to Dean's Hoosier heritage have already graced this book, more about their time together in New York helps to flesh out a fuller picture of the actor. The fun they had together was also a celebration of the city. Each day they spent time in Central Park, with Dean usually focusing on his bullfighting technique as Sheridan doubled as a charging bull. They would log hours at the main branch of the New York Public Library, at Fifth Avenue and Forty-second Street. The two enjoyed researching an assortment of subjects, from dance to bullfighting. But more than that, they simply savored the setting, an archive of knowledge. This same ambience of culture drew them to the Metropolitan Museum of Art, though they could not resist playing hide-and-seek in the wing devoted to ancient Egypt!

Sheridan had grown up in the city, so she often acted as guide. But Dean's awe over much of what they saw managed to recharge her interest anew.

Of course, in a great walking city such as New York, one need not have a fixed destination. Dean, a confirmed late-night wanderer, soon became very much at home prowling Manhattan. In addition, Sheridan and her transplanted Hoosier companion enjoyed just watching people and making up their biographies, such as the ice skaters at Rockefeller Center. Sheridan also introduced her boyfriend to one of the city's more famous street people, a formidable fellow in a Viking helmet and leather called Moondog. Usually to be found somewhere on what is now the Avenue of the Americas, near Fifty-first Street, he was a blind musician and poet. Moondog seemed to symbolize all of the city's struggling performers, and Sheridan had long ago adopted him as a friend and artistic guru.

A favorite eatery for the duo was Jerry's Bar and Restaurant, located on the Avenue of the Americas near West Fifty-fourth Street. The food and drink there were both good and inexpensive, with credit being extended to impoverished artistic types such as Sheridan and Dean. Whenever possible, Dean ordered spaghetti. This is where the couple celebrated his twenty-first birthday on February 8, 1952. Dean told Sheridan it was the "best birthday he had in years."[13] But a general lack of cash often meant the most creative of meal plans for Sheridan and Dean and other friends who were just getting by. At one point Sheridan was an usher at an art house theater that had an endless supply of coffee and doughnuts in its hospitality room. Whenever possible, she would sneak Dean and other starving friends in for a doughnut fest. Or the couple might have a romantic candlelight dinner where the main dish was shredded wheat.

The most entertaining aspect, however, of Sheridan's New York portrait of pre-fame Dean are the witticisms she recalled. While his mimicry skills have been well documented in this book, rare has been the profiler who kept track of Dean's ability to turn a phrase. Not so with Sheridan. For example, James' response to her question on whether he liked living at the YMCA was as follows: "Well, I wouldn't call it living, but it's an okay place to sleep. It'll be even more okay when I get the bedroom set I ordered."[14] On another occasion, Sheridan complained about how gangly she was at sixteen: "Yuck! I was stupid-looking. I was built like a ten-year-old boy—straight up and down. A skinny kid, and very obnoxious." Dean's rapid-fire response: "Well, it's nice to know some things never change."[15] Obviously, as even Brackett's friend Wilder later observed of Sheridan, "She was a wonderful girl, and an extremely good influence for Dean. He needed her. Whenever she was with him, he was calmer and more stable than usual."[16]

Dean and Sheridan's first crisis as a couple came when Rogers Brackett relocated to New York City. But in explaining his relationship with Brackett to Sheridan, Dean claimed their sexual history was limited to a one-time-only seduction by the older man: "He didn't threaten me or anything, but he gave me the impression that our relationship depended on this moment. I decided to go along with it. I succumbed to him. I felt bad afterward. Really strange, like a whore."[17]

The shock of this revelation was soon coupled with another bombshell. Dean wanted to continue mentor contact with Brackett, but strictly on a platonic level. Still, Sheridan agreed to accompany James to a meeting with Brackett at his hotel suite in the Algonquin. While a famous Dean would later have no qualms about cutting Brackett out of his life, at this point he needed Sheridan's help on two levels. First, the existence of a girlfriend underlined the fact that Dean wanted to void the sexual aspect of his relationship with Brackett. Second, beyond her mere physical presence at a meeting, Dean knew that the outspoken Sheridan would demonstrate both her commitment to him and show off her sophisticated background (from a famous father to Robert Benchley having been her sister's godfather). Why was this important? Dean seemed to have a predilection to establish Sheridan's credentials as a quasi-mentor. It was as if to say to Brackett, "I have now moved on to another personal guide/lover." Sheridan believes her meeting with Brackett accomplished Dean's goal, though it remains to be seen if the young actor broke off the physical relationship with the director. But Brackett did continue to assist James in finding some small roles.

With regard to Dean's bisexual nature, however, a more disturbing claim is made by biographer Paul Alexander. His book on the actor suggests Dean was much more homosexually active in New York, and that it was of a sadomasochistic nature.[18] But given both Dean's heavy involvement with Sheridan, and his ongoing ties to Brackett (whose homosexuality abhorred the sado-masochistic), Alexander's sensationalism seems unlikely. As Dean biographer John Howlett has said of Alexander, "Such claims read more like fantasies and have never been substantiated."[19] But one might also offer a final provocatively indirect argument against Dean's active involvement in New York's homosexual scene. The actor's fascination with Brando and Clift fueled an ongoing desire on his part to meet them. While Dean ultimately succeeded in talking to Brando several times, the closest he came to Clift was to leave countless messages with his answering service. All were along the lines of: "I'm a great actor and you're my idol and I need to see you because I need to communicate."[20] Clift was put off by this quasi-stalker approach and never contacted Dean, though their mutual friend, Dennis Hopper, claimed Clift later greatly regretted his action.[21] Regardless, Clift was a major player in New York's gay scene, regularly cruising a number of Manhattan's gay bars. If Dean had been so active along these lines, does it not stand to reason the two would have met under these circumstances? Or, at the bare minimum, would not Dean have come up with a more creative way of contacting Clift than leaving messages with his service?

While sexual questions about Dean will probably be debated until the end of time, there is much about his workaday life in New York that is definite. To help make ends meet, he had an endless supply of part-time jobs. These ranged from the menial, such as washing dishes and busing tables, to the previously mentioned position as a stunt tester on CBS's *Beat the Clock*, which had debuted the year before James had come to New York. Dean's cousin Marcus would say of his surrogate brother's life at this point: "He struggled in New York. Whenever he'd write he'd ask for $10. My father would also frequently send Jimmy cartons of cigarettes, which back then were prepackaged for mailing [a carryover from World War II]."[22] Acting jobs were thin to nonexistent for Dean. Indeed, at first he believed his career had regressed. James had fled bit parts in major movies, only, if he was lucky, to receive nonspeaking bit parts on television.

Dean's best early break, however, came from a neophyte agent, Jane Deacy, who became yet another mentoring mother figure in his life. As one biographer noted, "if Jimmy had talent, it was Jane Deacy's persistence that put him in places where he could reveal it . . . [and she had] the limitless faith to drive him."[23] To the actor, Deacy made a tough-love promise: "You're every bit as good as you think you are. But it's going to be a long time and hard work making other people understand that."[24] Ironically, she did not quite get it right; within two years of Dean's fall 1951 arrival in New York he was winning starring roles on television, such as a psychopathic killer in an installment titled "A Long Time Till Dawn," broadcast November 11, 1953, on the NBC dramatic anthology *Kraft Television Theatre* (1947–58). Author Rod Serling (now famous for his *Twilight Zone* series) said of Dean's performance, "I can't imagine anyone playing that particular role better."[25]

Many Dean biographers, including David Hofstede, credit "A Long Time Till Dawn" as the actor's first starring role on television, in part because of the Serling praise.[26] But a better case for the small-screen honor occurs in an episode of the NBC dramatic anthology *Campbell Soundstage* (1952–54), broadcast July 17, 1953. Titled "Something for an Empty Briefcase," the episode had Dean costarring with Susan Douglas as a juvenile delinquent trying to go straight. Moreover, their sensitive scenes together, as she helps Dean's character find his way, anticipates the moving give-and-take of the actor's starring film debut with Julie Harris in *East of Eden*. Interestingly enough, an early bit of Dean dialogue from this *Campbell Soundstage* installment even anticipates a classic scene from Brando's *On the Waterfront* (1954). A year before Brando's "I could've been somebody" speech, Dean proclaimed, "I want to do something. I want to be somebody."

An earlier supporting television role for Dean that meant a great deal to him occurred on the CBS docudrama *You Are There* (1953–57). Based upon the reenactments of major events, with newsman Walter Cronkite acting as an on-the-scene reporter, this particular installment was "The Capture of Jesse James," with major Western fan Dean playing the outlaw's killer. Fittingly, the episode was directed by Sidney Lumet, whose future films, such as *Dog Day Afternoon* (1975) and *The Verdict* (1982), often embraced antiheroic subjects in which Dean probably would have been most comfortable starring. Indeed, the lead for the former film was Al Pacino, who, early in his career, was often compared to Dean. And the latter picture starred Paul Newman, who, as previously noted, actually replaced Dean in two movies, *Somebody Up There Likes Me* (1956) and *The Left-Handed Gun* (as Billy the Kid, 1958), after Dean's death. "What if" situations like this bring home all the more the tragedy of Dean's death.

During Dean's New York days he engaged in some friendly competition with Newman for many of the same roles. Newman once affectionately told Dean's close friend William Bast, in Dean's presence, "Bill, so help me, every time I went to read for a part in New York this clown would be there. Got so's I couldn't turn around without seeing him." Dean chuckled and replied he was "haunting him."[27] Newman later noted, "I think he [Dean] would have surpassed both Marlon and me. I think he really would have gone into the classics."[28]

By the second half of 1953, Dean consistently obtained prominent parts in high-profile television productions, fueled in part by a well-received small role in the Broadway play *See the Jaguar*, which ran briefly in December 1952. Even when he appeared in small roles, Dean had a knack for stealing the show. My favorite such example occurs in an installment of NBC's *Armstrong Circle Theatre* (1950–63), broadcast November 17, 1953. Titled "The Bells of Cockaigne," the program had Dean playing a young married man with a sickly child. He works at a warehouse unloading railroad boxcars. Desperately in need of extra cash for medicine, he loses his paycheck in a lunchtime poker game. The production's nominal star, character actor Gene Lockhart (who had appeared with Dean in the Easter television special *Hill Number One*), is the wise, older mentor figure that often surfaced in Dean's real life.

James played the part against type, making his young man angry instead of initially sympathetic. Yet by the end

*James Dean practices some roping skills during
the production of* Giant *(1956).*

of this thirty-minute drama this overwhelmed husband and browbeaten worker, forced to gamble longer than he knows he should, has captured all of our empathy. In addition to the quiet intensity that pulls viewers in, he is a master of drawing one's attention through the use of inanimate objects. This would be most famously done by Dean in *Giant*, when he plays with a rope throughout the scene where he is informed of his inheritance. Just as Dean would steal this sequence in *Giant*, he keeps the viewers' attention during a poker game in "The Bells of Cockaigne" by being the only gambler lighting and handling a cigarette.

While "Bells" remains a treat, the amiable Lockhart had trouble with Dean, who had stayed in angry character for the part. The older actor complained to the director: "You've got to talk to that boy. He's very difficult to work with, and I never know what he's doing. He's very rude."[29] But Dean had established a reputation for being difficult early in his acting career, dating back to his "The Madman" speech in high school. The greater problem, however, in Dean's early television work involved looking for a Method-acting motivation in parts that hardly necessitated a motivation. One might compare this situation to the scene in Dustin Hoffman's *Tootsie* (1982), where his character is playing a piece of fruit in a Fruit-of-the-Loom underwear commercial and requests motivation tips. Though played for laughs and normally associated

Sydney Pollack (left) and Dustin Hoffman in Tootsie *(1982),
with Pollack both directing and costarring.*

with the Dean-like demands of the young Hoffman, one
should also bear in mind that *Tootsie* was directed by
Sydney Pollack. This contemporary of Dean, also from
Indiana, was a struggling actor in New York at the same
time as Dean. Moreover, in a late-night talk show appearance promoting the original release of *Tootsie*, he credited Hoffman's demanding character to a litany of
Method actors, including Dean.

Being a working actor in New York helped to define
Dean. Plus, he now felt most at home in the city. Though

he returned to Hollywood to become a movie star, New York was never out of his mind. Dean's final screen contract even made time for stage and television work in New York. But beyond that, the city was a place in which to both unwind and embrace life. After the 1955 race in Salinas, California, the one he died driving to, he was going to return to his adopted city. There were Broadway plays to consider and old haunts to visit. But three peaks to his New York story remain to be examined—acting validation by way of two Broadway plays and membership in post–World War II's most exclusive entertainment organization, the Actors Studio.

7

The Actors Studio and Broadway

*"The real problem for the actor . . . is how to create in each perform-
ance the same believable experiences and behavior, and yet include
what Stanislavsky called 'the illusion of the first time.'"*[1]

LEE STRASBERG

THE THREE HIGHLIGHTS OF JAMES DEAN'S LIFE IN NEW YORK
were qualifying for inclusion in the Actors Studio under
the leadership of Lee Strasberg and obtaining small but
much-praised parts in two Broadway plays, *See the Jaguar*
(1952) and *The Immoralist* (1954). But the most unlikely
of these accomplishments was gaining admittance to the
Actors Studio, which was normally just referred to as the
Studio. In the early 1950s it was the premier place to be if
you were a young actor. At that time it was heavily associated not only with Strasberg, but also director Elia Kazan,
a founding member (1947) of the Studio, and his protégé,
Marlon Brando. The latter duo had become the proverbial
toast of both Broadway and Hollywood, with their most
high-profile joint project at the time of Dean's entry into
the Studio (1952) being the stage and screen productions
of Tennessee Williams's play *A Streetcar Named Desire*.
These hugely influential works, particularly Brando's

animalistic characterization of Stanley Kowalski, helped to redefine the parameters of naturalistic acting.

In Foster Hirsch's history of the Actors Studio, *A Method to the Madness*, he insightfully reminds readers that many of Hollywood's top movie stars of the time, including Clark Gable, Gary Cooper (a special favorite of Dean's), Jimmy Stewart, and Spencer Tracy were much praised for their naturalism, too.[2] They seemed instinctive, without self-consciousness in their dialogue delivery or their physical movement. In other words, there was no distracting technique, and they seemed to be playing variations of their own personalities. Obviously, this is a gross simplification. Their art was making it look so natural. The Method simply pushed the envelope further for this phenomenon.

The approach is also sometimes called the "total immersion system," since the actor is asked to completely draw upon personal experience. If the actor can fully embrace this total involvement, he is rewarded not only by a great performance but also by a sense of freedom. Thus, Strasberg describes the Method as not having "the time to worry whether he [the actor] will be able to act his part or what the audience will think of him or how awful it feels to walk on the stage where everyone can see and criticize."[3] Consequently, there is often a greater intensity to the Method actor than what one expects from a Gable or a Cooper. Couple this with the fact that the Actors

Studio performer is an antihero, versus the leader-of-men type that is synonymous with Gable, Cooper, Stewart, and Tracy, and one has another Method component—inarticulateness and/or vulnerability. Consequently, the early 1950s Brando often mumbled, while Dean made a practice of stumbling over his words or introducing the awkward pause. Years ago Robin Williams had a Method-acting joke where an audience member complains, "I can't understand him," only to be shouted down by another playgoer, "Shutup, he *feels* it!"

As this bit of Williams comedy suggests, the Method has always been subject to ridicule. Some commentators likened it to the "itch-and-scratch" style, while others characterized it thus: "The Armpit, the Dirty Fingernail, and the Torn Shirt School, its reputation was that you were hissed unless you featured ratty jeans, wrinkled fatigues, and lumberjackets."[4] Not only did Dean have a good sense of humor about this rumble-mumble mindset, part of his joy in so frequently mimicking Brando was based in it. This was best demonstrated by Dean when the *Rebel Without a Cause* wardrobe tests were held on the Warner Brothers sets for *A Streetcar Named Desire*. Dean relished reportedly entertaining visitors with his overblown take on Brando's famous *Streetcar* staircase scene, in which he wails, "Stella!"[5]

Interestingly enough, this natural style of acting did not originate with the Actors Studio. Roughly two hundred years earlier, English actors Charles Macklin and David Garrick pioneered a similar performing style.[6] This involved everything from broken phrases to drawn-out pauses. Moreover, just as Brando's and Dean's rough and rude screen behaviors sometimes spilled over into real life, Macklin's comparable antics even antagonized some fans two centuries before the "itch-and-scratch" Method. But just as the passage of time often makes the old new again, Brando and Dean helped usher in a performing approach more natural than the standard cinema style of the period.

What makes Dean's summer 1952 admission to the Actors Studio most impressive is that at the time he had hardly made a ripple on the New York theater and television scene. Granted, Dean had a letter of introduction to Strasberg from James Whitmore and numerous entertainment contacts courtesy of Rogers Brackett. But ultimately it all came down to the level of one's Actors Studio audition piece. As if adding an extra challenge, Dean's chosen sketch, done with its author (Christine White), was the most nontraditional of audition properties; that is, the Studio strongly encouraged beginning actors to use well-established literary works, not unlike Dean's award-winning "The Madman" high school performance piece, which had been taken from Charles Dickens's *Pickwick Papers*.

Dean had happened upon his performance partner strictly by chance. The young actor made a habit of hanging out at the office of his agent, Jane Deacy. One lunch hour, Deacy was gone, but an attractive young blonde, Chris White, was there typing away on a script. She was also a Deacy client and had recently graduated from the University of North Carolina. White only had access to the typewriter at noon, so Dean's nonstop questions about the script initially had her pegging him as a pest. But when James discovered it was an audition piece for the Actors Studio, he turned on that little lost-boy charm.

Soon he had bamboozled himself into the short script, which had an F. Scott Fitzgerald ring to it. Set on a beach, it chronicled a meeting between a southern belle and a young intellectual outsider. With Dean's girlfriend Dizzy Sheridan playing summer stock in New Jersey, Chris and James became inseparable. Over the next two months, they continually tweaked the short (seven to ten pages) script and rehearsed it in front of anyone who would listen, including strangers in Central Park, their favorite "theater."

When the time came for their audition, Dean was so nervous he drank one of their props, a bottle of beer. When this and a second beer did not curb James' anxiety, Chris had to give him a pep talk. Ironically, it was only the normally simple stage entrances that proved to be a problem. Acting without his thick glasses, Dean had trouble finding her on center stage. But once they began their dialogue, it became one of those "bright moments" of life mentioned in the previous chapter.[7] Consistent with Dean's tendency to pack everything into a project, the collaboration with White went over the studio's time limitation, just as Dean's Dickens monologue had run long in high school. But while he was ultimately penalized for the earlier infraction, Strasberg was so taken with the sketch that he let Dean and White go well over the five-minute limit.

Impressively, of the 150 people auditioning that August 1952, Dean and White were among only fifteen to be accepted into the Studio. Moreover, at twenty-one years of age, Dean became the youngest person ever to gain membership. An overjoyed Dean wrote his surrogate parents, Uncle Marcus and Aunt Ortense, back in Indiana: "After months of . . . [work] I am very proud to announce that I am a member of the Actors Studio. The greatest school of theatre. It houses great people like Marlon Brando, Julie Harris, Arthur Kennedy, Elia Kazan . . . and on and on and on. Very few people get into it, and it's absolutely free. It's the best thing that can happen to an actor. . . . If I can keep this up . . . one of these days I might be able to contribute something to the world."[8] The same letter thanked his aunt and uncle for all they had done, as well as requesting that they send an appreciation to his high school drama instructor, Adeline Nall, too. Then, as is often the case when a youngster writes home, he requested money.[9]

As a comic footnote to Dean's acting talent, one should also add the fact that he was masterful in memorizing the position of everything and everybody on the set. His difficulty in initially finding White during the audition was a rare breakdown in his normally flawless knack for metaphorically "dancing in the dark," once his glasses came off. Still, it is my belief that Dean's legendary casualness about not hitting his acting "marks" on the floor, so cameramen and costars could plan their movements, had little to do with either non-professionalism or simply being lost in the Method approach. Instead, it was a cover for his near blindness without his glasses. (Along related lines, a later film critic suggested that his lack of glasses in the movies "might account for the distant naked look of his acting eyes."[10])

The unfortunate follow-up to Dean's arrival as a Studio actor came with a subsequent sketch he did for his self-described "greatest school of theatre." Drawing upon his ongoing fascination with bullfighting, Dean adapted a section of a novel he was then reading, titled *Matador*. This was to be a wordless piece about an aging bullfighter preparing to enter the ring. Like Dean's scenes as a middle-aged Jett Rink in *Giant*, Strasberg did not find Dean effective outside the security blanket of playing his own age. Worse yet, the Studio guru saw Dean's presentation as merely an exercise piece and not a legitimate sketch for consideration. Strasberg was merciless in his criticism;

that was the Strasberg style. (Why would he be that way? One is reminded of the comic tag line to the old vaudeville explanation by someone with ogre-like behavior, "That's what I do.") Behind his back, Strasberg was affectionately, and sometimes not so affectionately, known as the "high priest."[11]

Never one to take criticism well, Dean was devastated. His humiliation was heightened by a large Studio audience, with such high-profile people in attendance as Marilyn Monroe and Eli Wallach. Dean even threatened to never return to the Studio. He later shared a personal theory with his roommate, UCLA buddy Bill Bast, who had followed James to New York, about why Strasberg's aggressive criticism was so threatening: "I don't know what happens when I act—inside. But if I let them dissect me, like a rabbit in a clinical research laboratory or something, I might not be able to produce again. They might sterilize me!"[12]

Dean's position was not unusual. In fact, it has a long history in the arts, especially among humorists, who often fear they will lose their ability to make people laugh if they analyze their gift too much. For example, Algonquin Round Table wit Robert Benchley, a special favorite of Brackett, even did a special tongue-in-cheek spoof of such critiquing attempts: "In order to laugh at something, it is necessary (1) to know *what* you are laughing at, (2) to know why you are laughing, (3) to ask some people why

COLLECTION OF WES D. GEHRING

*Gifted comic essayist Robert Benchley was also one
of America's favorite film comedians.*

they think you are laughing, (4) to jot down a few notes,
(5) to laugh. Even then, the thing may not be cleared up
for days."[13] Given the total tutorial nature of Brackett's
relationship with Dean, with the older man also living at

149

the Algonquin Hotel, Dean might even have been aware of the Benchley quote when he formed his own thoughts on the subject.

Despite this tradition of questioning the merits of analysis, one aspect of Dean being upset by Strasberg does *not* fit the actor's profile. Here was a young man constantly driven by a minute curiosity about everything, from the traditional arts to motorcycles and bullfighting. Moreover, he had just joined an elite fraternity, the Actors Studio, based upon the premise that the performer has to dissect his own life for useable emotional experiences. So why was he so upset with Strasberg? Yes, Strasberg was brusque, but that was a given with the Studio. Indeed, that was supposed to be part of the training. To illustrate, one of Strasberg's biographers states, "Afterward [from your time with Strasberg at the Studio] premieres and critics hold no terror. Once you've worked for Lee nothing else can make you fearful."[14]

Probably the best explanation of why Dean was so put out by Strasberg, beyond not wanting to dissect the magic or the "high priest" being cruel, was that Dean was still a spoiled and somewhat naïve person. From his lovingly protective Indiana aunt and uncle (not to mention Fairmount in general), to being Brackett's kept boy, much of the world had treated him as though he was surrounded by eggshells. One must not upset Jimmy. Granted, some genuine struggling had gone on in New

York. But even here three caretaker-type women had eased the way immeasurably: his girlfriend Sheridan, his quasi-girlfriend White, and the agent he called "Mom," Deacy. Plus, Brackett had relocated to New York from his temporary base in Chicago. And though Dean seems to have cut some of the Brackett strings, the older man continued to help his young protégé.

Ultimately, Dean backed off his threat about never returning to the Actors Studio. While he did avoid taking part in any major performance pieces, he would periodically reappear to watch others in workshop sketches. And while participants remember him as rather an odd loner, Studio student and future star Carroll Baker believed this was unfair, since all the Method members were a bit odd. "None of us thought the others were peculiar because we all were," Baker recalled. "My hair was in a bun. I was dreary and desperately trying to be intellectual, Rod Steiger would always greet you with a French or German or Jewish accent. . . . So Jimmy was no weirder than the others of us."[15]

Baker further defended Dean by adding, "Behaving as you felt—not according to convention—was Lee Strasberg's [Studio] attitude and most of us mimicked him [along non-conformity lines]."[16] So Dean managed to grow both as a person and as a performer by returning to the Studio. In time he could even admit that Strasberg was "an incredible man, a walking encyclopedia, with fantastic insight."[17]

Dean's second New York milestone, after gaining membership in the Studio, was making the Broadway cast of *See the Jaguar*. As luck would have it, his aunt and uncle were able to witness Dean's exuberance over a pivotal preliminary step in the *Jaguar* process. Dean and his best friends, Sheridan and Bast, had hitchhiked back to Indiana for an early Thanksgiving in October 1952. After a week of overeating and showing off all his hometown haunts and habits, James received a phone call from Deacy. Lemuel Ayers, best known then for having coproduced the Cole Porter Broadway hit *Kiss Me Kate*, wanted Dean to audition for a small but pivotal part in *Jaguar*. Sheridan remembered James as literally "glowing" with the news and stating: "I have the strangest feeling. I can't explain it, but I know I'm gonna get it. It's the strangest feeling I ever had about a job."[18]

Now, whether this was confidence or just the knowledge that Ayers was a homosexual crony of Brackett is unclear. Moreover, Dean had no doubt helped his case for consideration by having crewed for Ayers on his yacht the preceding summer. But while his connections helped get him an audition, Dean needed another break to get the part. A second actor beat Dean out, but turned the role down.

Before further documenting the *Jaguar* experience, though, two entertaining incidents on the trek back to Indiana merit noting. First, call it serendipity, but maybe

Dean's "strangest feeling" about getting the role was part of a larger happy change of fortune for him. For example, what could have been a long and arduous hitchhiking trip home became a fun excursion when sports-conscious Dean and friends were picked up just outside of New York by major league player Clyde McCullough, a former Chicago Cubs catcher in the 1940s then playing for the Pittsburgh Pirates and on his way to Iowa for an exhibition game.[19] While Dizzy and Bill did not have a clue about McCullough's identity, James was in baseball heaven, telling his friends all about their diamond angel. What is impressive about this is that McCullough was merely a journeyman player, without any real claim to fame, yet Dean was still knowledgeable about him. Actors Studio or not, former athlete Dean kept up on his baseball. McCullough's baseball skills might have been limited, but his people skills were of hall-of-fame quality. Sensing his passengers were low on funds (the trio had less than ten dollars among them), McCullough covered meal expenses all the way to Indiana. Comically, it was not until this baseball-focused time with McCullough that it dawned on Sheridan that if she were to wed Dean her married name would be Dizzy Dean—à la the great St. Louis Cardinals pitcher and radio personality. Talk of this zany baseball star might initially have been triggered by the fact that his Hollywood film biography, *The Pride of St. Louis*, had appeared earlier that year.

COLLECTION OF WES D. GEHRING

*A disappointed hitchhiker (Clark Gable) before Claudette Colbert
shows him the power of the leg in* It Happened One Night *(1934).*

The second diverting episode of note on the way back
to Indiana involved Dean's sense of humor. If this biography
reinforces one point, beyond Dean's tendency to often be a
tortured teen poseur, it is that the young man had the heart
of a mimic. His impersonation skills were alive and well on
this journey. What's more, his repertoire of material was evi-
dently extensive enough that he could be very event specific.
For example, Sheridan documents that prior to their baseball ride, Dean regaled her and Bast with his inventive take
on the celebrated hitchhiking scene from Frank Capra's *It*

Happened One Night (1934).[20] The sequence in question had Clark Gable comically demonstrating various hitchhiking techniques to a bored Claudette Colbert. Unfortunately, nothing stops a car until Colbert demonstrates the power of a shapely leg. Dean, of course, played both parts. (*It Happened One Night* also had a major impact on another Hoosier-born entertainer, Red Skelton. His first classic comedy sketch, a donut-dunking routine, was probably extrapolated from Gable demonstrating the technique to Colbert. A 1930s photo of Skelton also captures the comedian spoofing Colbert's nicely turned leg.[21])

As a final corollary to the subject of Dean the comic, he was not limited to the various impersonations and amusing observations already noted in this book. He also had the ability for unvarnished barbed wit. To illustrate, Dean later complained to a reporter about always being likened to his acknowledged hero, Marlon Brando: "How would you like [forever being] compared to [legendary newsman] Walter Winchell?"[22]

Once back in New York, a very nervous Dean went to his *Jaguar* audition. As with many potentially breakthrough parts, the role James was contending for was an unusual one. The character was sixteen-year-old Wally Wilkins, an illiterate, backwards southern youth whose unstable mother, in an attempt to protect her son from life, has kept him locked in an old icehouse for years. Before the mother's death she lets a wholly unprepared

Wally out into the real world. Now, couple this abnormal character with a sadistic storeowner/local bully who uses caged animals with obvious signs, á la "See the Jaguar," to attract customers to his business. Predictably, wild child Wally becomes the hunted prey of this sick man, and by play's end the naïve youngster finds himself in the jaguar's cage.

Given this scenario, it was hardly a surprise that the *Jaguar* backers were having trouble casting the part. In fact, more than a hundred auditions had already been held for the role, both in Chicago and New York. Hollywood "legend has it that Dean [then] got the part after besting scores of other actors. In reality, he was not the first choice for the role; he got it only after another actor, Wright King, had turned it down."[23] King, like Paul Newman, was a performer Dean knew through frequent competition for other New York stage and live television parts. A decade older than Dean, King would probably have accepted the *Jaguar* role had it been promptly offered. But because of a mix-up, or maybe continued uncertainty with the play's backers, King moved on.

Ironically, Dean did *not* then get the part through some magical *A Star is Born* (1937) audition. Instead, his reading for the play did not go well. Worse yet, Dean's hard-won contact, *Jaguar* producer Ayers, was further put off by the young man's rough edges; that is, even at this pivotal junction of his young career, Dean was unwilling and/or incapable of playing the polite game of small talk. Conventional chronicles credit the persistence of both the *Jaguar* playwright, N. Richard Nash, and the director, Michael Gordon, in persuading Ayers to give Dean a second reading. But James' agent, Deacy, was convinced the deciding factor was her client's mix of moxie and his neglected sense of humor: "Dean walked into the producer's [Ayers] office for an interview. The producer told Dean he was too short. [The five-foot-eight] Dean walked over to the producer and told him to stand up. The producer came up to Dean's shoulders. That brash attitude landed him the job."[24] Regardless of what transpired, Dean made the most of his second chance, and the part was his.

Rehearsals started on October 20, 1952, and the Broadway-bound youngster quickly fell under the spell of actor Arthur Kennedy, whose *Jaguar* character attempts to protect the boy Dean played. Seventeen years James' senior, Kennedy was then splitting his time between West Coast films and East Coast theater. Though still in his thirties, he had already won a Tony Award for playing one of the sons in Arthur Miller's *Death of a Salesman* (1949) and had been twice nominated for an Oscar, once in the Best Supporting Actor category for *Champion* (1949), and as Best Actor for *Bright Victory* (1951). He was also a member of the Actors Studio and had appeared in Elia Kazan's film *Boomerang* (1947).

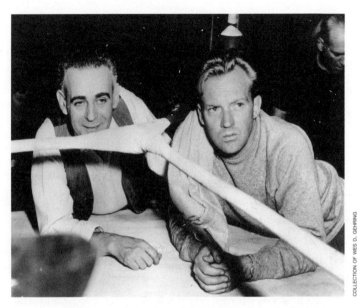

*Arthur Kennedy (right) in his Oscar-nominated role
from* Champion *(1949).*

While he would no doubt be a valuable mentor in many ways, there was a downside to this Dean discipleship to Kennedy: "nobody mattered except for the actor."[25] James had already witnessed a comic variation of this lesson on the set of *Sailor Beware* (1952), when Dean Martin and Jerry Lewis frequently disrupted production with their spontaneous practical jokes. But Kennedy took the actor-first mentality to a whole new level—a drawn-out, getting-in-character *method*. Undoubtedly, this influence would later contribute to Dean's reputation as a dif-

COLLECTION OF WES D. GEHRING

ficult actor with whom to work. An eerie footnote to this latest Dean mentorship was that the young actor's off-stage mannerisms were, for a time, reminiscent of Kennedy's. Apparently, Dean's mimicry skills were so innate that sometimes admiration unconsciously spilled over into impersonation.

As with many plays heading to Broadway, the out-of-town previews were buffeted about by two standard problems—funding frustrations and a nonstop call for script rewrites. Unfortunately, the complexities of this dark story were never effectively worked out. After *Jaguar* opened in New York on December 3, 1952, bad reviews caused the production to close after only four days. The *New York Daily News* reviewer was the most succinct on the subject: "If *See the Jaguar* had a reasonably credible story, it would be the best new piece on Broadway—but it hasn't, so it isn't."[26] In contrast, the *New York Journal-American* critic insightfully fleshed out its pan along the lines of a failed art-house production: "This is one of those intense, earthy dramas which reveals primitive love and conflict in the raw. Eugene O'Neil has been able to bring such characters to life, but [author] N. Richard Nash . . . was able only to produce confusion and bafflement."[27]

Although the critical consensus was not good for the play itself, there was another consensus of a more positive nature—Dean was someone to watch. The *New York World Telegram* said, "James Dean is gently awkward as

159

the ignorant boy," while the *New York Daily News* observed, "As the boy, James Dean is very good."[28] *Cue* noted, "The part of the feeble-minded boy from the ice-house is handled well . . . by a newcomer to Broadway, James Dean."[29] But the critical pièce de résistance on Dean's *Jaguar* performance came from the *New York Herald Tribune*'s acclaimed critic Walter F. Kerr, who later wrote for the *New York Times*. Kerr's comments were the kind of praise one puts at the front of the scrap-book, those special accolades which might have been ghostwritten by a mother: "James Dean adds an extraor-dinary performance in an almost impossible role: that of a bewildered lad who has been completely shut off from a vicious world . . . [but is now] coming upon both the beauty and the brutality of the mountain for the first time."[30]

Prior to *Jaguar* Dean had not worked in his chosen pro-fession for six months, other than a part in a one-night-only, off-Broadway dramatic reading of Franz Kafka's *The Metamorphosis*. But after Dean's sterling notices as Wally Wilkins in *Jaguar*, he was soon signed for small roles in three early 1953 high-profile television programs: a dramatic pres-entation of the "Hound of Heaven" on the daytime *Kate Smith Show* (1950–54), an episode of the action drama *Treasury Men in Action* (1950–55, from actual cases), and a Jesse James installment of *You Are There* (1953–57), a docu-drama with Walter Cronkite serving as a news anchorman for each recreated historical event. Dean's acting career was far from made, but he was on his way. As 1953 progressed, his television parts would increase in size. In fact, by the mid-July episode of the *Campbell Soundstage* (1952–54), "Something for an Empty Briefcase," Dean had reached star status on the small screen.

Dean's first Broadway turn had opened professional doors. The *Jaguar* part had represented a variation of his greatest strength and what he later rode to screen immortality—playing a confused teen trying to come to grips with the real world. In contrast, one could argue that James had inadvertently "researched" his next Broadway part, the homosexual houseboy (Bachir) of *The Immoralist*, during his relationship with Brackett. Whether or not art was actually imitating life, Dean was no stranger to the world of homosexual seduction, and Bachir was all about seduction. *The Immoralist* keys upon a young French archaeologist living in a North African village with his bride. The archaeologist, played by Louis Jourdan, is a long-repressed homosexual who has an affair with Dean's manipulative Bachir. Tortured by guilt, Jourdan's character attempts to make it up to his wife, played by Geraldine Page, with a night of passion. Predictably, she becomes pregnant. But unlike comedy's frequent use of a forthcoming birth as an upbeat promise of new beginnings, *The Immoralist* paints the pregnancy as a symbolic life sentence to a loveless union.

Unlike Dean's shaky first audition for *Jaguar*, he breezed through his reading for *The Immoralist*. This was doubly impressive, given that his select audience included the play's legendary producer, Billy Rose. Cowriter Ruth Goetz, who adapted the play (with Augustus Goetz) from Andre Gide's novel, fairly glowed in her praise of Dean's audition: "He began to read and he was marvelous. He was instinctively, absolutely right. He had the quality of sweetness and charming attractiveness, and at the same time, a nasty undercurrent of suggestiveness and sexuality. And he was smashing."[31] Dean started rehearsals in mid-December of 1953, almost exactly a year after the closing of *Jaguar*. *The Immoralist* experienced a stormy shakedown cruise before its February 8, 1954, opening, however, with much of the conflict centering on a difficult Dean. Former fan Goetz was most direct on the subject: "The little bastard would not learn the words, would not really try to give a performance, would not really rehearse. He drove us up the wall."[32] Tack on to this that Dean was often late, insulting, and never did a scene the same way twice, and one has an unhappy production. Moreover, the problem was exacerbated by the firing of director Herman Shumlin, who was not up to what was then seen as a controversial storyline.

Dean took the firing very personally, given that Shumlin had been his earliest *Immoralist* supporter, being a big fan of both James' *Jaguar* character as well as the young actor's television work. Ironically, another reason for Shumlin's sacking was that some people perceived his collaborative style as an inability to control Dean. Regardless of Shumlin's relative skills as a director, his often free exchange of ideas was an approach to which Dean responded best, not unlike Nicholas Ray on the later *Rebel Without a Cause*. Conversely, the no-nonsense Daniel Mann, who replaced Shumlin on *The Immoralist*, anticipated the constant conflicts Dean had with the traditionalist George Stevens on *Giant*. Indeed, Dean was said to have ever so briefly quit *The Immoralist* in anger, only to quickly swallow his pride and return.

Though a combination of ego and the Method were probably the pivotal source of Dean's disruptions, some biographers have also suggested that the actor was actually trying to get fired. Explanations range from a possible concern over how playing a gay character would affect his young career to some tempting film opportunities.[33] But *Immoralist* costar Page would probably have spoken against this hypothesis, since she believed Dean was constantly full of inventive suggestions for her character. Seven years older than Dean, she became a rare close friend on the production, and yet another protective mother figure to the actor. Given that she went on to be a seven-time Oscar-nominated actress (finally winning for *The Trip to Bountiful*, 1985), one could strongly suggest that Dean got at least one personal relationship right on his second and final Broadway play.

Along related lines, Dean's high school drama instructor, Adeline Nall, was briefly in New York during Dean's *Immoralist* rehearsals, and he invited her to the production at the Ziegfeld Theater. Whenever possible, he would slip into a seat near her and compare notes. "Once he asked, 'Are you learning anything?' Our roles as teacher and student were suddenly reversed," Nall said. "Now it was he who introduced me to new concepts and experiences. It meant a lot to me that he wanted me to learn."[34]

Dean's growing success was slowly pulling him away from his reliable old friends Bill Bast and Dizzy Sheridan. The process had started with *Jaguar* and was escalating with *The Immoralist*. Moreover, unlike the former play, his friends could offer little help. In *Jaguar* Dean had to sing part of a folk song composed by Alec Wilder. But Dean's Achilles heel was being nearly tone-deaf. Evening after evening Bast and Sheridan worked on making him, if not a singer, at least someone close to capable of carrying a tune. Nothing if not dedicated, Dean was relentless in his practice, though there was also a sense he enjoyed subjecting his two friends to his tone-deaf stylings.

Unlike *Jaguar*, *The Immoralist* opened to solid reviews. The *New York Times* said, "It is beautifully produced and acted," while the *New York World Telegram and Sun* described it as "a delicate, tender tragedy which is beautifully acted and exquisitely directed."[35] As he had with *Jaguar*, Dean stole the show with a small but flashy part. The *World Telegram and Sun* proclaimed, "It is James Dean as the houseboy who clearly and originally underlines the sleazy impertinence and the amoral opportunism which the husband must combat."[36] That Dean had perfectly created the villain an audience loved to hate is further documented in almost every other review. These notices would range from Walter Kerr's diplomatic praise in the *New York Herald Tribune*— "James Dean makes a colorfully insinuating scape-grace"—to a seemingly overwhelmed *New York Post* critic calling him "a particularly slimy young man, who taunts and tries to blackmail."[37]

The young actor was looking at a long, safe Broadway run. But Dean seldom played it safe. Besides, he had just been promised a plum part by the closest thing to a deity for an American actor of that era—director Elia Kazan. The unavoidable bait was a central role in the screen adaptation of John Steinbeck's best-selling 1952 novel *East of Eden*. The part was just a promise; Dean would have to fly to the West Coast and film a screen test. But this was good enough for Dean. Plus, abruptly quitting *The Immoralist* worked on two additional levels, besides being a basic career move. First, it fit Dean's affinity for shock. What could be more shocking than walking away from a hit Broadway play shortly after it opened? Second, Dean continued to have issues with the powers that be behind *The Immoralist*, from (to his mind) diminutive director Mann to pushy producer Rose. Depending upon one's source, Dean gave his notice either opening night or a mere two to three days later. No matter when he quit, the actor was headed back to the state—California—that had provided him with so much heartbreak earlier in his life.

8

East of Eden

> *"Cal wanted to throw his arms about his father, to hug him
> and to be hugged by him. He wanted some wild demonstration
> of sympathy and love."*[1]
>
> JOHN STEINBECK, *EAST OF EDEN* (1952)

JAMES DEAN'S FLIGHT TO CALIFORNIA WITH DIRECTOR
Elia Kazan to do a screen test for *East of Eden* was the
first time the young man had flown. Kazan was further
entertained by both Dean's "luggage" (two grocery sacks
tied with string) and the fact that the actor was glued to
the window watching the scenery far below. While Kazan
supposedly needed a studio-approved test to sign James
for *Eden*, the acclaim for the director's previous picture,
On the Waterfront (1954), essentially gave him carte
blanche on *Eden*. *Waterfront* had been an instantly recognized American classic and garnered a treasure trove of
Oscars, including statuettes for Best Picture, Best
Director (Kazan), Best Actor (Marlon Brando), Best
Supporting Actress (Eva Maria Saint), and Best Story and
Best Screenplay (Budd Schulberg).

The most telling incident to transpire between Kazan
and Dean during the *Eden* preproduction occurred just

*Elia Kazan and Marlon Brando discuss a scene
in* On the Waterfront *(1954).*

after their touchdown in Los Angeles. Dean requested that they stop at Winton Dean's Santa Monica home. When the director witnessed the extreme tension between the son and father, he realized *Eden* was a perfect match for the young actor. (Kazan was already well aware of the close rapport between James Dean and his surrogate parents, Marcus and Ortense Winslow. The director had seen it firsthand, since Dean's aunt and uncle had come to the New York opening of *The Immoralist*.)

The story that Kazan brought to the screen was the final section of John Steinbeck's sprawling 600-page novel, which covers several provocative generations in the life of a California family. The book culminates with a metaphorical Cain and Abel tale set on the eve of World War I. Two teenage brothers vie for the love of their puritanical father. In the film, Dean plays Cal Trask, the modern Cain, who never seems able to please his father, Adam, played by Raymond Massey. Richard Davalos is the good son, Aron. Julie Harris is the loyal girlfriend of Aron who finds herself increasingly attracted to Cal.

The director was drawn to this portion of the book because he saw it as a variation of his own story—Kazan's father, who owned a carpet store, thought that the future filmmaker would be a failure. When Kazan realized this was also a cross Dean had long been carrying, the director's job immediately became that much easier. With the

The Eden *(1955) rejection scene of Dean (left)*
by screen father Raymond Massey.

casting of veteran actor Massey as the quasi-biblical father, the *Eden* production was further blessed. Traditionalist Massey was put off by every Method actor nuance exhibited by Dean, and Dean, sensing the older man's hostility, was equally down on his screen father. Not surprisingly, Kazan used these volatile emotions. Indeed, he threw gasoline on them. The director confessed in his autobiography: "This was an antagonism I didn't try to heal; I aggravated it. I'm ashamed to say—well, not ashamed; everything goes in directing movies—I didn't conceal from Jimmy or Ray what they thought of each other, made it plain to each of them. The screen was alive with precisely what I wanted, they detested each other."[2]

As one Dean biographer comically observed, "Kazan's means of manipulating actors stopped just short of electric shock treatment."[3] More specifically, in one of the film's pivotal scenes, James' character purposely reads the Bible in a manner that is meant to upset his screen father. But when Kazan believed Massey remained too passive, the director secretly instructed Dean to quietly lace the reading with under-his-breath obscenities! Leonard Rosenman, who wrote the *Eden* score, was on the set that day and later described this ploy on Massey: "Well, the old man from the old school started to turn purple! He jumped up from the table and started to yell."[4] Kazan had his shot.

Of course, in Kazan's defense, directors have been movie manipulators since cinema was brand new. The great John Ford used subterfuge on every one of his productions. While making *The Informer* (1935), the first of four pictures for which he would win the Oscar for best director, he conveniently lied to leading man Victor McLaglen. On the eve of the film's pivotal scene, he told the alcoholic actor he had the next day off, knowing McLaglen would get drunk. But first thing the following morning the "painfully hung-over McLaglen was summoned to the studio. John went right to work on the [poignant confessional] court-of-inquiry scene, and McLaglen's thick-tongued, confused, anguished performance owed much to his very real hangover."[5] McLaglen flirted with retiring from acting, but he went on to win an Academy Award for best actor for the role and appeared in many future Ford films. As with Kazan's bag of tricks, such means are generally used to justify the ends.

Interestingly enough, Massey's autobiography provides a fascinating follow-up to the obscenity-laced Bible reading scene. Even though Kazan confessed to an upset Massey that he had put Dean up to the swearing, the older actor demanded an apology from Dean. Once that penitence was provided, Massey believed the production assumed a more professional tone. Moreover, he claimed this is what the majority of the cast wanted. To prove his point, Massey notes an entertaining observation by costar Burl Ives pertaining to a delay in shooting a relatively simple scene. An angry Cal was supposed to be wastefully sending blocks of ice down a chute from a summer storage loft. But Dean took a long time getting into his Method moment. When a frustrated Massey asked, "'What the hell goes on,' Burl Ives looked at his watch. 'Jimmy's got to get to hate the ice. . . . It takes time.'"[6]

Massey and Ives notwithstanding, one *Eden* performer strictly in Dean's corner was Harris, who played Aron's girlfriend. In his autobiography Kazan called her the "angel on our set," who was "goodness itself with

Dean, kind and patient and everlastingly sympathetic. She would adjust her performance to whatever the new kid did."⁷Moreover, a decade later Kazan elevated Harris's status on *Eden* further by observing, "If it hadn't been for Julie Harris I don't think he [Dean] would have gotten through the picture."⁸ This meant Harris was both a creatively flexible costar (her Method background allowed her to handle Dean's improvisations) and a stable offscreen friend who could help James through several current concerns, all revolving around his myriad creative interests. Undoubtedly, part of these alleged Dean needs can be equated to his assuming his "little boy lost" pose. Yet the gamesmanship played by both Dean and Kazan alienated enough people that a sympathetic friend would hardly go unappreciated. Harris later said, "That reputation of being 'difficult' arose from Jimmy's eagerness to keep his own integrity—a constant struggle to retain his own individuality—and to avoid being forced into the standard Hollywood mold. He succeeded magnificently in doing just that and it took tremendous courage."⁹ As a corollary to her courage comment, Harris was also impressed with Dean's physical bravery on *Eden*.He refused a stunt double, both in a scene that necessitated he jump off an express train and another sequence that required him to climb from one compartment to another on a Ferris wheel.

While such flirting with danger was good for *Eden*, Kazan much preferred that during the production Dean refrain from all things perilous in his personal life. The catalyst for the director's concern was the sports car and motorcycle James had bought with his *Eden* advance. Thus, in order to both monitor his protégé and even eliminate Dean's need to drive to work, Kazan left his lodging and "moved into one of those star dressing rooms on the Warner lot [where much of *Eden* was being shot] and put Dean into the one next door. I made sure that I would be with him night and day and take care of him. You don't do that with everybody."[10] Kazan also vetoed Dean's plan to ride his motorcycle to Salinas, California, when the *Eden* production went on location. James of course later died driving to Salinas for an automobile race.

Despite Kazan's babysitting claims, Dean still had time to begin a stormy relationship with Italian actress Pier Angeli, whom he had met during a break in filming from *Eden*, as she was also on the Warner lot making *The Silver Chalice* (1954) opposite Paul Newman. Dean visited their set, presumably to meet Newman, his friendly foe from live television days in New York. James had been offered Newman's *Chalice* part, but his New York agent, Jane Deacy, had wisely turned it down. *Chalice*, a biblical bomb and Newman's screen debut, had him wiring his agents before the production even wrapped, "You'd better have me [back] on stage when this thing is released or I'm dead!"[11] Conversely, Newman had tested to play Dean's brother, Aron, in *Eden*, but inexplicably did not get the part. One can only dream about what an electric pairing that would have made.

With regard to Angeli, those Dean biographers with a strictly homosexual agenda for the young Hoosier paint his relationship with the actress as strictly platonic.[12] But the evidence suggests otherwise. For example, the ever-present Kazan baldly states he could hear the young couple making love in the Warner dressing room that doubled as Dean's apartment during the production of *Eden*.[13] Of course, the director could also hear their frequent arguing, too. This was a microcosm, fire and ice, of their short, intense relationship.

A year younger than the twenty-three-year-old Dean, Angeli had been a film actress in Italy since the late 1940s. Legendary Italian filmmaker Vittorio De Sica said of Angeli, who starred in his *Tomorrow Is Too Late* (1949), "As soon as I saw the child, her fragile body, her sensitive face, I knew she was the right one."[14] Angeli made her Hollywood screen debut in *Teresa* (1951), a popular psychological drama. Fittingly, her modest career in American movies often showcased her as the young, fragile innocent. But neither film stardom nor a short marriage to singer Vic Damone panned out, and she returned to Europe and a series of forgettable films. Later calling Dean the love of her life, she committed suicide in 1971 at age thirty-nine.[15] The instability of this abbreviated life speaks directly to the stormy relationship

COLLECTION OF WES D. GEHRING

A lovesick Dean and Pier Angeli during the production of Eden.

she had with Dean during the production of *Eden*, but it does not acknowledge the key part her conservative Catholic stage-door mother had in undoubtedly breaking up the romance. There was nothing she liked about Dean, from his Quaker faith to his uncouth behavior. Even Dean admitted, "We're members of a totally different caste. She's the kind of girl you put on a shelf and look at. Anyway, her old lady doesn't dig me. Can't say I blame her."[16]

Beyond the cultural differences and an Italian mother's right to keep a hot-blooded American boy away from her daughter, there was also family breadwinner Angeli's screen image as the chaste young girl to protect. Dean's emerging antihero persona might easily tarnish her then-promising career, something even their studio (Warner Brothers) could appreciate, though the studio was also pleased over all the newspaper coverage generated by the romance. Ultimately, it was probably Dean's signature comic directness that doomed the relationship, at least as long as Angeli's mother was the power broker. On one occasion Angeli's mother read Dean the proverbial riot act over his lack of respect in bringing her daughter in so late. Piling on the verbal abuse, she finally added that in Rome no Italian boyfriend would keep a date out until the wee hours. Dean simply replied, "'When in Rome, do as the Romans do.' Welcome to Hollywood."[17]

Though there seems to have been genuine love between Dean and Angeli, a multitude of additional factors played out between them. First, with both Angeli's mother and Kazan so closely monitoring their every move, the romance was probably further fueled by a combination "let's play hooky" and "them against us" mentality. Nothing tastes better than forbidden fruit. Second, though romantic opposites often cannot sustain a relationship over time, differences are definitely diverting in the short term. This seemed especially true of Dean, whose one other serious Hollywood romance would be with Swiss-born bombshell Ursula Andress. The Indiana farm boy was definitely attracted to foreign-born film actresses. Was it love, or just James' innate sense of curiosity, that had him briefly studying Italian when linked to Angeli, and German when he was with Andress? Third, Dean and Angeli did have one moving component in common—both had lost a beloved parent at a young age. Like Dean's propensity to talk about his deceased mother, Angeli was often quick to discuss her late father. Fourth, one might just fall back on the old axiom that these youngsters were simply, "in love with being in love." And how easy that must be when one is a beautiful, twenty-something film star "working" in a dream factory.

When asked who might be labeled the love of Dean's life, the actor's surrogate brother, Marcus Winslow Jr., responded: "I think there were lots of girls in his life that he cared for. But I believe Pier Angeli was someone he really cared for. I think Jimmy really wanted to marry her. But [Angeli] let her mother dictate to her."[18] Asked if he believed the now almost mythic story about Dean allegedly waiting outside the Los Angeles church where Angeli and singer Damone were married on November 24, 1954, only to gun his motorcycle engine and race off when they appeared, Winslow replied: "I like to think it happened. It sounded like Jimmy."[19] Winslow also referred to the gold locket with Angeli's picture (now on display at Indiana's Fairmount Historical Society) that the actress gave Dean during their romance. Despite the actor's shock over her marriage, he continued to cherish this keepsake.

Providentially for Kazan, the roller-coaster nature of Dean's relationship with Angeli helped *Eden*. The director later confessed, "I was glad when she 'found' Vic Damone. Now I had Jimmy as I wanted him, alone and miserable."[20] Before one judges Kazan too harshly here, remember that this opportunist nature was just one more way he was like his young star. Besides a shared estrangement from their fathers, one additional parallel merits consideration. Kazan and Dean's approach to Method acting was on the same page. Furthermore, Kazan's take on directing was much more of a collaborative process, which is often the case with actors turned directors (Kazan had started out as an actor). More importantly, and central to what might be called his unique Method *directing*, was Kazan's approach of constantly feeding his performer new bits of business for each rehearsal in an attempt to keep the process fresh, despite set dialogue. This sounds perfectly logical now, but it was precisely this philosophy that often got Dean in trouble with more traditional actors and directors, with such criticisms as "He's not being professional!" "He never does it the same way twice!" "He's not hitting his marks!" How freeing it must have been for Dean to work with Kazan on *Eden*, even though some friction persisted with traditionalists such as Massey.

Earlier in this book a shared affinity by Kazan and Dean for an athleticism of acting was briefly noted. The director discussed how the body of former athlete James "was more expressive, actually, in free movement, than Brando's. . . . Brando's a genius. But Dean had a very vivid body, and I did play a lot with it in [*Eden*] long shots."[21] Kazan scholar Jeff Young recently brought an added dimension to the subject, which is analogous to what has just been described as Method directing. In Young's introduction to his book-length interview with Kazan, the historian likens his fascination with the director's style to a baseball hitter coming to the plate.[22] Each time up for the batter is similar to the last time, yet the player always makes various small adjustments. The catalyst for change might be any number of things, from a new relief pitcher to a runner suddenly being in scoring position. Along parallel lines, Method directors and actors such as Kazan and Dean are constantly awake to every new wrinkle in a given situation. If there is not a new wrinkle, they actively create one. Thus, the sports that were so important to a young Dean growing up in Indiana would seem to have provided him with an early arena for Method's encouragement of the improvisational touch.

Dean also used to warm up for a scene by either running around the set or doing something equally physical, such as jumping jacks or climbing the ladder to the scaffolding over the sound stage. This all would have meshed perfectly with Kazan, who forever mixed sports and art. The director "had a thing about his body. He kept in tip-top shape by playing a lot of tennis and walking tire-lessly."[23] Appropriately, Kazan's first pep talk to the Actors Studio keyed upon a sports metaphor, "This is not a club, this is a gym for actors to work out in. Everybody is expected to work hard."[24]

One could push this Kazan/Dean analogy between the Method and sports a step further by bringing in yet another entertainment development of the early 1950s— the Chicago School of Television. This was a period development in which Windy City television producers maximized the properties of the medium by bringing a more informal, intimate style to such television pioneers of the casual as Dave Garroway and Studs Terkel.[25] While sharing certain components with the New York scene, such as the belief in the superiority of live television to produce a more realistic viewing experience, the Chicago School essentially embraced one of sport's most funda-mental axioms—"You take what they give you."

Consequently, as the Chicago School turned early television's technical limitations into intimate positives, Kazan took some then-new movie developments such as CinemaScope and managed to use them to his advantage. This widescreen approach was not the ideal development for an intimate story such as *Eden*. But it was an unwrit-ten rule of early 1950s filmmaking, struggling to compete with the phenomenal popularity of television, that major movies were to be made in CinemaScope. The idea was to give the public something they could not get on the small screen. Thus, enter Kazan, no fan of CinemaScope. In fact, he enjoyed mocking the process and quoting director George Stevens's comic take on this technology, though the line has also been attributed to other filmmakers: "They finally found a way to photograph a snake."[26]

Still, Kazan used CinemaScope to further explore his fascination with the fluidity of Dean's movements in long shot. Moreover, the director embraced the process to emphasize the vulnerability of James' character through the actor's size. According to Kazan, "CinemaScope emphasized Dean's smallness. When he runs in the bean fields, there's a big thing [expanse] like that wide, and you see Dean running through it, looking like a little child."[27] The scenes in the bean field are all the more effective because Kazan allowed the Indiana farm boy to improvise his communion with nature, savoring the plants and soil he hopes will help him reconnect with his father. (Unbeknownst to this screen parent, Dean's character has made a large investment in a bean crop to defray an earlier financial loss suffered by his father.)

Not surprisingly, his Indiana friends and family found these CinemaScope farm scenes their favorite in the Dean oeuvre. His beloved father-figure uncle, Marcus Winslow, later reinforced this sentiment by saying, "I sup-

Dean as Cal in Eden. *Cal was the screen character reminiscent of the real Dean.*

COLLECTION OF WES D. GEHRING

pose in *East of Eden* he was closest to the way he actually was. He really didn't seem like he was acting to me."[28] His high school drama teacher and first major acting guru, Adeline Nall, indirectly supported this slant through her litany of Dean traits in the character of *Eden*'s Cal—"His funny little laugh that ripples with the slightest provocations . . . his sudden changes from frivolity to gloom"— these were all things she had seen in the halls of Fairmount High.[29] *Eden* was also a favorite of Dean's cousin Marcus Winslow Jr. for several often moving reasons: "I like the story and the timeframe. Jimmy didn't seem to be acting—the way he walked, talked, and laughed. Maybe I also liked it best because it was his first starring film. Plus, Jimmy's other two movies came out after his death. It was sad to see him on the screen and . . . [realize] he never got to see how the public responded to him. You know how family is."[30]

Since so much of Dean the person is recycled into Cal the character, it makes Steinbeck's original impression of the actor, also echoed by Kazan, all the more amazing. The director later described taking Dean to the novelist's New York apartment before the actor was even cast: "John liked him right away for the part. He said, 'Jesus Christ, he is Cal'; which is pretty close to the truth—he was."[31] The secret to this Dean-Cal connection might be found in Steinbeck's capsulization of *Eden*, by way of the seminal part of Cal in his novel: "The greatest terror a child can have is that he is not loved, and rejection is the hell he fears. I think everyone in the world to a large or small extent has felt rejection. And with rejection comes anger."[32]

While this book has already posited that Dean's sometimes angst-ridden posturing over both the death of his mother and the estrangement from his biological father was just that, posturing, it was a fairly polished persona by the time he met Steinbeck. Moreover, as this chapter has documented, Kazan stopped at nothing to get the performance he was after. Consequently, one has to assume that the director also dredged up painful Dean memories of a pre-Ortense and Marcus Winslow past. At times the democratic image of the collaborative Kazan falls away, and one simply sees a painful Pavlovian type: "Directing James was like directing the faithful Lassie. I either lectured him or terrorized him. . . . He was so instinctive and so stupid in so many ways."[33]

This unguarded moment by Kazan is probably not as representative of his many more mentor-sounding sentiments about Dean. Plus, it also further suggests the uncoiling anger behind much of who Kazan was in the early 1950s. This anger was not limited to a lack of love from his father. The director was in an undeclared fight to reclaim a tarnished reputation after being a 1952 friendly witness for the House Un-American Activities Committee and the now-infamous Senator Joseph McCarthy. Though the Communist-hunting paranoia of what has come to be called McCarthyism was on the wane by the 1954 production of *Eden*, the blacklisting of screen artists, fueled in part by friendly HUAC witnesses, continues to divide Hollywood even today. This was still most evident more than fifty years after *Eden* when Kazan accepted a lifetime achievement Oscar in 1998 from the Academy of Motion Picture Arts and Sciences. Half of the audience was either unresponsive or literally turned their back on the honoree.

Kazan's *On the Waterfront* (1954), done just prior to *Eden*, is often seen as the director's attempt to explain and justify his naming names. In the film, Brando's character testifies against crooked union leaders and essentially names names. Though a similar HUAC link to *Eden* is not as readily apparent, one still cannot read Kazan's comments about Cal and not think about a director trying to indirectly make amends and find acceptance. Calling *Eden* a more "personal" movie than *Waterfront*, Kazan observed, "I wanted to show that a boy whom people thought was bad was really good. . . . I was very like Cal, so *East of Eden* was for me a kind of self-defense. It was about people not understanding me."[34]

Dean's initial response to Kazan's HUAC appearance has gone unrecorded by history. Dean was not yet a personality to be cited. But Brando, according to the invariably sensitive critic, historian, and biographer Richard Schickel, "was stricken by the news . . . virtually in tears over Kazan's action, unable to believe that a man he loved and trusted could have done something of which he so deeply disapproved."[35] Still, Brando got over it. Kazan's case was complex, and the actor's friends and associates advised him to not judge quickly, to separate political activities from the artist. Moreover, the Brando of *Waterfront* wanted an Oscar as much as the Brando of *The Godfather* (1972) disdained the statuette. Brando knew going into *Waterfront* that Kazan would help make that Academy Award happen.

COLLECTION OF WES D. GEHRING

Kazan looking at the script for what is now considered his greatest picture, On the Waterfront *(1954).*

Since all things Brando were golden to him, Dean did not miss a beat in deciding to work with Kazan, then despised by the political left. In fact, Dean remained largely apolitical during his short adult life, with neither Kazan's friendly witness action nor the exiling of Dean's controversial comedy hero Charlie Chaplin (both in

1952) making him take a liberal stand. On the rare occasion when Dean was quoted on something then politically topical, such as communism, his remarks come across as simplistically safe. He once told the *Los Angeles Times*: "I hate anything that limits progress or growth. I hate institutions that do this, a way of acting that limits [creativity, or], a way of thinking. I hope this doesn't make me sound like a Communist. Communism is the most limiting factor of all today: if you really want to put the screws on yourself."[36] Paradoxically, in contrast to Kazan "singing" for HUAC, Dean was undoubtedly more upset with his director's order to both get a suntan and put on some weight for the part of Cal than he was about the director's politics. (Even during the production, Dean received instructions to drink a pint of cream a day to help maintain a healthy appearance.) The farm boy playing a farm boy had to still meet a city boy's (Kazan) notions of what constituted a healthy pastoral male.

As either a reward for jumping through all Kazan's metaphorical hoops or just a thoughtful gesture, the director made arrangements for Brando to visit Dean on the set of *Eden*. Angeli notwithstanding, this was James' most memorable moment on his first starring motion picture. The timing was appropriate, because Dean had never been so immersed in Brando as he was during this very Method shoot, especially late in the production of *Eden*. By then the industry buzz already had Dean as an emerging star, and he further aped Brando, assuming the older actor's bad-boy tendencies, from attending swank parties in jeans to ignoring and/or insulting Hollywood gossip columnists capable of making or breaking normal careers. Plus, Dean's lifelong pleasure at shocking friend and foe alike meshed perfectly with an axiom then synonymous with Brando but attributed to Brando's favorite acting coach, Stella Adler: "Be anything but dull."[37] However, it was a philosophy tailor-made for this Hoosier in Hollywood, too.

Though both Dean and *Eden* were projected to be hits by Hollywood insiders, the magnitude of the actor's impact surprised even Kazan. Confessing to be "totally unprepared," he chronicled a preview where "the instant he [Dean] appeared on the screen, hundreds of girls began to scream. They'd been waiting for him, it seemed-how come or why, I don't know."[38] While Dean's old friend Bill Bast did not scream, he was equally bowled over by an *Eden* preview experience: "I was shattered. . . . [I had] seen the irrefutable proof that Jimmy had achieved a degree of greatness in his acting."[39]

The majority of the reviews strongly embraced both *Eden* and Dean. The entertainment bible *Variety* observed, "It is a tour de force for the director's penchant for hard-hitting forays with life, and as such undoubtedly will be counted among his best screen efforts."[40] A second show-business staple, the *Hollywood Reporter*, said, "There can be no doubts as to the artistic merits of this picture. Beautifully acted, and superbly directed by Elia Kazan, it is bound to be one of the year's important contributions to screen literature."[41] *Time* magazine raved that the film "is a brilliant entertainment and more than that, it announces a new star, James Dean." The magazine described Dean as "a young man from Indiana, who is unquestionably the biggest news Hollywood has made in 1955." The actor possessed "the presence of a young lion and the same sense of danger about him . . . [yet] occasionally, he flicks a sly little look that seems to say, 'Well, all this is human, too—or had you forgotten?'"[42]

The *New York World Telegram and Sun* review had *Eden* as a rival to Kazan's much-honored *On the Waterfront*, adding, "James Dean makes a thunderclap impression in his movie debut. . . . He has resources of sympathy and affection along with impetuous emotional force."[43] The *New York Herald Tribune*'s praises indirectly acknowledged Kazan's use of CinemaScope: "Everything about Dean suggests the lonely, misunderstood nineteen-year-old. Even from a distance you know a lot about him by the way he walks—with his hands in his pockets and his head down, slinking like a dog waiting for a bone."[44] Other critical kudos ranged from the *New York Post* praising the "brilliant performances by the newcomers James Dean and Julie Harris" to the *Chicago Tribune* saying, "James Dean makes an impressive debut."[45] But credit for the most brilliantly prophetic *Eden* review returns one to the *Hollywood Reporter*, which had been the first major publication to critique the picture. Its assessment of Dean's performance poetically predicts the amazingly timeless hold this actor was about to exert on the disenfranchised young: "He is that rare thing, a young actor who is a great actor and the troubled eloquence with which he puts over the problems of misunderstood youth may lead to his being accepted by young audiences as a sort of symbol of their generation."[46]

Fittingly, back in Fairmount, Indiana, Dean was again on the front page, with the proud local critic noting, "Even if James Dean weren't a hometown boy, 'East of Eden' would be one of the most powerful productions ever released by Warner Brothers and it would be well worth the effort of and money of anyone."[47] The review added that the closest area screen, Marion's Indiana Theatre, had recently given a special performance of *Eden* for Dean's high school drama instructor Nall. Consistent with the ongoing populist support the actor had long received from Fairmount, the local critique credited the teacher, "together with the senior class, school officials and several others . . . [as being] enthusiastic with the picture, as most people who see it will be."[48]

The only modest fly in *Eden*'s critical hosannas was the common comment that Dean's acting was reminiscent of Kazan's earlier Method protégé, Brando. For example, the *New York Journal-American* reviewer said, "Performances throughout are effective, with young Dean giving a good account of himself in his first film role, even though his mannerisms and delivery are frequently remindful of Marlon Brando."[49] If a Brando parallel was noted in other *Eden* reviews, it tended to follow the pattern established by the *Journal-American*: praise for Dean mixed with a gentle suggestion to tone down any Brando acting affectations. Only the *New York Times*'s Bosley Crowther became cruel in his criticism: "Never have we seen a performer so clearly follow another's style. Mr. Kazan should be spanked for permitting him [Dean] to do such a sophomoric thing."[50] But one should add an insight here from the later award-winning *New Yorker* film critic, Pauline Kael, who once observed, "Bosley Crowther . . . can always be counted on to miss the point."[51]

Kael knew of which she spoke, since her criticism career was made, and Crowther's destroyed, by their opposing takes on *Bonnie and Clyde* (1967), another counterculture classic that even boasted a star (Warren Beatty) once described as "the next James Dean."[52] Crowther's blind spot to truly new-wave moments in the movies would be his downfall. But then as pianist, composer, actor, and celebrated wit Oscar Levant once said of his own criticism of Crowther, well before Kael weighed in against the reviewer, "It wasn't outlandish; most of the things I said were verifiable. I just mentioned the fact that he was opaque, murky, humorless and unperceptive."⁵³ Ironically, while Crowther, the critic for the mighty *New York Times*, managed to badly misread Dean's performance, the actor's modest hometown newspaper, the *Fairmount News*, gave a verdict on the Dean/Brando question for *Eden* that has insightfully survived the test of time: "This writer can see some . . . similarity . . . But Dean's is a warmer personality."⁵⁴

Today if the picture has a minor flaw, it is the less-than-believable closing reconciliation of Dean's Cal with his dying father Adam. When Cal's earlier gift of the bean money is rejected by Massey's Adam as so much war profiteering, Dean's character acts out against favored son Aron. Cal's revenge is to shatter his brother's spirit by revealing the dark family secret that the boys' mother, long claimed to have been dead by Adam, actually runs a brothel in a nearby community. Consequently, a quasi-suicidal Aron goes off to war and patriarchal Adam has a stroke. To then bring these melodramatic elements together in a feel-good finale often strikes the modern viewer as both forced and false to the cutting-edge realism that had come before. But Kazan's comforting close was consistent with an Eisenhower-era enthusiasm that was still reluctant to embrace an open ending. Thus, this homogeneous conclusion was not an issue in 1955.

As the movie mushroomed into a bicoastal media event, Dean fled from his newfound fame. Initially, he

used New York television work as a cover to avoid the
Hollywood hoopla of *Eden's* February 1955 sneak previews in the film capital. Then, as the picture's New York
opening began to build to the "most brilliant world premiere in recent Broadway history," Dean flew back to
Hollywood.[55] Skipping out on the latter event was a major
affront to both Warner Brothers and the Actors Studio,
since the premiere also doubled as a fund-raiser for
Kazan's performing school. Moreover, with major stars
such as Marlene Dietrich, Marilyn Monroe, Eva Marie
Saint, and others even consenting to serve as "ushers" for
the gala, despite no direct involvement with the picture,
it put no-show Dean in even a lesser light. But James was
now entering a final phase of his life in which controversy
became his calling card.

9

Rebel Without a Cause

"You are tearing me apart! You say one thing, he says another, and everybody changes back again."

JAMES DEAN'S TROUBLED TITLE CHARACTER IN *REBEL WITHOUT A CAUSE*

UNLIKE JAMES DEAN'S STRUGGLING TEEN IN *REBEL*, WHO just wanted to quietly fit in, the actor as perpetual poser enjoyed drawing attention to himself. For example, a Warner Brothers executive described Dean's typical 1955 studio shtick in the following manner: "You always knew when he was around. In the green room [cafeteria] he would hum, sing to himself, talk in a loud voice, drum on the table [Brando style] or with a spoon on a glass. Anything to attract attention."[1]

Sometimes these public displays could turn violent. For example, on one occasion he destroyed a picture of himself in the Warner Brothers cafeteria, where numerous portraits of studio stars, past and present, hung. It was also Dean's way of saying the studio did not own him. Naturally, the actor's antics resulted in bad press. The queen bee of Hollywood gossip columnists, Hedda Hopper, wrote of Dean, after seeing him misbehave on the Warner lot: "They've brought out from New York another dirty-shirt-tail [Method] actor. If this is the kind of talent they're importing, they can send it right back so far as I'm concerned."[2] With a self-deprecating sense of humor, Dean himself would admit at the time, through shades of his signature angst, "I'm intense. I'm so tense, I don't see how people stay in the same room with me. I wouldn't tolerate myself."[3] Not surprisingly, a familiar name surfaced during discussions of Dean's bad-boy behavior—Marlon Brando. One of Dean's late-night pals at the Sunset Boulevard café called Googies, Dean's favorite Hollywood hangout, observed, "I'd say that the best way to describe James Dean quickly is to say he is Marlon Brando . . . years ago. There's the refusal to conform to accepted patterns, right down to the motorcycle. Yet, somehow the comparison is unfair."[4] Actress Terry Moore, who dated Dean, added that on more than one occasion Dean would mutter to himself, "What would Marlon do in this situation?"[5] Of course, as one period critic suggested, "Making like [the minimal interview granting] Brando" also greatly simplified one's life.[6]

For all of Dean's allegedly random rebelling for the press, even though he was fully orchestrating this image with all the finesse of the most driven press agent, the persistence of the Brando clone comments hit home. Thus, even prior to the aforementioned crack at Googies, Dean uncharacteristically cornered a *Los Angeles Times* reporter in order to tell his side of the story. Under the headline, "Jimmy Dean Says He Isn't Flattered by Being Labeled 'Another Brando,'" the transplanted Hoosier was both polite and painfully honest about the parallels with Marlon: "It's true I am constantly reminding people of him. . . . They discover resemblances—we are both from farms, dress as we please, ride motorcycles and work for Elia Kazan. As an actor I have no desire to behave like Brando—and I don't attempt to. Nevertheless, it is very difficult not to be impressed, not to carry the image of a highly successful actor who is, so to speak, from the same [Method] school."[7]

This same *Los Angeles Times* piece also showed flashes of Dean's signature wit, with Dean noting, "I have my own personal rebellions and don't have to rely on Brando's."[8] It might be argued that sensitive lobbying like this, or an actual toning down of Dean's Brando tendencies, helped reduce the constant comparisons of the two actors, even before Dean's death. Even *New York Times* critic Bosley Crowther, who had been so bothered by Dean's alleged Brando mimicking in *East of Eden*, was suddenly much more appreciative of Dean by the time *Rebel Without a Cause* was released just a few months later.[9]

Though Brando was undoubtedly the figure that cast the greatest shadow on both the private and public Dean, another period personality probably lent additional coloring to Dean's provocative posing—Welsh poet Dylan

Thomas. Thomas was a controversial, nonconformist people's poet, whose life-in-the-fast-lane antics of drinking, chain-smoking, and womanizing were ultimately played out very publicly in Dean's own backyard, New York City. Moreover, this equally posturing poet made his well-documented exit precisely at a time (1953) in which the poetry loving Dean was most impressionable: on the eve of his own emergence as a major artist. Then couple these parallels with the fact that Thomas is sometimes seen as more actor than poet (his work "does not survive the amputation of the voice"[10]). Dean had yet another link to Thomas—as a performer. Regardless of how much Dean actually patterned himself after the poet, it was not unusual for later critics to compare the similar cults that quickly followed their premature fast-living deaths in the 1950s.[11]

Prior to the start of shooting *Rebel*, Dean made a final return visit to Fairmount. The catalyst for the trip was a *Life* magazine photo spread to be done by Dean's friend Dennis Stock. But before addressing this distinctive honor (for an actor whose first starring film had yet to even open!), one must restate the obvious: Dean frequently came home for the same reason most people come home—unconditional love. Dean's treks back to Indiana were also an ongoing tutorial in Midwestern reality, the Method notwithstanding. As his Fairmount High School drama instructor Adeline Nall once stated:

"Jimmy Dean loved the feel of Indiana soil under his feet, and I think that was the source of much of his strength. He knew about elemental simple folk and brought it to his acting."[12]

The *Life* pictorial, however, allowed the actor to further dabble in two special interests, photography and self-promotion. For all of Dean's alleged rejection of playing the Hollywood game, where one kowtows to members of the press, the actor loved generating his own publicity, from bad-boy behavior to a controlled photo shoot. Plus, photography in general had become, since his New York days, yet another Dean passion. Of course, whatever the latest hobby, his curiosity was seldom sustained long enough to make him a true student of the subject. For example, Dean's friend Leonard Rosenman, who composed the musical scores for both *Eden* and *Rebel*, recalled the actor's desire to study piano: "I felt he was gifted and sensitive but didn't have the patience or the rigor to practice. He never was able to figure out why he couldn't sit down and simply play the Beethoven sonatas without learning something about music."[13] Rosenman further added that the actor's "impatience with ordinary formal learning experiences resulted in what our friend Frank Corsaro called . . . [Dean's] 'chapter-heading knowledge of things.'"[14]

James never mastered photography, either. But since being photographed was second cousin to the one passion he conquered (acting), the countless stills of himself he helped stage speak volumes about him. Humor was often at the heart of this hobby, too. Dean's New York photography friend Roy Schatt once witnessed the actor making a pleasant pest of himself on a Manhattan sidewalk with an *empty* camera. Dean laughingly explained: "'It's a surrealist joke, like Dali's soft watches that can't work, yet tell the goddamned time, man.' He aimed the camera at two sour-faced tourists who were staring at him from a horse-drawn carriage and said, 'It's dear old Dali, Dali with a fringe on top.'"[15]

Dean's sense of humor is equally present in the aforementioned *Life* photo spread, especially the still captioned "Hamming It Up," with Dean burlesquing himself as the farmer-turned-actor in this stylized portrait beside a 700-pound hog on his uncle's 170-acre Indiana farm.[16] Dean's self-deprecating pose is reminiscent of Iowa Regionalist Grant Wood's *American Gothic*, the satirically hard-edged painting of a pitchfork-toting farm couple that has become one of the most spoofed images in American art history. Neither Dean nor Wood (also raised a Quaker) could resist the temptation to comically tweak serious situations and derail sentimentality. (Interestingly enough, Wood espoused an approach to painting from direct experience that anticipated the realistic core of Dean's Method.)

One should hasten to add, however, that while Wood sometimes exhibited a satirical love-hate relationship with a midwestern legacy not unlike that of Dean's, the actor was comfortable with his Hoosier heritage. This is underlined in the *Life* piece both by the text and additional still photos. The commentary states, "Back home in Indiana, he had hoped to come to an understanding of his roots, but he found something better—an awareness of his debts to the Quaker aunt and uncle who brought him up, encouraging his talents and accepting his eccentricities."[17] Fittingly, one of the *Life* photos celebrates the actor's beloved grandfather Charles Dean, from whom James was said to have inherited his interest in cars.

It was during this visit that Dean got his grandfather to perform some of the older man's signature auctioneer calling, which the actor secretly recorded. When Grandpa Dean comically complained, "Hey, you shouldn't have done that without telling me. I used some words there that maybe don't belong in polite society," James affectionately replied, "That's how I'm going to take you back to California with me—for now. But someday I'm going to have a nice house and I want you and Grandma to live with me."[18] James also believed that his grandfather's craft spoke directly to his own. Dean made this connection in a J. D. Salinger-like anecdote he later shared with acting friend Nick Adams: "Jimmy said . . . that his grandfather told him that what ruins a good auctioneer is when he gets a little too big for his breeches . . . and tries to fool the public and for a while he gets away with it, but sooner or later the public finds you out to be a phony and then you're through. Jimmy said, 'The same things hold true for an actor, Nick.'"[19]

All in all, photographer "Stock felt . . . the farm boy who had never grown completely away from home, fell easily back in the warm routine of life with Aunt Ortense and Uncle Marcus."[20] So much for that tortured-artist pose he enjoyed assuming in both New York and Hollywood.

That being said, however, does not mean Dean avoided the provocative back home. One of the photos which did not make the final *Life* spread had Dean laid out in a coffin at the local funeral parlor. Though later laughingly misread as a Dean death wish, it was just one more example of a prankster who liked to shock people. As a Fairmount friend said at the time, "It was the kind of joke Jimmy loved to play."[21] Amusingly, the comic-minded Dean also offered the mortuary director some unique feedback on his line of coffins—the actor informed him that when the lid was down it squished the nose!

Jokester notwithstanding, Dean was initially in hot water with his former drama instructor Adeline Nall for not searching her out, as was his habit. But she tracked James down at his grandparents' home, and this teacher-student duo quickly arranged for Dean to do a one-man show (part talk, part performance) at his old high school. These appearances had become a regular routine during his Indiana visits. Nall said of these occasions, "He was just a kid showing off for the hometown folks."[22] (Nall believed, however, that having a famous photographer in tow probably made this last Fairmount visit more self-conscious for Dean.)

Still, Dean put in an appearance at a school dance, where he briefly joined the band in order to play his Brando-inspired bongo drums. Not surprisingly, there were frequent autographs to sign. Indeed, the demand was so great for his signature, even back home, that the actor's always accommodating aunt and uncle, Ortense and Marcus Winslow, had accepted several autograph books in advance of their surrogate son's visit. Shortly after these Fairmount signings, Dean would be repeating the process on the set of *Rebel*. Costar Natalie Wood later described the rush to get Dean's autograph on location at Los Angeles's planetarium, where an extensive number of high school students had been hired as extras. Dean "busily signed autographs [while sitting in a trash can], exchanged stories unaware that he'd been pushed . . . [in a corner], and equally unaware of his [movie star] position or dignity," Wood recalled.[23]

As a final Fairmount footnote, the pervasiveness of the nation's interest in juvenile delinquency that soon fueled Dean's next screen production, *Rebel*, was even then apparent in his hometown newspaper. Articles ranged from a student essay contest on the "prevention of juvenile

James Dean signing autographs during the production of Rebel.

delinquency," to a PTA meeting that examined both local teen problems and a national *Saturday Evening Post* perspective titled, "The Shame of America."[24] Not only that, Fairmount had also just been selected to be "one of the first localities of its size" to have the opportunity to see a production of *Julius Caesar* starring Marlon Brando.[25] Hollywood seemed to have a pipeline to Dean's hometown.

After the comfort zone that was Fairmount, Dean's angst-ridden posing returned in the film capital. But he was smart enough to make peace with some of the publicity power brokers, such as Hopper. Thus, the month after his visit to Indiana, he was on his best behavior for an interview with the gossip columnist. This turnaround, and his acting in *Eden*, garnered him high-profile praise from Hopper: "I had seen Dean only once—in the studio commissary, slumped, surly-looking, carelessly dressed, and I was not impressed. But after watching his [*Eden*] performance I granted that he was worth all the praise that had been given him."[26] Given Hopper's large syndicated newspaper audience, Dean, the "rebel *with* a cause," was moved to share his long-term goals: "Acting is wonderful, and immediately satisfying, but it is not the be-all, end-all of my existence. My talent lies in directing even more than in acting. And, beyond directing, my great hope is writing."[27]

The collaborative *Eden* working arrangement between director Elia Kazan and Dean had no doubt helped fuel the actor's behind-the-screen interests. These aims escalated with the production of *Rebel*. But then, *Rebel* was, in many ways, a continuation of Dean's *Eden* experience. First, while *Rebel* director Nicholas Ray was not in a class with Kazan as a director, the two had a great deal in

COLLECTION OF WES D. GEHRING

*Dean (looking through the viewfinder) as a force
behind the camera on* Rebel.

common, besides being very close friends. Like Kazan, Ray
was a former actor with Method instincts. Plus, Ray started
his directing tutelage under Kazan as an assistant on *A Tree
Grows in Brooklyn* (1945), but he took the collaborator
philosophy even further than his mentor. Indeed, Dean's
Rebel screen father, Jim Backus, was later moved to write,
"May I say that this is the first time in the history of motion
pictures that a twenty-four-year-old boy, with only one
movie to his credit, was practically the co-director."[28] While
Backus neglected to take into account another twenty-

something film prodigy, Orson Welles, whose first picture was the acclaimed *Citizen Kane* (1941), Dean was still proving to be an amazing talent.

Ray basically gave Dean total creative freedom on *Rebel*. Consequently, it went beyond just indulging Dean's Method-acting needs. For example, the young performer was often allowed to improvise scenes, such as the poignant opening drunk sequence, where Dean's troubled teen rolls around on the street holding a stuffed animal. Cast member Beverly Long later recalled that the segment was shot at four in the morning on Sunset Boulevard: "And Jimmy said to Nick, 'I have an idea. Let me try something.' And Nick said, 'Fine.' So when Jimmy did that, all of it, he just shot it. It wasn't even rehearsed. And I remember sitting there and just being blown away. I remember thinking, 'Oh, my God. I'm working with a genius. He's crazy, but he's really, really talented.'"[29]

Ray later observed, "To work with him [Dean] meant exploring his nature, trying to understand it; without this, his powers of expression were frozen."[30] *Rebel* costar Wood added, "Jimmy trusted Nick a great deal, and I think Nick was very fatherly towards Jimmy."[31] More importantly, Ray and Dean were essentially cut from the same posing cloth. Kazan later described his director friend in the following manner: "Nick was, if the opprobrium could be lifted from the word, a poseur. He had never been just one man, but had been many different men at different times, matching where he was and whom he was with and what the scene needed."[32] Had Dean lived, this might have been his capsule review, too. As it is, when people ponder the James career that might have been, positing arguments for either the longevity of Paul Newman or the riveting-in-ruin fate of Brando, the well-rounded biographer might also put forward the name of Ray, because they were so much alike.

A second way in which Dean's *Rebel* experience was similar to *Eden* involved story parallels. Granted, *Eden* was adapted from a best-selling novel by the celebrated author John Steinbeck (a future winner of the Nobel Prize), while *Rebel* was simply drawn from a brief original story treatment by Ray, but the heart of both pictures is about a distressed boy/man trying to forge a relationship with his father. Of course, one should hasten to add that Backus's father figure was much more accessible than Raymond Massey's stern quasi-Biblical parent in *Eden*.

A third similarity between the films involves Dean's love interest. In each picture the young woman is initially with someone else at the beginning of the story. But circumstances and the vulnerability of each Dean character inevitably draw them to him. Moreover, in each case the young couple comes to represent a metaphorical family that is more real to them than their actual biological family. Interestingly enough, each of the actresses playing these love interests (Julie Harris on *Eden* and Wood on

Rebel) became fiercely supportive of Dean. Wood described him as "so inspiring, always so patient and kind. He didn't act as though he were a star at all. We all gave each other suggestions and he was very critical of himself, never satisfied with his work, and worried about how every scene would turn out."[33]

The closeness between Dean and Wood was fueled by several factors beyond that little-boy frailty he was so good at manifesting. For openers, Wood had appeared with James the previous November (1954) in a television drama on CBS's *General Electric Theater* (1953–62, with Ronald Reagan acting as host for much of the anthology's long run). What made this initial teaming with Dean so memorable for Wood was that it both included her first love scene and her simple excitement at working with this rising star. Ironically, Wood was yet another period person to initially describe Dean in Brando terms: "He was exactly what I expected. A junior version of Marlon Brando. He mumbled so you could hardly hear what he was saying, and he seemed very exotic and eccentric and attractive."[34] Second, Dean and Wood's rapport was probably further assisted by the actress' uncanny resemblance to James' former lover, Pier Angeli. (Even today, movie memorabilia shops in New York and Los Angeles often mislabel stills of the two actresses.) And when Angeli had suddenly and unexpectedly married singer Vic Damone, Wood had helped the inconsolable Dean through the

*Dean (right), Natalie Wood, and Nicholas Ray during one
of* Rebel's *many night shoots.*

shock. Third, James and Natalie were also drawn together
by her acting needs. Unlike Julie Harris, Wood was not a
Method actor. Thus, she frequently felt intimidated by an
Actors Studio alumnus such as Dean. In addition, while
he thrived on the freedom of Ray's improvisational style,
Wood was intimidated by the lack of structure. Although
Dean would sometimes affectionately kid her, as was his
nature, about these insecurities, he generally helped her
explore this new (to Wood) acting domain. Yet for all their
closeness, they forever remained platonic friends. In fact,

during the production of *Rebel*, the teenage Wood was romantically involved with forty-three-year-old director Ray. Fourth, Wood was bowled over by Dean's sense of humor. She later wrote of life on the *Rebel* set, "I can still remember how I doubled up from laughing so much . . . as Jimmy continued to go on with that . . . [comic] dialect changing every eight words. Everything from German to Japanese."[35]

One might add that a final parallel between *Eden* and *Rebel* was that they were both major Warner Brothers productions. However, the latter film had not started out that way. Initially slated to be a black and white "B" picture, the advance word was so strong on Dean's *Eden* performance that *Rebel* suddenly became an "A" vehicle, shot in both color and CinemaScope. The production's added cost also included the scrapping of a week's worth of footage already shot in black and white. *Rebel's* improved status could not, however, eliminate certain time constraints. Dean had earlier been signed to star in the epic screen adaptation of Edna Ferber's best-selling novel *Giant* (1956). Given both Ray's improvisational nature and Dean's increasing need for preparation time on major scenes, the *Rebel* shooting schedule courted overrun problems on a daily basis.

What is seldom noted, however, is that there could be a certain efficiency in Dean's Method madness. For example, much has been made through the years of a

Rebel scene in which the young actor kept the company waiting for an hour. The sequence involved his appearance at Juvenile Hall on a drunk and disorderly charge. During the course of the scene he has an aggressive argument with the duty officer and goes on to hysterically hit a desk in frustrated anger. To prepare, Dean remained in his dressing room drinking red wine and listening to a recording of the "Ride of the Valkyrie." Yet, after this long delay, Dean managed the nearly seven-minute scene in a single, inspired take, completely winning over a formerly exasperated crew. As costar Backus later wrote, "he saved the production department money with his method of making them wait while preparing himself for his one-take perfection . . . [because] on the average 'A' picture, seven minutes of film is considered a pretty fine full day's work."[36]

For all of the similarities between *Eden* and *Rebel*, there were some basic differences. First, despite both films keying upon a troubled teen played by Dean, *Rebel* attempted to embrace the then-contemporary phenomenon of juvenile delinquency. Historically, Brando's popular *The Wild One*, about a motorcycle gang terrorizing a small town, had gone into general release the year (1954) before *Rebel*. And 1954 was also the year Congress began investigating the comic book industry as a possible catalyst for juvenile delinquency. The federal action would, for a time, all but destroy this pulp-fiction industry. The

COLLECTION OF WES D. GEHRING

Dean (center) as a near victim of gang violence in Rebel.

message was clear, however; juvenile delinquency was serious business. (After a gang member in *Rebel* slashes a tire on Dean's car, Dean tells him, "You read too many comic books.")

Hollywood, never shy about capitalizing on headlines, had writer/director Richard Brooks's screen adaptation of Evan Hunter's novel *Blackboard Jungle* (1955) hit theaters in March, even *before Eden* opened. *Jungle* chronicled the frightening experiences of a teacher in a tough, inner-city high school. Naturally, Dean's death shortly before *Rebel*'s October premiere made it the more "must-see" movie. But *Rebel* would undoubtedly have drawn a larger youth audience than *Jungle* anyway, given that its focus figure was a student, instead of a teacher. Still, Sidney Poitier and Vic Morrow are especially memorable as troubled teens in *Jungle*. It was also the first mainstream movie to use rock and roll music—the 1950s anthem "Rock Around the Clock" by Bill Haley and his Comets is heard over the opening credits. One might also add that *Jungle* set the juvenile delinquency table for Dean, because as will soon be examined, rare was the *Rebel* review that did not draw a comparison with the earlier picture.

Though the stylized *Rebel* plays more effectively today as family melodrama than a problem film about juvenile delinquency, both Ray and the period audience were most fascinated with the picture's ties to 1950s youth. With that in mind, the director had his cast doing extra homework on the subject. Whereas Dean had not even read *East of Eden* in preparing for its screen adaptation, Ray had him and other *Rebel* cast members studying related nonfiction literature, including a text titled *Delinquents in the Making*. Dean also hung out with former Los Angeles gang member Frank Mazzola, whom Ray had hired as *Rebel* consultant and bit player for the picture. With Mazzola, Dean spent some time with real-life area gangs on their own turf. The young actor also met with Los Angeles social workers and juvenile authorities.

While screenwriters Irving Shulman and Stewart Stern were largely responsible for turning Ray's short treatment, *The Blind Run*, into the story now known as *Rebel Without a Cause*, the provocative *Rebel* title actually dated from a decade earlier. In the mid-1940s Warner Brothers had purchased a clinical study of a young delinquent. The serious tome by Dr. Robert Lindner had few selling points other than a great title, which Ray proposed lifting for his film. Since the book had already sat on the Warner inactive shelf for years (though it had once been considered for Brando!), the studio was more than happy to comply with Ray's request.

To Ray's credit, his *Blind Run* foundation story provided something not to be found in either Dr. Lindner's original book or in Brooks's *Jungle*. As Ray later explained, "I thought the material [in Lindner's book] was good, but I did not want to do a story about a boy who had been caught. I also did not want to do a picture which inferred that delinquency breeds in low income groups [as the *Blackboard Jungle* was doing] or in slum areas."[37] By making *Rebel* about a dysfunctional middle-class family, Brooks was getting at the heart of the then-current fascination with delinquency. After all, juveniles had been getting into trouble since the beginning of time. What made it topical in the 1950s was that a greater number of these delinquents were now coming from the middle class. One could liken this phenomenon to 1970s America awakening

COLLECTION OF WES D. GEHRING

*Dean receives knife fight choreography tips during
the production of* Rebel.

to an alleged drug problem. Substance abuse had been an
inner-city problem for *decades*, but only when middle-
class teens were involved did the country suddenly have a
problem. Ray was bright enough to realize this dynamic
back in the 1950s, and he ran with it.

Ray's greatest coup, of course, was just landing America's hottest young actor for the title character in *Rebel*. Like Kazan before *Eden*, Ray actively courted Dean prior to *Rebel* by spending a great deal of time with the groundbreaking performer. But then the general consensus in Hollywood was that the maverick Ray was the youngest forty-plus "player" in the film capital. Moreover, unlike earlier statements by Kazan that are sometimes contradictory in their take on Dean, one senses that Ray had a more genuine interest in the young actor beyond just getting a performance out of him. Ironically, one might best demonstrate this by noting a rare example of Dean anger directed at Ray during the shooting of *Rebel*. The scene in question involved the knife fight between James' character and Corey Allen's gang leader, Buzz. With Dean's passion for realism, Allen's real knife actually cut James. Supporting player Dennis Hopper, as another gang member, remembered a concerned Ray yelling: "'Cut, cut, cut.' And Jimmy came out of his shoes [in anger], man. He said, 'Don't ever say cut when something real happens in the scene. Don't ever do that.' He really flipped out. He said, 'It's one thing for me to be cut, but it's another thing for you to say cut' . . . so needless to say, Nick Ray never said 'cut' again unless he knew Jimmy was through."[38]

I posit that Kazan would never have stopped the scene for Dean's wound. My evidence would be a comparable situation at the Actors Studio the year before (1954). Dean was involved in a sketch with future two-time Oscar-winning actress Shelley Winters, under the direction of Kazan's Method mate, Lee Strasberg. As Dean prepared for the scene, which involved a knife, his intensity resulted in a nasty nick: "Lee never moved, but Shelley Winters jumped up. 'Stop the scene,' she cried. 'I can't stand this.' Lee wanted to kill her. 'Shelley,' he said, 'he's an unstable boy. He was just now working something through and you may well have stopped the one thing that could have helped him forever.'"[39]

Strasberg and Kazan were all about the end product, which is probably why Ray's directing marks never compared to Kazan's. But as simply a caring person, Ray would clearly get the better grade. As a footnote to this Actors Studio scene, it demonstrates that despite the aforementioned differences between Dean and Strasberg (see chapter 7), they were still often on the same metaphorical Method page.

The off-camera Dean on *Rebel* was still frequently edgy, but there was less melancholia (both real and posed) than during the *Eden* shoot. Indeed, at one point he even hosted a barbecue for the *Rebel* cast and crew, courtesy of his aunt and uncle sending him some farm-fresh ham, perhaps as an affectionate kidding of their beloved nephew. Dean's pleasantness was probably fueled by both a director who let him be a codirector, and

COLLECTION OF WES D. GEHRING

Shelley Winters and Nicholas Ray on the town during the 1950s.

a cast clearly in awe of him. Besides the close rapport already addressed in these pages between Dean and his *Rebel* screen father Backus, it was only logical that the mainly youthful cast would largely fall under his spell. With *Eden*, he had clearly arrived as an actor, and Dean was now someone for the *Rebel* teens to emulate, just as Dean had done earlier with Brando. Supporting player Hopper, who has gone on to a successful, if sporadic, acting and sometimes directing career, most synonymous with another alienated youth picture, *Easy Rider* (1969), later recalled confessing to Dean, "I don't have a clue what you are doing, but I know how great you are. What should I do?" Dean advised Hopper against having "any preconceived ideas about how the scene is going to play. Just go on a moment-to-moment reality level and don't presuppose anything."[40]

While Hopper never quite fulfilled Warner Brothers' promise that he would be "the next James Dean," no one else ever did either. Moreover, Hopper did come to represent another acclaimed iconic antihero, thanks to *Easy Rider*. Of course, not all of Dean's young *Rebel* alumni would be as successful as Hopper. James' friend and fellow mimic Adams, who often teamed with Dean to entertain the *Rebel* cast and crew with their impressions, never really got over his fixation on the young Hoosier. Ironically, probably his most memorable post-*Rebel* part traded upon his former association with Dean; that is, he played an ex-Confederate soldier in the popular Western television series *The Rebel* (1959–62, with Johnny Cash singing "The Ballad of Johnny Yuma" theme song). As a footnote to frustration for Adams, the young actor would later movingly share what Dean had said to encourage him on *Rebel*, even though Adams' part was tiny: "when you were on screen you contributed what was expected of you and then some. Sure it was a small part but someday you'll be starring in a picture and you'll know then how much I appreciate the hard work and the cooperation of

Dean and Sal Mineo at the planetarium in Rebel.

all the other actors. If we all work hard it'll be a good picture and then we'll all look good."[41] Fittingly, Adams
added, "He made us all feel good."[42]

Another young *Rebel* cast member who idolized
Dean was Sal Mineo, who played the sad-eyed Plato, the
fifteen-year-old all but abandoned by his wealthy screen
parents. Mineo later described that his work with Dean
was "the most significant experience of his life."[43] This
was doubly impressive coming from Mineo, since at the
time of *Rebel* he was already (unlike Hopper and Adams)
an established stage and screen actor. And his showy

221

Rebel performance, dying in Dean's arms at the picture's close, a victim of a policeman's bullet, garnered him an Oscar nomination as Best Supporting Actor.

The youth focus of *Rebel* centered upon Dean, Mineo, and Wood, the three potential delinquents who find themselves at the police station when the movie opens, all for unrelated minor crimes. As previous Wood comments in this book have suggested, she was very much a Dean disciple, too. As if summarizing the feelings of the youthful *Rebel* cast, she later observed, "All of us were touched by Jimmy and he was touched by greatness."[44]

Wood went on to the major star status that Dean would have known, had he lived. Sadly, Wood, Mineo, and Adams shared something else with Dean—all died tragically before their time. For the superstitious, Dean's fatal car wreck, before *Rebel* was even released, forever jinxed the impressionable young cast. Adams died of a drug overdose in 1968. A possible suicide, Adams was only thirty-seven years old. Mineo was murdered in 1976 at age thirty-seven, stabbed to death outside his Hollywood home. His killer was never caught. Wood drowned in a 1981 boating accident, a death still covered with controversy. She was forty-three. (As a macabre added twist, the actress had feared a dark, watery death since childhood.)

Rebel's reviews were dominated, naturally, by Dean's death. The *New York Post* stated, "Foremost, unfortunately [in the *Rebel* experience] is the constant remembrance of the tragic death of the star, James Dean. Again and again you are reminded of what a good, strong actor he was. He was strong enough to carry his audiences to the edge of extreme personal idiom without losing their belief."[45] The *New York Journal-American* said, *Rebel* "stars the late James Dean whose young life and brilliant career were cut so tragically short a few weeks ago in an automobile crash. In sensitivity and understanding, his performance even surpasses the one that brought him stardom in 'East of Eden.'"[46] Given that Dean's *Rebel* character constantly flirts with death, from a knife fight to a "chicken run" (where he and a rival race stolen cars toward a cliff to see who will jump from his vehicle first), *Variety*'s review take on Dean's death is provocatively insightful: "The performance of the star, James Dean, will excite discussion, especially in connection with the irony of his own recent crash death under real-life conditions of recklessness which form a macabre press agent frame as the picture goes into release."[47] Along similar lines, the *Saturday Review* stated, "He [Dean] stands as a remarkable talent, and he was cut down, it would seem, by the very passions he exposes so tellingly in this strange and forceful picture."[48]

Running such *Rebel* review commentary a close second were comparisons to the tough teen picture *Blackboard Jungle*, released earlier that year (1955). The

New York Times said, "It [*Rebel*] is a violent, brutal and disturbing picture of modern teen-agers. . . . Like 'Blackboard Jungle' before it, it is a picture to make the hair stand on end."[49] The *Hollywood Reporter* added, "The [*Rebel*] exhibitor can expect this story of juvenile delinquency to capture the 'Blackboard Jungle' type of audience and be a real money picture."[50] The *New Yorker*'s critic zeroed in on Ray's attempt to break from the *Jungle*'s slum slant: "Having exploited juvenile delinquency with some degree of perception in 'Blackboard Jungle,' Hollywood now offers another aspect of the trouble in 'Rebel Without a Cause.' In this one, we have delinquents of a higher social order than those in 'Blackboard Jungle.'"[51]

In examining a plethora of *Rebel* reviews, however, what is most telling now is the general lack of period recognition as to why we continue to honor the picture today, beyond the cult connection to Dean. As previously noted in this book, *Rebel* was instrumental in helping to redefine the genre parameters of *family melodrama*. The pre-1950s norm for this domestic dilemma invariably made the children the source of the problem, be it director Leo McCarey's memorable *Make Way for Tomorrow* (1937, where adult children thoughtlessly separate their impoverished retirement-age parents) or Michael Curtiz's *Mildred Pierce* (1945, with Joan Crawford's Oscar-winning turn as a working mother victimized by an ungrateful daughter). In contrast, *Rebel* suggested the problem was with the parents. This was a bold move, though anyone involved in genre study realizes that the general formula for any given type of movie is a work in progress; that is, genre analysis frequently operates on a contradiction. It is very much formulaic but at the same time must be flexible enough to incorporate the ongoing changes affecting all genres.[52]

A rare 1955 review that sympathetically acknowledged *Rebel*'s reconfiguration of the melodrama model came from *Time*: "The strong implication of this picture is that the real delinquency is not juvenile but parental. This may be obvious and only a part of the problem, but it is well worth propounding."[53] Dean's dominating mother (Ann Doran) and henpecked father (Backus) in *Rebel* constantly counsel noninvolvement and appear to always avoid controversy (real or imagined) by running away—relocating the family. Yet, as critic Andrew Sarris later noted in the counterculture 1960s, "We are all involved, as James Dean cries out in *Rebel Without a Cause*, and whatever is done or not done for whatever reason affects us all."[54]

Yet, 1955 *Rebel* reviewers, *Time* notwithstanding, generally rejected the parents as problem formula. Some critics, such as the *Nation*'s Robert Hatch, were ever so crass: "It is easy to explain delinquency if you assume that parents are howling idiots, but the supposition is neither true nor very interesting."[55] Other reviewers, such as The *New Yorker*'s John McCarten, turned simpleminded: "what really ails them [youngsters] is the lack of some sound discipline."[56] But there were critics, like the *Hollywood Reporter*'s Jack Meffitt, who sympathetically wrestled with the issue of parents as villains and ultimately gave *Rebel* a qualified recommendation: "So, in my opinion, this is a superficial treatment of a vital problem that has been staged brilliantly."[57] Meffitt also offers an explanation for an underdeveloped conflict in the picture, why Wood's screen father (William Hopper) constantly rebuffs her: "As these scenes are played, they seem to imply that he is resisting an incestuous interest in his pretty daughter."[58] While I would call this an overstatement—Hopper seems more befuddled than incestuous about a daddy's girl who has suddenly become a sexy young woman—Meffitt was still that rare 1955 critic who addressed the topic.

Regardless of how period critics read or misread *Rebel*, family melodrama today routinely posits that parents are most often the source of the problems, from Robert Duvall's Marine father in *The Great Santini* (1979) or Mary Tyler Moore's against-type, witchy mother in *Ordinary People* (1980), to the disconnected parental couple of Kevin Spacey and Annette Benning in *American Beauty* (1999). Thus, the dysfunctional screen family has very much followed the lead of *Rebel*, though the roots were also there in *Eden*, too. It is just that *Rebel* provided a three-way exclamation on the subject of parental neglect, keying upon the movie families of Dean, Wood, and Mineo. But in fairness to the initial *Rebel* reviewers, change is never easy to assimilate, even in the arts. As the influential genre author John G. Cawelti has observed, "When genre critics forget that their supertexts are critical artifacts and start treating them as prescriptions for artistic creation, the concept of genre becomes stultifying and limiting."[59]

With both Dean's death and *Rebel's* provocative subject matter, the picture was a major box office hit, outgrossing such other 1955–56 hits as Frank Sinatra's then-daring drug addiction film *The Man with the Golden Arm*, Marilyn Monroe's acting validation picture *Bus Stop*, Alfred Hitchcock's *The Man Who Knew Too Much*, and the moving Civil War story *Friendly Persuasion*, with Gary Cooper as the head of a struggling Quaker family.[60] A star's death does not, however, always guarantee success. In fact, when Dean died with two movies yet to be released (*Rebel* and *Giant*), Warner Brothers saw possible catastrophe. Jack Warner bluntly observed, "Nobody will come and see a corpse."[61] He could not have been more wrong, but historically, Warner was right to worry. A number of posthumous releases, such as Hoosier Carole Lombard's final film, *To Be or Not to Be* (1942), proved financially disappointing.[62] In having written on the phenomenon of posthumous pictures, I would postulate one rule of thumb: the most popular of these final films showcased a star in a typical role.[63] To illustrate, Dean's standard antihero in *Rebel* helped fuel its success, while Clark Gable's movingly atypical (for him) antihero in the posthumous *The Misfits* (1961) probably contributed to its less-than-stellar box office, despite good reviews. Regardless, *Rebel*'s sizable financial success still did not match the commercial grosses of *Eden*, which, both then and now, is generally considered the superior film. Yet *Rebel* remains Dean's signature role, the one an army of young fans have embraced through the years.

More importantly, among this army of disciples, numerous performers felt a call to artistic arms via Dean's *Rebel*. Four-time Oscar-nominated actress Marsha Mason has described her teenage viewing of *Rebel* in the follow-ing manner: "It is at this moment that my life takes an extraordinary turn. . . . I couldn't put my adolescent feelings into words until that moment. . . . I am James Dean. I have met myself. Someone who is just like me."[64] Even more dra-matic was *Rebel*'s impact on Emmy Award–winning actor Martin Sheen, who claimed, "James Dean was the strongest influence of any actor that ever stepped in front of the cam-era. Ever!"[65]

Like all great art, however, *Rebel* offers different angles of vision for different eras. As a teenager who came of age in the cause-oriented 1960s, a "rebel *without* a cause" did not immediately resonate with me. What did draw me to the actor in *Rebel* was the naturalness of so many of the movie's small nonverbal moments. Historian Foster Hirsch has described one such scene I admire: "Before he [Dean] leaves the house for the chicken run, Jim cuts himself a thick slice of chocolate cake. . . . [It] seems improvised. . . . Halfway out the door, he turns abruptly, goes to the table, and slices. [It] has a wonderful freshness and intimacy that tells us, through movement, how Jim thinks. In another passing action, Dean hugs a milk bottle to his cheek. . . . It's a private moment that registers the character's sensitivity."[66] As a former athlete I am drawn to this entertainingly casual athleticism of Dean. And like a marathoner, Dean would be severely tested by the epic production of his last film, *Giant*.

10

Giant

"Leslie glimpsed this Jett Rink in the doorway now—a muscular young fellow. . . . He wore the dust-colored canvas and the high-heeled boots of the region, his big sweat-stained hat was pushed back from his forehead. . . . His attitude, his tone were belligerent."[1]

EDNA FERBER, *GIANT* (1952)

THE FILM PRODUCTIONS OF *REBEL WITHOUT A CAUSE* AND *Giant* (1956) overlapped, so a tired and overworked James Dean found himself being rushed to the Marfa, Texas, location of *Giant* as soon as *Rebel* wrapped. But whereas the earlier shoot had been an exhilarating experience for James, given the almost codirector status its director, Nicholas Ray, had accorded the actor, *Giant* would be an entirely different proposition. The director of the latter picture, George Stevens, was a Hollywood traditionalist whose personal and professional agenda left little wiggle room for the improvisational tendencies of a Method actor. Moreover, one must add that the detail-conscious Stevens had been involved in the preproduction minutia of *Giant* since 1953. Thus, his sense of this screen adaptation being clearly his movie was greater than one would expect on the standard Hollywood picture, regardless of how traditional the working arrangement.

Dean and director George Stevens on location in Texas for Giant *(1956).*

The artistic conflict that came to define the Dean-Stevens "collaboration" on *Giant* was grounded, however, in a basic irony. Each man began the production as the other's allegedly biggest fan. In a Warner Brothers press release, Dean said, "George Stevens, for my money, is the greatest director of them all—even greater than Kazan. . . . This Stevens was born for the movies. He's so real, so unassuming, and he doesn't miss a thing."[2] Although Dean actively campaigned for the part of Jett Rink, spending a great deal of time hanging out at Stevens's Warner Brothers office, period articles document a director especially taken with the actor's television work. Indeed, Stevens claimed he picked Dean for the part by watching him on a television show. "It was the first time that I ever waited anxiously for the credits so I could find out who this brilliant, sensitive young actor was," Stevens recalled. "His was an extraordinary talent."[3]

Beyond this not uncommon paradox of two artists having creative differences, there are several additional ironies that Dean literature has failed to address. First, Stevens had not always been such a rigid, by-the-Hollywood-book director. He began his film career as Leo McCarey's cameraman on the inspired and often improvisational Stan Laurel and Oliver Hardy short subjects of the late 1920s.[4] When Stevens moved to directing during the 1930s, he often continued these off-the-cuff ways. This tendency was encouraged by the fact that his early features involved another popular comedy team, Wheeler and Woolsey.[5]

In the years prior to Stevens's involvement in World War II, he explored several film genres but remained at his best in the realm of multifaceted comedy. These Stevens movies included three exceptional romantic comedies (*Alice Adams*, 1935; *Penny Serenade*, 1941; and *Woman of the Year*, 1942), two splendid screwball comedies (*Vivacious Lady*, 1938; and *The More the Merrier*, 1943), and an affectionate parody of action adventure films (*Gunga Din*, 1939).[6] Unlike his mentor McCarey, however, Stevens was inclined to shoot increasing amounts of film footage. Still, he invariably left room for improvisational sequences, such as the Laurel and Hardy-like conclusion to *Woman of the Year*, when Katharine Hepburn becomes a physical comedy victim of the modern kitchen. Most significantly, by the early 1940s Stevens's artistic vision had even labeled him a Hollywood rebel. For example, "To ensure his independence, he once had a contract [circa 1941] forbidding Columbia [Studio] Boss Harry Cohn to so much as speak to him about his pictures."[7]

The second Dean-Stevens paradox, beyond the director's once seemingly Method-friendly improvisational ways, was that Stevens's original catalyst for shooting miles of footage was simply, "I really rehearse on film; you know, your film stock is the cheapest thing you have."[8] Yet in the 1930s and early 1940s, his "rehearsing" was open to experimenting with the actor. Actor Joel McCrea remembered on *The More the Merrier*, "I'd do some little gag. I had to take a shower in that picture while I was rooming with Charles Coburn. . . . So I got in the shower and I was squirting water with my hands, and Stevens said, 'Do that, do that in the scene.' [I did] A lot of little things like that. Well, this adds confidence and everything [for the actor]."[9] Unfortunately, by the 1950s Stevens's collaborative rehearsals had atrophied into a mechanical exercise where each scene was simply filmed from as many angles as possible, with little creative input from the performer. This situation was especially frustrating for Dean, the aspiring director, forever bursting with scene embellishments.

The third Dean-Stevens irony was that while World War II helped fuel a friendly climate for the naturalism of Dean's Method acting, Stevens's personal experiences as head of an Army Signal Corps film unit (including filming the freeing of the prisoners of Dachau concentration camp) made the director much more rigid about getting his, and his alone, cinematic vision on the screen. (He also later directed the first film adaptation of *The Diary of Anne Frank* in 1959.) This more arbitrary development in Stevens's directing was evident during his initial post-war picture, the populist classic *I Remember Mama* (1948).[10] The title character is played by Irene Dunne, an actress responsible for bringing Stevens onto the project, given her earlier teaming with him on *Penny Serenade*. While she remained a loyal fan of his talent, Dunne noticed a less collaborative tone to his work on *Mama*.[11] For example, Stevens could be dictatorial in the simple blocking of a scene: "I [Dunne] said, why? He said, '*Do* as I say. Ten steps, then cross [the room].' Well I didn't like that. I have to know *why* I'm doing something. As it turned out, it was just for the cutting. But he wanted to be stubborn, to make me do it without telling me why. So we had a kind of upset [argument]."[12] Despite Dunne's quasi-Method acting need for motivation in this scene,

The invariably upbeat Indiana-raised Irene Dunne after a screening of the George Stevens-directed Penny Serenade *(1941).*

she was normally the most even-tempered professional. Thus, if Stevens could upset an actress also known as the "first lady of Hollywood," was it any wonder that there would be fireworks between Stevens and the short-fused Method fanatic Dean on *Giant*?[13]

A fourth Dean-Stevens paradox is that the director's 1950s American epic trilogy of *A Place in the Sun* (1951),

Shane (1953), and *Giant* "that once seemed accomplished now seems labored."[14] While Stevens was much honored for these pictures, winning best director Oscars for both *Sun* and *Giant*, as well as taking home the Academy of Motion Picture Arts and Sciences' Irving Thalberg Award the same year (1953) *Shane* opened, Stevens's best work is now generally seen as the earlier, simpler pictures. One might recycle an observation made by critic and documentary producer John Grierson about director Josef von Sternberg: "When a director dies—he becomes a cameraman."[15] Grierson meant that when von Sternberg's films became more focused on creating pretty pictures of his protégé/lover, actress Marlene Dietrich, than on addressing traditional character and story points, he ceased to be a true director. The same complaint might be made of Stevens's epic 1950s pictorial style. (The Laurel and Hardy cameraman had reverted to type, though those short subjects were actually comic character studies.)

That being said, however, there is still much that is poignant about the tragic love story of Montgomery Clift and Elizabeth Taylor in *Sun*, a film which so fascinated a young Dean. And the simple Western fable nature of *Shane* remains especially moving, despite its sometimes overly mythic presentation of Alan Ladd's knight-like cowboy. But for today's viewer, *Giant* has little, beyond Dean's performance, to recommend it. As revisionist critic David Thomson observed, "*Giant* is bloated, seldom plausible, with actors who never settle into the story or the idea of Texas."[16]

One should quickly add, of course, that the screen adaptation of *Giant* was a huge critical and commercial hit in 1956. While this will be addressed in depth later in the chapter, it bears noting that the film was the third grossing movie of 1957, finishing just behind *The Ten Commandments* and *Around the World in 80 Days* (both released in 1956).[17] (The 1957 fiscal focus was the result of all three pictures being released late the preceding year.) So what was the period attraction for *Giant*, if revisionist critics now denigrate the movie? The answer lies in the challenges to filmmaking in the 1950s. With the phenomenal fascination for the new medium of television during this decade, general movie attendance plummeted. In fact, Marlon Brando biographer Patricia Bosworth described 1955, the year *Giant* was shot, as "one of the worst years in the motion-pictures business. . . . Millions of families now sat in their living rooms, hypnotized in front of flickering sets watching *I Love Lucy* [and other small-screen classics]."[18] Film studios were scrambling just to survive. Thus, to get people away from that mesmerizing small screen at home, filmmakers had to give the public something that television could not. *Giant* is a classic example of the studios' solution to this dilemma.

First, the technical presentation of movies during the 1950s underwent a radical change. Various widescreen processes became the norm. *Newsweek*'s review of *Giant* would call it "the time of the mastodon movie, visually immense."[19] Moreover, films were more likely to appear in color, with enhanced sound. Needless to say, all of these developments were applied to *Giant*. Who would not occasionally be tempted to leave their tiny twelve-inch, black-and-white screen for a "colorful" widescreen spectacle, regardless of the story? Second, the epic is the genre that best lends itself to such a splashy presentation. Again, *Giant* perfectly fits the bill. In addition to being a complex tale of a powerful family told over decades, the picture was coupled with the standard epic backdrop, a historical panorama of a bigger-than-life place—Texas through time. Third, the 1950s "A" film was often an adaptation of a commercial hit from another medium. Again, to get people away from the small screen, the thinking was to go with the safe bet—a proven product. This brings out both the curious and the established fan of the earlier success. If the original property was adapted from a hit Broadway play or a best-selling novel, that fan base might be huge. Ferber's novel *Giant* was one such publishing gold mine. Within the first five years of its publication in 1952, the novel sold twenty-five million copies![20] Indeed, the book was beyond the proverbial king's ransom, given that Ferber mixed her Pulitzer Prize–winning reputation with a provocative topic. As Ferber biographer Julie Goldsmith Gilbert noted: "To say that in 1952 the impact of *Giant* created a tumult not only in the book world but in the real world of the United States would not be an exaggeration. It was a much-talked-about book not only from the standpoint of readability but of controversy. The entire state of Texas felt impugned by it, and it created in displaced Texans a surge of nationalistic nastiness."[21]

The notes for the Perennial Classics 2000 edition of *Giant* added, "Considering its enduring popularity, it is hard to imagine the furor that erupted when Edna Ferber published *Giant*—at least in Texas, where its author was reviled. Banner headlines in Texas newspapers called for nothing short of Ferber's hanging."[22] This initial Lone Star state response to the novel might be likened to the later controversy attached to television's popular evening melodrama *Dallas*, which premiered in 1978. Like *Giant*, *Dallas* also chronicled a Texas family's empire in oil and cattle. (The picture is sometimes credited as the inspiration for *Dallas*. One could further argue that the initials of its central villain, J. R. Ewing, are taken from Dean's *Giant* character, Jett Rink.)

Besides the print controversy ultimately contributing to the commercial success of the movie *Giant*, Dean's death also added to the film's box office. Though the actor's passing had occurred more than a year before the late 1956 release of the film, America became obsessed with Dean. Even Ferber was fascinated with the actor, writing in her autobiography: "[He] was spectacularly talented; handsome in a fragile sort of way; and absolutely outrageous. He was an original. Impish, compelling, magnetic; utterly winning one moment, obnoxious the next. Definitely gifted. Frequently maddening."[23]

Strangely enough, Dean's accident-waiting-to-happen nature also made Ferber and several other Dean contacts appear slightly psychic about his death. Ferber later wrote, "Occasionally—rarely—one encounters a dazzling human being who is obviously marked for destruction. Such a one was this young Jimmy Dean. . . . [He had] the complete absence of the sense of caution . . . the quality that prevents them from observing ordinary precaution; the common sense, really, of everyday physical behavior."[24] Even more chilling was actor Alec Guinness's pronouncement after Dean showed him his new sports car: "'Please, never get in it.' I looked at my watch. 'It is now ten o'clock, Friday the 23rd of September, 1955. If you get in that car you will be found dead in it by this time next week.' He [Dean] laughed. 'Oh, shucks! Don't be so mean!'"[25] Sadly, Guinness's prediction, something he normally never did, was right on target.

An on-location (Marfa, Texas) decision by the *Giant* studio manager provided yet another foreshadowing of Dean's self-destructive tendencies. Each of the film's primary cast members was provided with his or her own car during the shoot. But the young actor lost his vehicle privileges after amassing several speeding violations and shooting out the windows of his own car with a BB gun. This story comes courtesy of Dean's close friend during the *Giant* production, actress Mercedes McCambridge, who played Rock Hudson's domineering sister in the picture.[26] McCambridge also provided a possible catalyst for another example of Dean's outrageousness during the epic production. James had gone through several takes of his first scene with Elizabeth Taylor, where her *Giant* character comes to "tea" at Dean's cabin after his Rink character has inherited some land. A nervous James walked away from the set to a nearby field where, in full view of a crowd of onlookers, he casually urinated. Now, the time-honored take on this bizarre behavior has been provided by *Giant* costar Dennis Hopper, who played Rock Hudson's screen son in the picture. When Hopper asked his hero why he had done this "way out" thing, Dean allegedly replied: "I was nervous. I'm a Method actor. I work through my senses. If you're nervous, your senses can't reach your subconscious and that's that—you just can't work. So I figured if I could piss in front of those two thousand people, man, and I could be cool, I figured if I could do that, I could get in front of that camera and do just anything, anything at all."[27]

While Dean might have been just that articulate to the idolizing Hopper (who also appeared in *Rebel*),

COLLECTION OF WES D. GEHRING

Dean and Elizabeth Taylor on the set of Giant. *Note that Dean is wearing his coat from* Rebel.

McCambridge's autobiography suggests Dean was moved to perform this public act by a Winston Churchill story she had shared with him. It seems that the then-elderly statesman was on holiday in France pursuing his landscape painting passion. A respectful crowd had gathered at a distance to watch. Given Churchill's healthy appetite for brandy, he soon needed to relieve himself. Thus, Churchill put down his ever-present cigar and "walked over to the seawall and let spray . . . at great length! When he had finished, the villagers applauded! As he walked back to his easel, they shouted, *'Magnifique!'* and *'Formidable!'* Sir Winston stopped, took off his hat, and bowed!"[28] Given Dean's fondness for shock effect, I would posit (with McCambridge) that the Churchill story was the real instigator of Dean's action, particularly since he picked a situation not limited to cast and crew.

While Taylor's thoughts on this particular action have not been recorded, she became, after McCambridge, Dean's other pivotal acting ally on *Giant*. Initially, however, she had been put off by Dean's scene stealing and cool behavior, something her screen husband (Hudson) forever resented. "[Dean] never smiled. He was sulky, and he had no manners," said Hudson. "I'm not that concerned with manners—I'll take them where I find them—but Dean didn't have 'em. And he was rough to do a scene with . . . in the giving and taking, he was just a taker. He would suck everything out and never give back."[29]

Of course, Phyllis Gates, Hudson's wife at the time, later revealed that her insecure husband had told her, "Stevens is throwing the picture to Dean, I know he is. Dammit, he spends all his time talking to Dean, and he hardly tells me a thing."[30] She also believed Hudson was jealous of both Dean's talent and the attention he was getting from the press.[31] Regardless, as happened on both *Rebel* and *East of Eden*, Dean's little-boy-lost posturing soon had another leading lady mothering him, despite the fact that twenty-three-year-old Taylor was a year younger than Dean. Besides, just as Dean savored these nurturing maternal situations, Taylor's track record at this late date (2005) has long proven a proclivity for the underdog and/or antihero, which was Dean in a nutshell. Consequently, before long the two of them were staying up late sharing life histories.

Undoubtedly, other factors probably drew Dean and Taylor together. For example, while confident Dean merely enjoyed posturing as the waif type, Taylor was not without real underdog feelings on *Giant*. To illustrate, despite starring in Stevens's *A Place in the Sun*, she had not been his first choice as *Giant*'s female lead. (The director would have preferred Grace Kelly, who was unavailable.) Plus, as a Taylor biographer later wrote, the actress soon realized "how well-protected she had been when making *A Place in the Sun* for him [Stevens]. No longer a minor, and without chaperones, she was exposed to her director's professional ruthlessness."[32] In addition, Stevens was rather like the stereotypical "play with pain" football coach. Thus, part of his apparent "distaste" for the actress was grounded in the belief she was "altogether too prone to a bad back when the [*Giant*] shooting got rough."[33] Moreover, though we now approach the picture as starring the great Elizabeth Taylor, in 1955 her two Best Actress Oscars were still years away. At the time she was perceived as more of a beauty than an actress. Yet Taylor's part, one of the most coveted roles of the decade, would ask her to be convincing in a story that covered thirty years. For added Hollywood irony, her screen daughter (Carroll Baker) was actually slightly older than Taylor.

Another component pulling Dean and Taylor together was Stevens's autocratic behavior. On separate occasions he reprimanded both performers in front of the cast and crew. (Dean's crime was disagreeing with Stevens's direction, while hers was being too concerned with her appearance—the aforementioned knock of being a beauty, not an actress.) Regardless, joint doghouse victimization tends to bring people together. But in all honesty, Dean's ongoing creative differences with Stevens made Dean the real outsider on *Giant*. That caused Dean to be all the more attractive as someone to defend for both Taylor and McCambridge. Recently, Dean's cousin Marcus Winslow Jr. summarized Dean's frustration on his last film: "Nicholas Ray gave Jimmy a lot of [improvisational] leeway [on *Rebel*]. Then when he [Dean] got to *Giant*, George Stevens wanted it his way. He'd shoot from every angle. Jimmy called it the 'round the clock' method. And Stevens would make Jimmy sit there all day if he was in the scene or not. Jimmy felt he wasn't a machine, that he couldn't turn it [his acting] on and off. He felt a good director should know what he wanted and not have all that [film] coverage."[34]

Interestingly enough, Winslow also believed, unlike any other source, that Stevens might have manufactured some of the conflict with Dean in order to get a performance out of him. For example, Winslow shared a story originally related to him by former cowboy Bob Hinkle, the "Texas" dialogue coach on *Giant*. In the scene where Dean was to pace off the territory he had inherited, Stevens had put down scraps of paper for each step. An angry Dean said, "I don't need somebody to step off my paces with paper!" But Winslow's take on this revelation from Hinkle was to suggest, "Maybe Stevens was just doing it to get Jimmy mad! Because Stevens got what he wanted. . . . [An assertive Dean] is what the scene called for."[35] Certainly, as noted earlier in the book (see Chapter 8), directors have frequently been more manipulative than this in order to get a performance they want from an actor.

Possibly the greatest single factor feeding the fire between Dean and the director, however, was simply that

Dean was not the star of *Giant*. Though the later marketing of the picture would put him on an equal status with Taylor and Hudson, his was essentially a supporting character. This was new ground for Dean, who had been the focus figure in both *Eden* and *Rebel*. Consequently, Stevens's *Giant* not only negated Dean's need to collaborate, but the picture also removed him from his coveted center ring. Given Dean's often-spoiled background, from the idyllic Indiana childhood to his earlier indulged and pampered pictures, the young actor's anger at Stevens was to be expected.

Dean's perspective notwithstanding, *Giant* would have been a better film had Dean's part been embellished. At the very least, the character aura of Rink should have been established at the onset, as it was in the novel. Ferber's book does not necessarily give Rink more space than does the film, but his character looms large over the book from page one: "All Texas was flying to Jett Rink's party."[36] Like Joseph Conrad's teasing talk about the character Kurtz in his celebrated novella *Heart of Darkness* (1902), one's curiosity about Rink is piqued long before he surfaces in *Giant*. Granted, Ferber's novel is neither in a class with *Darkness* nor does she hold Rink out until the end (as Conrad does of Kurtz). But if her novel works at all, the book functions because of one's inquisitiveness about Rink.

That Stevens should choose to somewhat mute this outsider character is ironic, given that a variation of the figure occupies a strong presence in the director's oeuvre, be it Hepburn's funny/sad attempt to put on a proper dinner party in the summer heat of *Alice Adams* or Clift's deadly desperation to also escape his economic station in *A Place in the Sun*. Indeed, Stevens scholar Donald Richie makes a direct link between Rink and another of the director's pivotal characters: "In *Giant* we find the little boy from *Shane* grown up. He is now Jett Rink, as played by James Dean, and has remained innocent. In this film, we find that we are looking at the Benedict [Rock Hudson and Elizabeth Taylor] family not directly but, in the manner of *Shane*, through the eyes of innocence. . . . Then, James Dean, just like [little] Brandon de Wilde, discovers that his heroes are not ideals. He also discovers that he is not ideal."[37] *Giant*'s closing image of Dean's Rink, a drunken middle-aged millionaire, passed out at his own banquet, is ultimately a cautionary tale about a sympathetic outsider undone by a truth which, at best, bewilders him.

Of course, at face value the picture remains a Texas epic about a cattle empire (the Benedict family) versus an upstart oil king (Rink) that dovetails into a more traditional story about old money versus new. But just as *Giant* would have been strengthened with more attention to Dean's character at the beginning, Stevens's film might also have taken a constructive cue from Elia Kazan's adaptation of the epic novel *East of Eden*; that is, Kazan only keyed upon a portion of John Steinbeck's sprawling family melodrama. Stevens's *Giant* is hurt by the abrupt jump in time, where Dean goes from his late teens to his mid-forties. Moreover, just as Dean's Method-acting realism often makes it seem as if he is performing in a different movie than his costars, Dean's character is the only one that radically ages. As Dean aficionado Randall Riese later noted, "To audiences the on-screen evolution of Jett Rink is startling, difficult to adjust to and accept . . . and perhaps most debilitating, was the unlikely, blatantly artificial makeup that Dean wore as the elder Rink."[38] This was partly a result of Dean joining the *Giant* shoot late, due to *Rebel*. But besides this lack of preproduction preparation was the questionable decision to accent his newfound years. Whereas other "aging" principals, such as Taylor and Hudson, seemed to merely acquire blue-gray hair, Dean's hair was shaved back to simulate a receding hairline, and his face was given enough bags and wrinkle lines to be reminiscent of an Iowa road map. Entertainer Eartha Kitt, a close Dean friend, remembered him complaining about *Giant*, "I had nothing to grow on. . . . I could not gradually mature the character as I wanted to because the others were not maturing with me."[39]

Tragically, given Dean's death prior to the completion of the picture (though he had finished his scenes), questions of his movie aging were not an issue for years. In fact, there was almost a macabre appropriateness to the

The radically aged Dean (foreground) of Giant, *with a still-youthful Rock Hudson.*

fact that the young actor who was taken too early still looked old, his artificially shaved receding hairline having not yet grown back. Paradoxically, in death he caused Stevens one more production delay on *Giant*. The day after Dean's fatal accident the director expected Taylor to complete "reaction shots of a scene she had done with Dean. . . . She realized, with anguish, that she would now be 'reacting' to a man who lay in a funeral home at Paso Robles."[40] The grieving actress collapsed with stomach cramps and was hospitalized.

The deification of Dean was almost immediate. While 3,000 people attended his October 8, 1955, funeral at Back Creek Friends Church in Fairmount, Indiana, millions of movie fans mourned his death. Not since the passing of film icon Rudolph Valentino had there been such a public response. By January 1956 Dean fan letters requesting photographs had reached a volume of 7,000 a month.[41] For three years his movie mail would top that of all *living* stars. While this unprecedented response, which has yet to disappear, will be addressed further in the epilogue, suffice it to say that a threatening aspect of this Dean hysteria affected Stevens. The director of *Giant*, busy editing his epic, received countless threatening letters from fans, soon to be nicknamed "Deaners," with warnings "not to cut out as much as one single frame of Dean. . . . 'It's absolutely weird,' Stevens said, 'the most uncomfortable stuff I've ever read.'"[42]

A year after Dean's death, *Giant* opened to almost universal acclaim. The title for the *Hollywood Reporter*'s review provides a suggestion of the nearly total critical kudos: "George Stevens' '*Giant*' an Epic Film in a Class with the All-Time Greats."[43] *Time* said, "*Giant* is something the film colony often claims but seldom achieves: an epic."[44] And *Variety* called it "an excellent film which registers strongly on all levels, whether it's in its breathtaking panoramic shots of the dusty Texas plains; the personal, dramatic impact of the story itself, or the resounding message it has to impart."[45]

Other than the star turn often accorded director Stevens, praise for Dean's final role dominated the reviews. *Newsweek*'s critique, entitled "Young Dean's Legacy," observed: "If the picture can be said to belong to any of the actors . . . it belongs to the late James Dean; he gives the part of a local black sheep such memorable life of its own that the young actor's death last year now emerges as a much more significant theatrical loss to the mature moviegoer than it is to the adolescent cultists who have mourned so noisily."[46]

The *New York Times* added, "it is the late James Dean who makes the malignant role of the surly ranch hand who becomes an oil baron the most tangy and corrosive in the film. Mr. Dean plays this curious villain with a stylized spookiness. . . . This is a haunting capstone to the brief career of Mr. Dean."[47] Even the *New Yorker*, which recorded a rare pan of *Giant* (satirically entitled "Southwestern Primitives"), said of the actor, "The exception to the standardized scheme of things is provided by the late James Dean, who plays the role of an ambitious cowpoke with lunatic cuteness. Muttering to himself, and wearing a large Stetson . . . he proves that Stanislavsky is just as much at home among the cattle as he ever was off Broadway."[48]

As with the production, however, the *Giant* reviews and accompanying articles recorded several ironies. The most paradoxical, given their production differences, was the fact that Stevens came forward to champion the image of Dean as a normal working actor. In an interview with the *New York World-Telegram*, Stevens said one should forget all this "ghoulish nonsense . . . about his [Dean] being a wild one, wandering aimlessly in search of an indefinable something . . . [which] is pure poppycock. Dean knew exactly where he was going. He always had a goal and he was determined to reach his goal of being a top-notch movie star at any price."[49] Some *Giant* scenes praised by critics for their collaborative nature we now know were produced under artistic duress. The *Hollywood Reporter* noted, "Stevens has directed him [Dean] beautifully. . . . A single scene, where Dean paces out the first land he has ever owned, is unforgettable."[50] (As noted earlier in the chapter, this is the scene in which Stevens provoked Dean by putting down pieces of paper to mark the actor's pacing steps.)

For all the general lionizing of *Giant*, several period reviews hinted at modern concerns with the picture. For example, many critiques gently hinted that the movie's three-hour-plus length was excessive; the *Nation* described it as "tedium," adding "the second half is drudgery."[51] Plus, the *Nation* was the first publication to suggest that Dean stumbled as the middle-aged Rink: "Dean doesn't do this very well; he becomes careful and leans heavily on props and cliché gestures."[52] Decades later Kazan seconded this position on Dean's characterization of an over-forty Rink: "Dean had no technique to speak of. When he tried to play an older man in the last reels of *Giant*, he looked like what he was: a beginner."[53] Costar Carroll Baker later confessed, "Jimmy . . . had great difficulty relating to the older Jett. He agonized over his last scene."[54] (This remains a sometimes knock against Dean—that he only successfully played his age. Yet, one assumes he would have grown into older parts, just as Brando did.)

Interestingly enough, the *Nation*'s original detracting crack on Dean's aging Rink did offer the actor a creative out, suggesting maybe those "cliché gestures" were done on purpose as a satirical take on what was ultimately a "corny" character.[55] Though this is an overly generous explanation, Dean's natural tendency was often to embrace the comic. Regardless, another period complaint which now seems revisionist is the *New York Post*'s review that Dean "emerges as an extremely mannered actor, too much so for the Jett Rink of the novel, but still an eye-catcher as himself immersed in his own act."[56] This could be filed in the current school of thought that feels Dean was acting in a different movie than everyone else, a criticism that is more a problem of poor directing than of poor acting.

These complaints notwithstanding, *Giant* was a critical and commercial smash and garnered ten Oscar nominations, including Best Picture, Stevens as Best Director, Dean and Hudson as Best Actor, and Mercedes McCambridge as Best Supporting Actress. But Stevens was the only Academy Award winner. Best Picture went to *Around the World in 80 Days*, produced by the man (Michael Todd) who became Taylor's second husband the month before the Oscars. *The King and I*'s Yul Brynner took home the Best Actor statuette, with Dean and Hudson probably taking votes from each other. Moreover, many believe Dean might have won had he been nominated in the more logical Best Supporting Actor category. McCambridge lost the Supporting Actress statuette to *Written on the Wind*'s Dorothy Malone.

A legion of Dean fans believed the actor should have been given a posthumous Oscar at the Academy ceremony (March 27, 1957) honoring the film artistry of 1956. Surprisingly, this included the influential Hollywood columnist Hedda Hopper, who also offered the startling suggestion "that Warner Brothers [which produced *Giant*] could mount the Oscar on a granite shaft over Dean's grave."[57] The Golden Globe Awards, however, did honor Dean's *Giant* performance with a statuette in a new category, "World Film Favorite–Male." And Dean's performance as Rink also garnered France's Winged Victory Award as Best Actor.

For the naïve movie fan, Dean's career now seemed over—but it had only just begun.

COLLECTION OF WES D. GEHRING

If Dean was the epitome of 1950s cool, Humphrey Bogart wore that title for the 1940s. Here he is in his defining film, Casablanca *(1943).*

EPILOGUE

"Dean died at just the right time. Had he lived, he'd never have been able to live up to his publicity."[1]

—HUMPHREY BOGART

FOR ALL THE DARKLY COMIC WISDOM IN HUMPHREY BOGART'S take on James Dean's ongoing iconic fame, there is no easy answer to the "why" of the enduring legend of the Hoosier-born "rebel." Otherwise, Hollywood would have produced an army of James Deans since the young actor's 1955 death. Ironically, during the cult hysteria that first followed his passing (which ranged from numerous global teen suicides to the establishment of three hundred fan clubs in Japan alone[2]), many believed Dean's home studio (Warner Brothers) was manufacturing this mass mourning. Paradoxically, Warner's was more concerned that viewers would not turn out to see a dead actor, since Dean died before both *Rebel Without a Cause* (1955) and *Giant* (1956) were released.

Cultural historian Adam Gopnik has written, "It always takes a while to look back and see on what point the significant lines of history converge—that's why they call it perspective."[3] So what would now be the reasons why Dean, with only three starring roles, remains one of the most celebrated of film stars, with "Deaner" fans still making his hometown (Fairmount, Indiana) a movie Mecca, not to mention memorabilia marketing schemes that are still with us? First, it begins with talent. Coupled with his heroes, Marlon Brando and Montgomery Clift, Dean "helped revolutionize the finely-honed art of film acting by making it less finely honed, ruffling it up with rough edges."[4] Second, taking a cue from the equally iconic Bogart, the timing of Dean's death fueled the fame. But this point is contingent upon a third component of Dean's legacy—being a "symbol of frustrated youth, of mixed-up kiddery, revolt, and loneliness."[5] For instance, shortly before the world saw Dean's screen persona test fate by entering a potentially fatal automobile "chicken run" in *Rebel*, the young actor's real-life racing recklessness led to his death. A foolish waste, yes, but that "life on the edge" consistency legitimized the poignancy of Dean's screen characters. Like the signature fictional figure of the 1950s, novelist J. D. Salinger's Holden Caulfield, Dean was all about fighting phoniness. Indeed, Holden's complaint, "I was surrounded by phonies. . . . They were coming in the goddamn window," sounds just like something Dean's *Rebel* character might have said.[6]

The nature of Dean's death is also linked to a fourth factor in the mythology of the actor—the public's perverse fascination with the self-destructive artist, be it poet Dylan Thomas or rocker Janis Joplin. Why does such interest persist? Biographers and critics alike have long enjoyed romanticizing the creative process. For example, even Val Holley's superior chronicle of Dean's life finds the need to close with the most simple sentimentality: "Dean's earthy records were achieved because of—not in spite of—his self-destructiveness, insecurity, and vulnerability. The gift of artistry can be a curse as well as a blessing."[7] This is an entertainingly romantic take on Dean, but ultimately neglects so much, such as the points delineated here.

A fifth item elevating him to movie deity was Dean's duplicity in suggesting he completely mirrored the troubled teens he played. Yes, Dean was every bit as passionate as these screen characters, and the actor suffered neither fools nor phonies in real life. But Dean was *not* the aimless, angst-ridden youth he played in the movies. His beloved cousin and surrogate brother, Marcus Winslow Jr., has suggested Dean knowingly let elements of this wounded film persona "rub off" on his accepted biography.[8] Dean instinctively realized that for the public, this would add poignancy to his performances; that is, he seemingly replicated his reality. Put another way, his "fans have sighed and said, 'He didn't need to act, only to remember.' It is a compliment to his art. But it is also a fallacy."[9] Granted, his Method acting was sometimes fueled by tapping into painful memories, such as the childhood loss of his mother. But this was simply a performing technique for his art; he was not that suffering, rudderless figure in real life. His friend and pivotal early mentor, high school drama teacher Adeline Nall, was probably the most passionate of his inner circle to attempt to set the record straight. Her refreshing response to the misleading image of Dean as a melancholy boy always mourning his mother was: "Hogwash. It just wasn't so. Jim had as much, in fact more, love and affection than almost any one boy in Fairmount."[10] As *Giant* director George Stevens later noted: "Dean wanted success badly and he had a concrete plan to achieve it. . . . He worked hard to get publicity and always had a photographer with him. He had a fine concept of how [the screen persona] Jimmy Dean could be made popular."[11]

A sixth component in Dean's emergence as a cinema immortal is the total wild card of chance. An overly modest Marlon Brando later discussed in his autobiography how this fortuitous yet totally random sense of timing swept both him and Dean along in its very public wake: "Because we were around when it [counterculture beginnings] happened, Jimmy Dean and I were sometimes cast as symbols of this transformation—and in some cases as instigators of alienation. But the sea change in society had nothing to do with us; it would have occurred with or without us. Our movies didn't precipitate the new attitudes, but the response to them mirrored the changes bubbling to the surface."[12]

Brando's reality check here also reminds the reader that a pivotal point of the memoir or biography is to preserve the humanity of the subject. To illustrate, when Dean's close friend and biographer William Bast later did a television documentary on the actor, he told the *Christian Science Monitor*, "If I don't tell them [the public] who he was on a more realistic personal level, they'll forget that he was anybody. He'll just become their instrument, the instrument of their fantasies."[13] Of course, one should hasten to add that the humility of Brando's views in no way lessens the great gift both he and Dean had to share. But Brando prompts us to keep things in cultural perspective.

Interestingly, Dean would undoubtedly have shared these sentiments. Though Brando based his autobiographical insights upon the wisdom of a then-stormy seventy years of life, Dean was already leaning in this direction at age twenty-four. In pianist/composer/actor Oscar Levant's comic memoir, *The Unimportance of Being Oscar*, this Hollywood wit described a gracious Dean coming for a visit, largely because one of Levant's daughters was an ardent fan. Levant, who also did not suffer fools or phonies, was completely charmed by Dean, and they talked until dawn. But the pianist revealed "a strange thing . . . [upon] seeing my daughter's room filled with dozens of pictures of him in various poses, did not seem to please Dean. On the contrary, it depressed him. He said he felt crushed under the weight of such adulation."[14]

Paradoxically for Brando, though he predated Dean, the younger actor's death pushed him to the front of the iconic rebel line. Brando's innocent desertion was not about just surviving, or even getting old and overweight; it also involved moving on to merely traditional parts. One passionate student of the 1950s described it in the following manner: "At first the [counterculture] hero could have been Brando, until he put on a suit and sang songs just like Dad [in *Guys and Dolls*, 1955]. That was a betrayal. It had to be someone else, someone who would remain permanently young, permanently rebellious . . . James Dean"[15]

A seventh possible enduring fame factor for Dean was Warner Brothers' sale of both *East of Eden* and *Rebel Without a Cause* to television in 1960. The thinking here is that just as repeated small-screen appearances of *The Wizard of Oz* (1939) and *It's a Wonderful Life* (1946) turned those pictures into cherished classics (almost rite-of-passage pictures), the sudden easy availability of Dean's two most antiheroic films at the beginning of the antiestablishment 1960s helped solidify his status as the patron saint of the misfit and the misunderstood. A 1971 *Chicago Sun-Times* article went so far as to suggest that "without these two movies on television, the Dean legend might have dimmed and finally died."[16] An overstatement or not, the real irony here was that Warner Brothers had made the sale because the studio felt the obsession with Dean was finally fading!

An eighth element feeding the phenomenon of James Dean is youth culture itself. One might call the actor a hymn to youth itself. But this goes beyond a simplistic recycling of Rod Stewart's recording of "Forever Young." Yes, Dean's death will keep him forever young. But I am referring to the nostalgia most people have for that early time in their lives when they are burning with curiosity about *everything*. Thus, besides being moved by Dean's attempts to reconnect with his screen fathers, I am equally drawn to the boy/man fascinated by the young plants in *Eden* or the nurturing friend to Plato (Sal Mineo) in *Rebel*. I am reminded of a passage from S. E. Hinton's coming-of-age novel *The Outsiders* (1967), a 1950s tale saturated with the spirit of Dean. The dying boy Johnny has written a letter to his friend, Ponyboy. He describes, in part, what he thinks a poem noted earlier in the text, Robert Frost's "Nothing Gold Can Stay," means: "I've been thinking about . . . that poem, that guy that wrote it, he meant you're gold when you're a kid. . . . When you're a kid everything's new, dawn. It's just when you get used to everything that it's day."[17] Though Frost's title warns, "Nothing Gold Can Stay," the image of Dean represents a capsulization of Johnny's implied advice to Ponyboy, which was to stay golden—young at heart.

A final puzzle piece to the deification of Dean might be the pity factor—bemoaning what might have been. Would he have maintained the youthful diversity of his old New York stage and television rival, Paul Newman? Or, would he have gone the riveting-in-ruin route of his hero, Brando? I could not resist asking Marcus Winslow Jr. where Dean might be today, had he avoided that sports car death. Marcus answered with one word: "director."[18] It is a good and knowing answer. So should we mourn what might have been? My answer is drawn from a biography of the inspired French director Jean Vigo, whose iconoclastic *Zero for Conduct* (1933), about a boarding school where the authorities cannot regiment the most spontaneous of children, reminds me of Dean. Vigo also died in his twenties, after only four films. Biographer P. E. Salles Gomes observed, "To dwell on the brevity of Vigo's career, and to speculate on what might have been if he had lived, is to dismiss the scale of his achievement."[19] Along similar lines, I would advise forgetting the shortness of Dean's career and instead celebrating "the scale of his achievement." It is, after all, remarkable under any time frame.

Marlon Brando's title character in The Godfather *(1972) with Al Pacino (sitting).*

Filmography

Bit Parts

November 1951

Fixed Bayonets (Twentieth Century Fox, 92 minutes)
Director/Screenplay: Samuel Fuller, from the John Brophy novel. Stars: Richard Basehart, Gene Evans, Michael O'Shea, Richard Hylton. (James Dean briefly appears as a GI.)

February 1952°

Sailor Beware (Paramount, 108 minutes)
Director: Hal Walker. Screenplay: James Allardice and Martin Rackin, additional dialogue John Grant, from the Kenyon Nicholson play. Stars: Dean Martin, Jerry Lewis, Corinne Calvet, Marion Marshall, Robert Strauss. (Dean appears as a corner man for Lewis's boxing opponent.)

July 1952

Has Anybody Seen My Gal? (Universal, 88 minutes)
Director: Douglas Sirk. Screenplay: Joseph Hoffman, from the Eleanor H. Porter story. Stars: Piper Laurie, Rock Hudson, Charles Coburn, Gigi Perreau. (Dean orders ice cream in a scene with Coburn.)

°General release was 1952 but sometimes listed as a late 1951 picture.

Starring Roles

March 1955   *East of Eden* (Warner Brothers, 115 minutes)
Director: Elia Kazan. Screenplay: Paul Osborn, from the John Steinbeck novel. Stars: Julie Harris, James Dean, Raymond Massey, Richard Davalos, Burl Ives.

October 1955   *Rebel Without a Cause* (Warner Brothers, 111 minutes)
Director: Nicholas Ray. Screenplay: Stewart Stern, from an Irving Shulman adaptation of a Ray story inspired by Dr. Robert M. Lindner's book *The Blind Run*. Stars: James Dean, Natalie Wood, Sal Mineo, Jim Backus, Ann Doran, Corey Allen, William Hopper, Rochelle Hudson, Virginia Brissac, Nick Adams, Jack Simmons, Dennis Hopper.

October 1956   *Giant* (Warner Brothers, 201 minutes)
Director: George Stevens. Screenplay: Fred Guiol and Ivan Moffat, from the Edna Ferber novel. Stars: Elizabeth Taylor, Rock Hudson, James Dean, Carroll Baker, Jane Withers, Chill Wills, Mercedes McCambridge, Sal Mineo, Dennis Hopper.

Preface

1. Frank Friedrichsen, "The Short Tragic Life of Jimmy Dean," *Movie Stars Parade*, December 1955, 42.

2. Paul Hendrickson, "JD: The Legend That Won't Go Away," *Philadelphia Inquirer*, July 22, 1973.

3. Marcus Winslow Jr., interview with author, July 23, 2004.

4. John Williams, "The Strange Love-Making of James Dean," *Movie Star Parade*, October 1955, 70.

5. Natalie Wood, "I Can't Forget Jimmy," *Movie Life*, December 1956, 28.

6. Pauline Kael, *I Lost It at the Movies* (Boston: Little, Brown and Company, 1965), 56.

7. Don Larsen (with Mark Shaw), *The Perfect Yankee: The Incredible Story of the Greatest Miracle in Baseball History* (Champaign, IL: Sagamore Publishing, 1996), 202.

Prologue

1. Antoine de Saint Exupéry, *The Little Prince* (1943; reprint, New York: Harcourt Brace and World, Inc., 1971), 4.

2. Donald Spoto, *Rebel: The Life and Legend of James Dean* (1996; reprint, New York: Cooper Square Press, 2000), 182.

3. David Dalton, *James Dean, The Mutant King: A Biography* (1974; reprint, Chicago: Cappella, 2001), 271.

4. Val Holley, *James Dean: The Biography* (London: Robson Books, 1995), 10.

5. John Gilmore, *Live Fast, Die Young: Remembering the Short Life of James Dean* (New York: Thunder's Mouth Press, 1997), 216.

6. "Dean Kin Grant Rare Interview," *Indianapolis Star*, September 22, 1985.

7. Ernest Hemingway, *Death in the Afternoon* (1932; reprint, New York: Scribner, 2003), 2.

8. Paul Alexander, *Boulevard of Broken Dreams: The Life, Times, and Legend of James Dean* (New York: Plume, 1997), 192.

9. Ernest Hemingway, *The Old Man and the Sea* (New York: Charles Scribner's Sons, 1952), 68.

10. Vincent Canby, *The Natural* review, *New York Times*, May 11, 1984.

11. Gilmore, *Live Fast, Die Young*, 2.

12. John Howlett, *James Dean: A Biography* (1975; reprint, London: Plexus, 1997), 143.

13. Warren Newton Beath, *The Death of James Dean* (New York: Grove Press, 1986), 39.

14. Seymour Korman, "The Last Hours of James Dean," *Chicago Tribune Magazine*, February 5, 1956, 41.

15. For example, see Alexander, *Boulevard of Broken Dreams*, 239.

16. David Loehr's James Dean Gallery, Gas City, Indiana, includes a facsimile of the Porsche death car.

17. There are several sources. For example, see Howlett, *James Dean: A Biography*, 143.

18. Gilmore, *Live Fast, Die Young*, 232.

19. Francois Truffaut, *The Films in My Life* (1975; reprint, New York: Da Capo Press, 1994), 299.

Chapter 1

1. John Gilmore, *Live Fast, Die Young: Remembering the Short Life of James Dean* (New York: Thunder's Mouth Press, 1997), 9.

2. See Ronald Martinetti, *The James Dean Story* (London: Michael O'Mara Books Limited, 1996), 4.

3. Val Holley, *James Dean: The Biography* (1995; reprint, London: Robson Books, 1999), 17.

4. Donald Spoto, *Rebel: The Life and Legend of James Dean* (1996; reprint, New York: Cooper Square Press, 2000), 14.

5. Wes Gehring, *Carole Lombard: The Hoosier Tornado* (Indianapolis: Indiana Historical Society Press, 2003).

6. David Dalton, *James Dean: American Icon* (New York: St. Martin's Press, 1984), 234.

7. Randall Riese, *The Unabridged James Dean: His Life and Legacy from A to Z* (Chicago: Contemporary Books, 1991), 92.

8. Jim Backus, *Rocks on the Roof* (New York: G. P. Putnam's Sons, 1958), 156.

9. Riese, *James Dean*, 91.

10. Gilmore, *Live Fast, Die Young*, 35.

11. David Dalton, *James Dean, The Mutant King: A Biography* (1974; reprint, Chicago: Cappella, 2001), 5.

12. Eleanor Gehrig and Joseph Durso, *My Luke and I* (New York: Thomas Y. Crowell Company, 1976), 224.

13. Frank Graham, *Lou Gehrig: A Quiet Hero* (New York: G. P. Putnam's Sons, 1942), 211.

14. Paul Alexander, *Boulevard of Broken Dreams: The Life, Times, and Legend of James Dean* (New York: Plume, 1997), 21, 23.

15. John Howlett, *James Dean: A Biography* (1975; reprint, London: Plexus, 1997), 13.

16. Gehring, *Leo McCarey: "From Marx to McCarthy"* (Lanham, MD: Scarecrow Press, forthcoming).

17. Holley, *James Dean*, 18.

18. Hedda Hopper, "Keep Your Eyes on James Dean," *Chicago Tribune Magazine*, March 27, 1955, 40.

19. Dalton, *James Dean*, 6.

20. Liz Sheridan, *Dizzy and Jimmy: My Life with James Dean* (New York: Regan Books, 2000), 66.

21. Spoto, *The Life and Legend of James Dean*, 25.

22. George Scullin, "James Dean: The Legend and the Facts," *Look*, October 16, 1956, 123.

23. Riese, *James Dean*, 414.

24. Holley, *James Dean*, 201.

25. William Russo, *The Next James Dean* (New York: Xlibris Corporation, 2003), 10.

26. William Bast, *James Dean: A Biography* (New York: Ballantine Books, 1956), 41.

27. Alexander, *Boulevard of Broken Dreams*, 27.

Chapter 2

1. Randall Riese, *The Unabridged James Dean: His Life and Legacy from A to Z* (Chicago: Contemporary Books, 1991), 408.

2. *The James Dean Story*, 1957. A George W. George and Robert Altman Film (82 minutes).

3. William Bast, *James Dean: A Biography* (New York: Ballantine Books, 1956), 79.

4. Liz Sheridan, *Dizzy & Jimmy: My Life with James Dean* (New York: Regan Books, 2000), 224.

5. Emma Woolen Dean, "James Dean—The Boy I Loved," *Photoplay*, March 1956, 84.

6. Val Holley, *James Dean: The Biography* (1995; reprint, London: Robson Books, 1999), 19.

7. David Dalton, *James Dean: The Mutant King: A Biography* (1974; reprint, Chicago: Cappella, 2001), 47.

8. Bast, *James Dean*, 41.

9. Holley, *James Dean*, 191.

10. Jeff Young, *Kazan: The Master Director Discusses His Films: Interviews with Elia Kazan* (New York: Newmarket Press, 1999), 198.

11. Wes Gehring, *Carole Lombard: The Hoosier Tornado* (Indianapolis: Indiana Historical Society Press, 2003).

12. Holley, *James Dean*, 174.

13. Riese, *The Unabridged James Dean*, 408.

14. B-Western film historian Ray White, telephone interview with author, May 6, 2004.

15. Jon Tuska, *Billy the Kid: His Life and Legend* (Westport, CT: Greenwood Press, 1994), 189.

16. Ibid., 1.

17. Frederick Elkin, "The Psychological Appeal for Children of the Hollywood B Western," in Jack Nachbar, ed., *Focus on the Western* (Englewood Cliffs, NJ: Prentice Hall, 1974), 75.

18. "Dean Kin Grant Rare Interview," *Indianapolis Star*, September 22, 1985.

19. Bast, *James Dean*, 47.

20. Donald Spoto, *Rebel: The Life and Legend of James Dean* (1996; reprint, New York: Cooper Square Press, 2000), 33.

21. Evelyn Washburn Nielsen, "The TRUTH about James Dean," *Chicago Tribune Magazine*, September 9, 1956, 23.

22. *The James Dean Story*, 1957.

23. Antoine de Saint Exupéry, *The Little Prince* (1943; reprint, New York: Harcourt, Brace and World, Inc., 1971), 4.

24. David Dalton, *James Dean: American Icon* (New York: St. Martin's Press, 1984), 16.

25. Gehring, *American Dark Comedy: Beyond Satire* (Westport, CT: Greenwood Press, 1996), 91.

26. Marcus Winslow Jr., interview with author, July 23, 2004.

27. *James Dean and Me*, 1995. A Tom Cochran and Tom Alvarez Film (approximately 90 minutes).

28. James R. Mellow, *Hemingway: A Life without Consequences* (Boston: Houghton Mifflin, 1992), 438.

29. Paul Alexander, *Boulevard of Broken Dreams: The Life, Times, and Legend of James Dean* (New York: Plume, 1997), 34.

30. John Howlett, *James Dean: A Biography* (1975; reprint, London: Plexus, 1997), 20.

31. Ibid.

32. Charles Dickens, "A Madman's Manuscript" [Chapter XI], in *Pickwick Papers: Part One* (New York: P. F. Collier and Son, 1837), 158–59.

33. George H. Ford, *Dickens and His Readers: Aspects of Novel-Criticism Since 1836* (1955; reprint, New York: W. W. Norton and Company, 1965), 18.

34. Ronald Martinetti, *The James Dean Story* (1975; reprint, London: Michael O'Mara Books, 1996), 16.

35. Ibid., 15.

36. Various sources, such as Holley, *James Dean*, 25.

37. "James Dean First Place Winner in Dramatic Speaking," *Fairmount News*, April 14, 1949.

38. "Good Luck at Longmont—Jim," *Fairmount News*, April 28, 1949.

39. Ibid.

40. "James Dean," *Fairmount News*, October 13, 1955.

Chapter 3

1. *The James Dean Story*, 1957. A George W. George and Robert Altman Film. (82 minutes).

2. Donald Spoto, *Rebel: The Life and Legend of James Dean* (1996; reprint, New York: Cooper Square Press, 2000), 49.

3. Randall Riese, *The Unabridged James Dean: His Life and Legacy from A to Z* (Chicago: Contemporary Books, 1991), 351.

4. Adeline Nall (as told to Val Holley), "Grant County's Own [James Dean]," *Traces of Indiana and Midwestern History*, Fall 1989, 19.

5. Earl L. Conn, "Coach Remembers 'Jimmy' as a Pretty Fair Athlete," *Muncie Star*, September 28, 1975.

6. Conn, "At Guard for Fairmount—James Dean," unpublished, 1957–58, author's files.

7. Conn, "The Faces of James Dean," *Muncie Star*, June 24, 1996.

8. Conn, "At Guard for Fairmount—James Dean."

9. Ed Breen, "James Dean's Indiana: The Stage Along Sand Pike," *Traces of Indiana and Midwestern History*, Fall 1989, 9, and Conn, "Coach Remembers 'Jimmy' as Pretty Fair Athlete."

10. Conn, interview with author, April 2003.

11. David Dalton, *James Dean: American Icon* (New York: St. Martin's Press, 1984), 15.

12. Howard Thompson, "Another Dean Hits the Big Leagues," *New York Times*, March 13, 1955.

13. Val Holley, *James Dean: The Biography* (1995; reprint, London: Robson Books, 1999), 253.

14. Alice Packard, "The Real Jimmy Dean," *Movie Star Parade*, May 1956, 41, 56.

15. "Rev. James DeWeerd Heads Kletzing College," *Fairmount News*, June 23, 1949.

16. Emma Woolen Dean, "James Dean—The Boy I Loved," *Photoplay*, March 1956, 84.

17. John Howlett, *James Dean: A Biography* (1975; reprint, London: Plexus, 1997), 19.

18. Evelyn Washburn Nielsen, "The TRUTH about James Dean," *Chicago Tribune Magazine*, September 9, 1956, 23.

19. Joyce Carol Oates, "Do You Love Me?," *New York Times Book Review*, May 16, 2004.

20. Ronald Martinetti, *The James Dean Story* (1975; reprint, London: Michael O'Mara Books, 1996), 12.

21. Joe Hyams (with Jay Hyams), *James Dean: Little Boy Lost* (New York: Warner Books, 1992), 18–20.

22. Holley, *James Dean*, 28.

23. Ibid., and Joe Hyams, "James Dean," *Redbook*, September 1956, 28.

24. For example, see Hyams, "When James Dean Lost Pier Angeli to Vic Damone," *National Enquirer*, November 4, 1973.

25. Marcus Winslow Jr., interview with author, July 23, 2004.

26. Paul Alexander, *Boulevard of Broken Dreams: The Life, Times and Legend of James Dean* (New York: Plume, 1997), 43.

27. Tom Shaks, "TV Film on JD Tries to Ignore the Myth," *Louisville Courier*, February 15, 1976.

28. Rosanne Cash, "Janis Joplin," *Rolling Stone*, April 15, 2004, 136.

29. For example, see William Russo's *The Next James Dean* (New York: Xlibris, 2003), 10.

30. Riese, *The Unabridged James Dean*, 44.

31. David Dalton, *James Dean: The Mutant King* (1974; reprint, Chicago: Cappella, 2001), 333.

32. William Hall, *James Dean* (Gloucestershire, UK: Sutton Publishing, 1999), 17.

33. Spoto, *Rebel: The Life and Legend of James Dean*, 42.

34. "Jimmy Dean: The Star Who Never Died," *Movieland*, October 1956, 42, 81.

35. "James Dean Placed Sixth in National Forensic Meet," *Fairmount News*, May 5, 1949.

36. "James Dean Presents 'The Mad Man' at Lions Club Meeting," *Fairmount News*, May 26, 1949.

37. "James Dean Placed Sixth in National Forensic Meet."

38. "James Dean Killed as Result of California Car Accident," *Fairmount News*, October 6, 1955.

39. "Footsteps on the Sands of Time," in *Black and Gold '49* (Fairmount, IN: Fairmount Journalism Department, 1949), n.p.

40. "Senior Class," in *Black and Gold*, n.p.

41. Paul Hendrickson, "J D: The Legend That Won't Go Away," *Philadelphia Inquirer*, July 22, 1973.

42. Natalie Wood, "You Haven't Heard the Half about Jimmy!," *Photoplay*, November 1955, 82.

43. Ibid.

Chapter 4

1. Emma Woolen Dean, "James Dean—The Boy I Loved," *Photoplay*, March 1956, 84.

2. David Dalton, *James Dean: The Mutant King* (1974; reprint, Chicago: Cappella, 2001), 36.

3. Joseph Humphreys, consultant, *Jimmy Dean on Jimmy Dean* (London: Plexus, 1990), 14.

4. Ronald Martinetti, *The James Dean Story* (1975; reprint, London: Michael O'Mara Books, 1996), 19.

5. Donald Spoto, *Rebel: The Life and Legend of James Dean* (1996; reprint, New York: Cooper Square Press, 2000), 40.

6. See chapters two and three of this book.

7. John Howlett, *James Dean: A Biography* (1975; reprint, London: Plexus, 1997), 23.

8. Paul Alexander, *Boulevard of Broken Dreams: The Life, Times, and Legend of James Dean* (New York: Plume, 1997), 58.

9. Val Holley, *James Dean: The Biography* (1995; reprint, London: Robson Books, 1999), 38.

10. Joe Hyams, "James Dean," *Redbook*, September 1956, 74.

11. John Gilmore, *Live Fast, Die Young: Remembering the Short Life of James Dean* (New York: Thunder's Mouth Press, 1997), 50.

12. *James Dean and Me*, 1995. A Tom Cochrun and Tom Alvarez Film (approximately 90 minutes).

13. Late night television talk show circuit, circa 1975.

14. Joseph Humphreys, consultant, *Jimmy Dean on Jimmy Dean*, 8.

15. For example, see Venable Herndon's *James Dean: A Short Life* (Garden City, NY: Doubleday and Company, 1974), 66.

16. Val Holley, *James Dean*, 56.

17. Randall Riese, *The Unabridged James Dean: His Life and Legacy From A to Z* (Chicago: Contemporary Books, 1991), 95.

18. Ibid., 96.

19. Mercedes McCambridge, *The Quality of Mercy: An Autobiography* (New York: Times Books, 1981), 208–9.

20. David Halberstam, *The Teammates* (New York: Hyperion, 2003), 112.

21. Holley, *James Dean*, 47.

22. William Bast, *James Dean: A Biography* (New York: Ballantine Books, 1956), 13.

23. Ibid.

24. Joe Hyams (with Jay Hyams), *James Dean: Little Boy Lost* (New York: Warner Books, 1992), 32.

25. William Hall, *James Dean* (Gloucestershire, UK: Sutton Publishing, 1999), 28.

26. Bast, *James Dean*, 21.

27. William Hall's *James Dean* is one of the texts that gets the discovery story (p. 28) wrong.

28. Riese, *The Unabridged James Dean*, 386.

29. Howlett, *James Dean*, 28.

30. Spoto, *Rebel: The Life and Legend of James Dean*, 71.

31. "But He Soon Learned How to Attract Attention," *Marion Chronicle*, September 20, 1956.

Chapter 5

1. Hedda Hopper, "Keep Your Eyes on James Dean," *Chicago Tribune Magazine*, March 27, 1955, 40.

2. William Bast, *James Dean: A Biography* (New York: Ballantine Books, 1956), 24–25.

3. Tim Brooks and Earle Marsh, *The Complete Directory to Prime Time Network TV Shows, 1946–Present* (New York: Ballantine Books, 1979), 54.

4. Val Holley, *James Dean: The Biography* (1995; reprint, London: Robson Books, 1999), 95.

5. Liz Sheridan, *Dizzy & Jimmy: My Life with James Dean* (New York: Regan Books, 2000), 27.

6. Lynette Clemetson, "From Doodles to Clintons: Simmie Lee Knox," *New York Times*, June 15, 2004.

7. Holley, *James Dean*, 63.

8. Bast, *James Dean*, 28–29.

9. Peter Evans, *Peter Sellers: The Mask behind the Mask* (New York: Signet, 1980), 158.

10. Ronald Martinetti, *The James Dean Story* (London: Michael O'Mara Books Limited, 1996), 30.

11. Donald Spoto, *Rebel: The Life and Legend of James Dean* (1996; reprint, New York: Cooper Square Press, 2000), 78.

12. Chris Murray, ed., "Salvadore Dali" entry, in the *Dictionary of the Arts* (London: Brockhampton Press, 1997), 135.

13. Gretchen Rubin, *Forty Ways to Look at Winston Churchill: A Brief Account of a Long Life* (New York: Ballantine Books, 2003), 56.

14. Randall Riese, *James Dean: His Life and Legacy From A to Z* (Chicago: Contemporary Books, 1991), 60.

15. Gretchin Rubin, *Forty Ways to Look at Winston Churchill*, 147.

16. William Knowlton Zinsser, ed., *Extraordinary Lives: The Art and Craft of American Biography* (Boston: Houghton Mifflin Company, 1986), 13.

17. For example, see Martinetti, *The James Dean Story*, 37.

18. Doris Kearns, "Angles of Vision," in Marc Pachter, ed., *Telling Lives: The Biographer's Art* (1979; reprint, Philadelphia: University of Pennsylvania Press, 1985), 90–103.

19. Rubin, *Forty Ways to Look at Winston Churchill*.

20. Holley, *James Dean*, 3.

21. John Howlett, *James Dean: A Biography* (1975; reprint, London: Plexus, 1997), 33.

22. Holley, *James Dean*, 236.

23. Paul Alexander, *Boulevard of Broken Dreams: The Life, Times, and Legend of James Dean* (New York: Plume, 1997), 89.

24. Cobbett Steinberg, *Reel Facts: The Movie Book of Records* (New York: Vintage Books, 1978), 345.

25. Ibid., 405.

26. Sheridan, *Dizzy & Jimmy*, 71.

27. For example, see Nick Tosches, *Dino: Living High in the Dirty Business of Dreams* (New York: Dell, 1992), 247.

Chapter 6

1. Hedda Hopper, "Keep Your Eyes on James Dean," *Chicago Tribune Magazine*, March 27, 1955, 40.

2. Wes Gehring, *"Mr. B" or Comforting Thoughts About the Bison: A Critical Biography of Robert Benchley* (Westport, CT: Greenwood Press, 1992), 37.

3. Val Holley, *James Dean: The Biography* (1995; reprint, London: Robson Books, 1999), 85.

4. Michael Chabon, *Wonder Boys* (New York: Picador, 1995), 251.

5. Liz Sheridan, *Dizzy & Jimmy: My Life with James Dean* (New York: Regan Books, 2000), 140.

6. David Dalton, *James Dean: American Icon* (New York: St. Martin's Press, 1984), 201.

7. Marlon Brando, with Robert Lindsey, *Brando: Songs My Mother Taught Me* (New York: Random House, 1994), 220–21.

8. Ibid., 224.

9. Sheridan, *Dizzy & Jimmy*, 140–41.

10. Dalton, *James Dean*, 60.

11. Jim Knipfel, *Slackjaw* (1999; reprint, New York: Berkley Books, 2000), 12.

12. Ibid., 170.

13. Ronald Martinetti, *The James Dean Story* (London: Michael O'Mara Books Limited, 1996), 50.

14. Sheridan, *Dizzy & Jimmy*, 13.

15. Ibid., 57.

16. Martinetti, *The James Dean Story*, 52.

17. Sheridan, *Dizzy & Jimmy*, 145.

18. Paul Alexander, *Boulevard of Broken Dreams: The Life, Times, and Legend of James Dean* (New York: Plume, 1997), 129–34, 146–47.

19. John Howlett, *James Dean: A Biography* (1975; reprint, London: Plexus, 1997), 39.

20. Randall Riese, *The Unabridged James Dean: His Life and Legacy from A to Z* (Chicago: Contemporary Books, 1991), 88.

21. Ibid.

22. Marcus Winslow Jr., interview with author, July 23, 2004.

23. David Dalton, *James Dean: The Mutant King* (1974; reprint, Chicago: Cappella, 2001), 89.

24. Howlett, *James Dean*, 36.

25. David Hofstede, *James Dean: A Bio-Bibliography* (Westport, CT: Greenwood Press, 1996), 7.

26. Ibid.

27. William Bast, *James Dean: A Biography* (New York: Ballantine Books, 1956), 103.

28. Riese, *The Unabridged James Dean*, 361.

29. Ibid., 304.

Chapter 7

1. Lee Strasberg, *A Dream of Passion: The Development of the Method* (Boston: Little, Brown and Company, 1987), 35.

2. Foster Hirsch, *A Method to Their Madness: A History of the Actors Studio* (New York: W. W. Norton, 1984), 294.

3. Strasberg, *A Dream of Passion*, 57.

4. Cindy Adams, *Lee Strasberg: The Imperfect Genius of the Actors Studio* (Garden City, NY: Doubleday and Company, 1980), 214–15.

5. Randall Riese, *The Unabridged James Dean: His Life and Legacy from A to Z* (Chicago: Contemporary Books, 1991), 514.

6. Ball State University theatre professor Roger Smith, interview with author, June 17, 2004.

7. Jim Knipfel, *Slackjaw* (1999; reprint, New York: Berkley Books, 2000), 12.

8. Joseph Humphreys, consultant, *Jimmy Dean on Jimmy Dean* (London: Plexus, 1990), 39.

9. Venable Herndon, *James Dean: A Short Life* (Garden City, NY: Doubleday and Company, 1974), 106.

10. C. A. Lejeune, "The Dean Legend," *London Observer*, November 10, 1957.

11. "Lee Strasberg," in Charles Moritz, ed., *Current Biography Yearbook: 1960* (New York: H. W. Wilson Company, 1960), 406.

12. William Bast, *James Dean: A Biography* (New York: Ballantine Books, 1956), 66.

13. Wes Gehring, *"Mr. B" or Comforting Thoughts about the Bison: A Critical Biography of Robert Benchley* (Westport, CT: Greenwood Press, 1992), xiii.

14. Adams, *Lee Strasberg*, 210.

15. Ibid., 218.

16. Carroll Baker, *Baby Doll: An Autobiography* (New York: Arbor House, 1983), 85.

17. Howard Thompson, "Another Dean Hits the Big Leagues," *New York Times*, March 13, 1955.

18. Liz Sheridan, *Dizzy & Jimmy: My Life with James Dean* (New York: Regan Books, 2000), 224.

19. "Clyde McCullough," in John Thorn and Pete Palmer, with David Reuther, eds., *Total Baseball* (New York: Warner Books, 1989), 1297.

20. Sheridan, *Dizzy & Jimmy*, 208.

21. Wes Gehring, *Seeing Red: The Skelton in Hollywood's Closet: An Analytical Biography* (Davenport, IA: Robin Vincent, 2001), 37.

22. "'Sensitive'; To Whom? Himself!," *Variety*, September 11, 1974.

23. Val Holley, *James Dean: The Biography* (1995; reprint, London: Robson Books, 1999), 128.

24. Riese, *The Unabridged James Dean*, 481.

25. Ronald Martinetti, *The James Dean Story* (London: Michael O'Mara Books Limited, 1996), 66.

26. *See the Jaguar* review, *New York Daily News*, December 4, 1952.

27. John McClain, "Play Is Baffling and Confusing," *New York Journal-American*, December 4, 1952.

28. William Hawkins, "'Jaguar' Has Obscure Spots," *New York World Telegram*, December 4, 1952, and *See the Jaguar* review, *New York Daily News*.

29. *See the Jaguar* review, *Cue*, December 13, 1952.

30. Walter F. Kerr, "The Theaters: 'See the Jaguar'," *New York Herald Tribune*, December 4, 1952.

31. David Hofstede, *James Dean: A Bio-Bibliography* (Westport, CT: Greenwood Press, 1996), 33.

32. Donald Spoto, *Rebel: The Life and Legend of James Dean* (1996; reprint, New York: Cooper Square Press, 2000), 141.

33. See Spoto, *Rebel*, 142–44.

34. Adeline Nall (as told to Val Holley), "Grant County's Own [James Dean]," *Traces of Indiana and Midwestern History*, Fall 1989, 21.

35. *The Immoralist* review, *New York Times*, February 9, 1954, and William Hawkins, "'Immoralist' Marked by Tender Tragedy," *New York World Telegram and Sun*, February 9, 1954.

36. Hawkins, "'Immoralist' Marked by Tender Tragedy," 22.

37. Walter F. Kerr, "Theater: 'The Immoralist,'" *New York Herald Tribune*, February 9, 1954, and Richard Watts Jr., "Two on the Aisle: A Grave Drama about Abnormality," *New York Post*, February 9, 1954.

Chapter 8

1. John Steinbeck, *East of Eden* (1952; reprint, New York: Penguin Books, 2002), 450.

2. Elia Kazan, *Elia Kazan: A Life* (New York: Alfred A. Knopf, 1988), 535–36.

3. David Dalton, *James Dean: American Icon* (New York: St. Martin's Press, 1984), 60.

4. Dalton, *James Dean: The Mutant King* (1974; reprint, Chicago: Cappella, 2001), 166.

5. Dan Ford, *Pappy: The Life of John Ford* (Englewood Cliffs, NJ: Prentice Hall, 1979), 86.

6. Raymond Massey, *A Hundred Different Lives: An Autobiography* (Boston: Little, Brown and Company, 1979), 377.

7. Kazan, *Elia Kazan*, 538.

8. Jeff Young, *Kazan: The Master Director Discusses His Films: Interviews with Elia Kazan* (New York: Newmarket Press, 1999), 199.

9. Julie Harris, "How I Remember James Dean," *Picturegoer*, June 16, 1956, 10.

10. Young, *Kazan*, 199.

11. Elena Oumano, *Paul Newman* (New York: St. Martin's Press, 1989), 50.

12. For example, see Paul Alexander's *Boulevard of Broken Dreams: The Life, Times, and Legend of James Dean* (New York: Plume, 1997), 160, 163, 169.

13. Kazan, *Elia Kazan*, 537.

14. Venable Herndon, *James Dean: A Short Life* (Garden City, NY: Doubleday and Company, Inc., 1974), 149–50.

15. Randall Riese, *The Unabridged James Dean: His Life and Legacy from A to Z* (Chicago: Contemporary Books, 1991), 23–24.

16. Joseph Humphreys, consultant, *Jimmy Dean on Jimmy Dean* (London: Plexus, 1990), 75.

17. Ibid.

18. Marcus Winslow Jr., interview with author, July 23, 2004.

19. Ibid.

20. Kazan, *Elia Kazan*, 537.

21. Michel Ciment, *Kazan on Kazan* (New York: Viking Press, 1974), 125–26.

22. Young, *Kazan*, 7.

23. Patricia Bosworth, *Marlon Brando* (New York: Viking, 2001), 30.

24. Ibid., 33.

25. Douglas Martin, "Charles Andrews, 88, Writer for Garroway and Other TV Pioneers," *New York Times*, July 8, 2004.

26. Young, *Kazan*, 201.

27. Ciment, *Kazan on Kazan*, 126.

28. "Dean Kin Grant Rare Interview," *Indianapolis Star*, September 22, 1985.

29. Donald Spoto, *Rebel: The Life and Legend of James Dean* (1996; reprint, New York: Cooper Square Press, 2000), 157.

30. Winslow, interview with author, July 23, 2004.

31. Herndon, *James Dean*, 138.

32. William Hall, *James Dean* (Gloucester, UK: Sutton Publishing, 1999), 58.

33. Dalton, *James Dean*, 60.

34. Young, *Kazan*, 197.

35. Richard Schickel, *Brando: A Life in Our Times* (New York: Athaneum, 1991), 108.

36. Philip K. Scheuer, "Jimmy Dean Says He Isn't Flattered by Being Labeled 'Another Brando,'" *Los Angeles Times*, November 7, 1954.

37. Adam Bernstein, "Brando: 1924–2004," *Des Moines Register*, July 3, 2004.

38. Kazan, *Elia Kazan*, 538.

39. William Bast, *James Dean: A Biography* (New York: Ballantine Books, 1956), 110.

40. *East of Eden* review, *Variety*, February 16, 1955.

41. "'East of Eden' Combines Artistry with Boxoffice," *Hollywood Reporter*, February 16, 1955.

42. "The New Pictures: 'East of Eden,'" *Time*, March 21, 1955, 98, 102.

43. Alton Cook, "Kazan Rivals Best in 'Eden,'" *New York World Telegram and Sun*, March 10, 1955.

44. William K. Zinsser, "Screen: 'East of Eden,'" *New York Herald Tribune*, March 10, 1955.

45. Archer Winsten, "Reviewing Stand: 'East of Eden' Opens at Astor," *New York Post*, March 10, 1955, and Mae Tinée, "'East of Eden' Has Some Sins as Film Art," *Chicago Tribune*, April 13, 1955.

46. "'East of Eden' Combines Artistry With Boxoffice."

47. "Dean's 'Eden' Proves to Be Powerful," *Fairmount News*, April 7, 1955.

48. Ibid.

49. Rose Pelswick, "A Saga of Emotions," *New York Journal-American*, March 10, 1955.

50. Bosley Crowther, *East of Eden* review, *New York Times*, March 10, 1955.

51. Pauline Kael, *I Lost It at the Movies* (Boston: Little, Brown and Company, 1965), 206.

52. William Russo, *The Next James Dean* (New York: Xlibris, 2003), 187.

53. Oscar Levant, *Oscar Levant: The Memoirs of an Amnesiac* (1965; reprint, New York: Bantam, 1966), 195.

54. "Dean's 'Eden' Proves to Be Powerful."

55. "Festive 'Eden' Preem Nets $34,000 for Actors Studio," *Hollywood Reporter*, March 10, 1955.

Chapter 9

1. "But He Soon Learned to Attract Attention," *Marion Chronicle*, September 20, 1956.

2. Randall Riese, *The Unabridged James Dean: His Life and Legacy from A to Z* (Chicago: Contemporary Books, 1991), 242.

3. "Demon Dean," *Photoplay*, July 1955, 78.

4. Ibid.

5. Merry Louis, "James Dean: The Boy Who'd Like to Be Brando," *Movie Play*, January 1956, 64.

6. Ibid., 13.

7. Philip K. Scheuer, "Jimmy Dean Says He Isn't Flattered by Being Labeled 'Another Brando,'" *Los Angeles Times*, November 7, 1954.

8. Ibid.

9. Bosley Crowther, *East of Eden* review, *New York Times*, March 10, 1955, and Bosley Crowther, *Rebel Without a Cause* review, *New York Times*, October 27, 1955.

10. Kenneth McLeigh, *Arts in the Twentieth Century* (1985; reprint, Middlesex, UK: Penguin Books, 1986), 185.

11. For example, see the article "Undying Voice," *Newsweek*, January 27, 1964, 58–59.

12. Paul Hendrickson, "Remembering James Dean Back in Indiana," *Los Angeles Times*, July 22, 1973.

13. Leonard Roseman, "Jimmy Dean: Giant Legend, Cult Rebel," *Los Angeles Times*, December 18, 1977.

14. Ibid.

15. Roy Schatt, *James Dean: A Portrait* (1982; reprint, New York: Ruggles de Latour, 1990), 42.

16. "Moody New Star: Hoosier James Dean Excites Hollywood," *Life*, March 7, 1955, 126.

17. Ibid.

18. Emma Woolen Dean, "James Dean—The Boy I Loved," *Photoplay*, March 1956, 57, 84.

19. Nick Adams, "What Dean Told His Best Friends," *Movie Life*, October 1956, 40.

20. "The Real Jimmy Dean," *Movie Star Parade*, May 1956, 41, 56.

21. Ronald Martinetti, *The James Dean Story* (1975; reprint, London: Michael O'Mara Books, 1996), 106.

22. Hendrickson, "Remembering James Dean Back in Indiana," 22.

23. Natalie Wood, "You Haven't Heard the Half About Jimmy," *Photoplay*, November 1955, 82.

24. "Fairmount High School Students Invited to Enter Contest on Prevention of Juvenile Delinquency," *Fairmount News*, February 17, 1955, and "Second PTA Meeting on Juvenile Delinquency Slated for Monday," *Fairmount News*, February 3, 1955.

25. "Julius Caesar," *Fairmount News*, January 27, 1955.

26. Hedda Hopper, "Keep Your Eyes on James Dean," *Chicago Tribune Magazine*, March 27, 1955, 40.

27. Ibid.

28. Jim Backus, *Rocks on the Roof* (New York: G. P. Putnam's Sons, 1958), 153.

29. Riese, *The Unabridged James Dean*, 435.

30. Val Holley, *James Dean: The Biography* (1995; reprint, London: Robson Books, 1999), 259.

31. Suzanne Finstad, *Natasha: The Biography of Natalie Wood* (New York: Harmony Books, 2001), 154.

32. Elia Kazan, *Elia Kazan: A Life* (New York: Alfred A. Knopf, 1988), 789.

33. John Howlett, *James Dean: A Biography* (1975; reprint, London: Plexus, 1997), 112.

34. Finstad, *Natasha*, 136.

35. Natalie Wood, "I Can't Forget Jimmy," *Movie Life*, December 1956, 28.

36. Backus, *Rocks on the Roof*, 155.

37. Riese, *The Unabridged James Dean*, 425–26.

38. Susan King, "Now They're Rebels with a Cause: A Reunion," *Los Angeles Times*, October 25, 2000.

39. Cindy Adams, *Lee Strasberg: The Imperfect Genius of the Actors Studio* (Garden City, NY: Doubleday and Company, 1980), 210.

40. King, "Now They're Rebels with a Cause: A Reunion."

41. Nick Adams, "Jimmy Dean—Why We Loved Him," *Movie Life*, September 1956, 39.

42. Ibid.

43. Howlett, *James Dean*, 113.

44. Joseph Humphreys, consultant, *Jimmy Dean on Jimmy Dean* (London: Plexus, 1990), 97.

45. Archer Winsten, "Reviewing Stand: 'Rebel without a Cause' at Astor," *New York Post*, October 27, 1955.

46. Rose Pelswick, "'Rebel Without a Cause': Wild Teen Film," *New York Journal-American*, October 27, 1955.

47. *Rebel Without a Cause* review, *Variety*, October 26, 1955.

48. *Rebel Without a Cause* review, *Saturday Review*, October 1955.

49. Crowther, *Rebel Without a Cause* review.

50. Jack Meffitt, "'Rebel without A Cause' Real Money Attraction," *Hollywood Reporter*, October 21, 1955.

51. John McCarten, "The Current Cinema," *New Yorker*, November 5, 1955.

52. Wes Gehring, *Handbook of American Film Genres* (Westport, CT: Greenwood Press, 1988), 3.

53. *Rebel Without a Cause* review, *Time*, November 28, 1955.

54. Andrew Sarris, *Confessions of a Cultist: On the Cinema, 1955–1969* (1970; reprint, New York: Simon and Schuster, 1971), 63.

55. Robert Hatch, "Theater and Films," *Nation*, December 3, 1955, 486.

56. McCarten, "The Current Cinema," 119.

57. Meffitt, "'Rebel Without a Cause' Real Money Attraction," 3.

58. Ibid.

59. John G. Cawelti, "The Question of Popular Genres," *Journal of Popular Film and Television*, Summer 1985, 55–56.

60. Cobbett Steinberg, *Reel Facts: The Movie Book of Records* (New York: Vintage Books, 1978), 347.

61. Wes Gehring, "Hollywood's Dilemma about Posthumous Releases," *USA Today Magazine*, May 2003, 64.

62. Wes Gehring, *Carole Lombard: The Hoosier Tornado* (Indianapolis: Indiana Historical Society Press, 2003), 221–24.

63. Wes Gehring, "Hollywood's Dilemma about Posthumous Releases," 69.

64. American Film Institute (with Duane Byrge), *Private Screenings: Insiders Share a Century of Great Movie Moments* (Atlanta, GA: Turner Publishing, Inc., 1995), 115–16.

65. David Dalton, *James Dean: American Icon* (New York: St. Martin's Press, 1984), 7.

66. Foster Hirsch, *A Method to Their Madness* (New York: W. W. Norton, 1984), 310.

Chapter 10

1. Edna Ferber, *Giant* (1952; reprint, New York: Perennial Classics, 2000), 107.

2. David Hofstede, *James Dean: A Bio-Bibliography* (Westport, CT: Greenwood Press, 1996), 54.

3. "James Dean, Bright Film Career Ended by Death, to Make Last Trip to Indiana," *Indianapolis Star*, October 2, 1955.

4. Wes Gehring, *Leo McCarey: From Marx to McCarthy* (Lanham, MD: Scarecrow Press, 2004).

5. Wes Gehring, *Personality Comedian as Genre: Selected Players* (Westport, CT: Greenwood Press, 1997).

6. Wes Gehring, *Screwball Comedy: A Genre of Madcap Romance* (Westport, CT: Greenwood Press, 1986); *Parody as Film Genre: "Never Give a Saga an Even Break"* (Westport, CT: Greenwood Press, 1999); and *Romantic vs. Screwball Comedy: Charting the Difference* (Lanham, MD: Scarecrow Press, 2002).

7. "The New Pictures: Giant," *Time*, October 22, 1956, 112.

8. Patrick McGilligan, *Film Crazy: Interviews with Hollywood Legends* (New York: St. Martin's Press, 2000), 83.

9. Ibid., 117–18.

10. Gehring, *Populism and the Capra Legacy* (Westport, CT: Greenwood Press, 1995).

11. Gehring, *Irene Dunne: First Lady of Hollywood* (Lanham, MD: Scarecrow Press, 2003).

12. James Harvey, "Irene Dunne Interviewed by James Harvey," *Film Comment*, January–February 1980, 31.

13. Gehring, *Irene Dunne: First Lady of Hollywood*.

14. Andrew Sarris, *The American Cinema: Directors and Directions, 1929–1968* (New York: E. P. Dutton and Co., 1968), 111.

15. Josef von Sternberg, *Fun in a Chinese Laundry* (1965; reprint, New York: Collier Books, 1973), 316.

16. David Thomson, "George Stevens," in Thomson, ed., *The New Biographical Dictionary of Film* (New York: Alfred A. Knopf, 2003), 834–35.

17. Cobbett Steinberg, *Reel Facts: The Movie Book of Records* (New York: Vintage Books, 1978), 347.

18. Patricia Bosworth, *Marlon Brando* (New York: Penguin, 2001), 123.

19. "Young Dean's Legacy," *Newsweek*, October 22, 1956, 112.

20. Paul Alexander, *Boulevard of Broken Dreams: The Life, Times, and Legend of James Dean* (New York: Plume, 1997), 208.

21. Julie Goldsmith Gilbert, *Ferber: A Biography* (Garden City, NY: Doubleday and Company, 1978), 177–78.

22. "Giant: 1952 [Notes]," in *Giant*, Edna Ferber, 407.

23. Edna Ferber, *A Kind of Magic* (Garden City, NY: Doubleday and Company, 1963), 266.

24. Ibid.

25. Alec Guinness, *Blessings in Disguise* (1985; reprint, Glasgow, UK: Fontana/Collins, 1988), 61.

26. Mercedes McCambridge, *The Quality of Mercy: An Autobiography* (New York: Times Books, 1981), 209.

27. David Dalton, *James Dean: The Mutant King* (1974; reprint, Chicago: Cappella, 2001), 302.

28. McCambridge, *The Quality of Mercy*, 209.

29. Ray Loynd, "Some Unsentimental Memories of James Dean by Rock Hudson," *Hollywood Reporter*, August 9, 1968.

30. Phyllis Gates and Bob Thomas, *My Husband, Rock Hudson: The Real Story of Rock Hudson's Marriage to Phyllis Gates* (Garden City, NY: Doubleday, 1987), 64.

31. Ibid.

32. Alexander Walker, *Elizabeth* (1990; reprint, New York: Grove Press, 1997), 161.

33. Sheridan Morley, *Elizabeth Taylor* (London: Pavilion Books, 1989), 79.

34. Marcus Winslow Jr., interview with the author, July 23, 2004.

35. Ibid.

36. Ferber, *Giant*, 1.

37. Donald Richie, *George Stevens: An American Romantic* (1970; reprint, New York: Garland Publishing, 1985), 68.

38. Randall Riese, *The Unabridged James Dean: His Life and Legacy from A to Z* (Chicago: Contemporary Books, 1991), 207.

39. Eartha Kitt, *Confessions of a Sex Kitten* (New York: Barricade Books, 1989), 150.

40. Walker, *Elizabeth*, 163.

41. George Scullin, "James Dean: The Legend and the Facts," *Look*, October 16, 1956, 121.

42. Hofstede, *James Dean*, 18.

43. "George Stevens' 'Giant' an Epic Film in a Class with the All-Time Greats," *Hollywood Reporter*, October 10, 1956.

44. "The New Pictures: Giant," *Time*, 108.

45. *Giant* review, *Variety*, October 10, 1956.

46. "Young Dean's Legacy," *Newsweek*, 112.

47. Bosley Crowther, *Giant* review, *New York Times*, October 11, 1956.

48. John McCarten, "The Current Cinema: Southwestern Primitives," *New Yorker*, October 20, 1956, 178–79.

49. Alfred C. Roller, "The James Dean Myth Blows Up," *New York World-Telegram*, November 3, 1956.

50. "George Stevens' 'Giant' an Epic Film in a Class with the All-Time Greats," *Hollywood Reporter*.

51. Robert Hatch, "Films," *Nation*, October 20, 1956, 334.

52. Ibid.

53. Elia Kazan, *Elia Kazan: A Life* (New York: Alfred A. Knopf, 1988), 538.

54. Carroll Baker, *Baby Doll: An Autobiography* (New York: Arbor House, 1983), 139.

55. Hatch, "Films," *Nation*, 334.

56. Archer Winsten, "Reviewing Stand: 'Giant' Takes Over Roxy Screen," *New York Post*, October 11, 1956.

57. Mason Wiley and Damien Bona, *Inside Oscar: The Unofficial History of the Academy Awards* (New York: Ballantine Books, 1993), 271.

Epilogue

1. Donald Spoto, *Rebel: The Life and Legend of James Dean* (1996; reprint, New York: Cooper Square Press, 2000), 256.

2. "Jimmy Dean: The Star Who Never Died," *Movieland*, October 1956, 42.

3. Adam Gopnik, "A Critic at Large: The Big One," *The New Yorker*, August 23, 2004, 84.

4. Harry Haun, "James Dean," *New York Daily News*, September 28, 1980.

5. C. A. Lejeune, "The Dean Legend," *London Observer*, November 10, 1957.

6. J. D. Salinger, *The Catcher in the Rye* (Boston: Little, Brown and Company, 1951), 14.

7. Val Holley, *James Dean: The Biography* (1995; reprint, London: Robson Books, 1999), 279.

8. Marcus Winslow Jr., interview with author, July 23, 2004.

9. "Does the Legend Betray the Man?," *Movieland*, 1957 Annual, 9.

10. Beverly Limet, "The Secret Happiness of Jimmy Dean," *Movie Life*, August 1956, 22.

11. Alfred C. Roller, "The James Dean Myth Blows Up," *New York World-Telegram*, November 3, 1956.

12. Marlon Brando (with Robert Lindsey), *Brando: Songs My Mother Taught Me* (New York: Random House, 1994), 222.

13. David Sterritt, "TV's Biographer with a Golden Pen," *Christian Science Monitor*, September 22, 1975.

14. Oscar Levant, *The Unimportance of Being Oscar* (1968; reprint, New York: Pocket Books, 1969), 90.

15. Derek Marlowe, "Soliloquy on JD's Forty-Fifth Birthday," *New York Magazine*, November 8, 1976.

16. "Old at all . . . for a legend," *Chicago Sun-Times Midwest Magazine*, January 24, 1971, 19.

17. S. E. Hinton, *The Outsiders* (1967; reprint, New York: Dell Publishing, 1989), 154.

18. Winslow, interview with author, July 23, 2004.

19. P. E. Salles Gomes, *Jean Vigo* (1957; reprint, London: Faber and Faber, 1998), 239.

SELECT BIBLIOGRAPHY

Special Collections

"James Dean Clipping Files." Fairmount Public Library, Fairmount, Indiana.

"James Dean Clipping Files." Margaret Herrick Library, Academy of Motion Picture Arts and Sciences, Beverly Hills, California.

"James Dean Clipping Files." Performing Arts Library, New York Public Library at Lincoln Center, New York, New York.

"James Dean Library." James Dean Gallery, Gas City, Indiana.

Individual clipping files for *East of Eden* (1955), *Rebel Without a Cause* (1955), and *Giant* (1956) at both the Academy Library and New York's Performing Arts Library.

Books

Adams, Cindy Heller. *Lee Strasberg: The Imperfect Genius of the Actors Studio*. Garden City, NY: Doubleday and Company, 1980.

Alexander, Paul. *Boulevard of Broken Dreams: The Life, Times, and Legend of James Dean*. New York: Plume, 1997.

American Film Institute (with Duane Byrge). *Private Screenings: Insiders Share a Century of Great Movie Moments*. Atlanta, GA: Turner Publishing, Inc., 1995.

Backus, Jim. *Rocks on the Roof*. New York: G. P. Putnam's Sons, 1958.

Baker, Carroll. *Baby Doll: An Autobiography*. New York: Arbor House, 1983.

Bast, William. *James Dean: A Biography*. New York: Ballantine Books, 1956.

Bosworth, Patricia. *Marlon Brando*. New York: Viking, 2001.

———. *Montgomery Clift: A Biography*. New York: Harcourt, 1978.

Brando, Marlon (with Robert Lindsey). *Brando: Songs My Mother Taught Me*. New York: Random House, 1994.

Brooks, Tim, and Earle Marsh. *The Complete Directory to Prime Time Network TV Shows, 1946–Present*. New York: Ballantine Books, 1979.

Chabon, Michael. *Wonder Boys*. New York: Picador, 1995.

Ciment, Michael. *Kazan on Kazan*. New York: Viking Press, 1974.

Dalton, David. *James Dean: American Icon*. New York: St. Martin's Press, 1984.

———. *James Dean: The Mutant King*. 1974. Reprint, Chicago: Cappella, 2001.

Davis, Sammy Jr. *Yes I Can*. New York: Farrar, Straus, 1965.

Douglas, Kirk. *The Ragman's Son: An Autobiography*. New York: Simon and Schuster, 1988.

Evans, Peter. *Peter Sellers: The Mask behind the Mask*. New York: Signet, 1980.

Exupéry, Antoine de Saint. *The Little Prince*. 1943. Reprint, New York: Harcourt Brace and World, Inc., 1971.

Ferber, Edna, *Giant*. 1952. Reprint, New York: Perennial Classics, 2000.

———. *A Kind of Magic*. Garden City, NY: Doubleday and Company, 1963.

Finstad, Suzanne. *Natasha: The Biography of Natalie Wood*. New York: Harmony Books, 2001.

Ford, Dan. *Pappy: The Life of John Ford*. Englewood Cliffs, NJ: Prentice Hall, 1979.

Ford, George H. *Dickens and His Readers: Aspects of Novel-Criticism since 1836*. 1955. Reprint, New York: W. W. Norton and Company, 1965.

Gates, Phyllis, and Bob Thomas. *My Husband, Rock Hudson: The Real Story of Rock Hudson's Marriage to Phyllis Gates*. Garden City, NY: Doubleday, 1987.

Gehrig, Eleanor, and Joseph Durso. *My Luke and I*. New York: Thomas Y. Crowell Company, 1976.

Gehring, Wes D. *American Dark Comedy: Beyond Satire*. Westport, CT: Greenwood Press, 1996.

———. *Carole Lombard: The Hoosier Tornado*. Indianapolis: Indiana Historical Society Press, 2003.

———. *Handbook of American Film Genres*. Westport, CT: Greenwood Press, 1988.

———. *Irene Dunne: First Lady of Hollywood*. Lanham, MD: Scarecrow Press, 2003.

———. *Leo McCarey: "From Marx to McCarthy."* Lanham, MD: Scarecrow Press, 2004.

———. *"Mr. B" Or Comforting Thoughts about the Bison: A Critical Biography of Robert Benchley*. Westport, CT: Greenwood Press, 1992.

———. *Parody as Film Genre: "Never Give a Saga an Even Break."* Westport, CT: Greenwood Press, 1999.

———. *Personality Comedian as Genre: Selected Players*. Westport, CT: Greenwood Press, 1997.

———. *Populism and the Capra Legacy*. Westport, CT: Greenwood Press, 1995.

———. *Romantic vs. Screwball Comedy: Charting the Difference*. Lanham, MD: Scarecrow Press, 2002.

———. *Screwball Comedy: A Genre of Madcap Romance*. Westport, CT: Greenwood Press, 1986.

———. *Seeing Red: The Skelton in Hollywood's Closet: An Analytical Biography*. Davenport, IA: Robin Vincent, 2001.

Gilmore, John. *Live Fast, Die Young: Remembering the Short Life of James Dean*. New York: Thunder's Mouth Press, 1997.

Gomes, P. E. Salles. *Jean Vigo*. 1957. Reprint, London: Faber and Faber, 1998.

Graham, Frank. *Lou Gehrig: A Quiet Hero*. New York: G. P. Putnam's Sons, 1942.

Guinness, Alec. *Blessings in Disguise*. 1985. Reprint, Glasgow, UK: Fontana/Collins, 1988.

Halberstam, David. *The Teammates*. New York: Hyperion, 2003.

Hall, William. *James Dean*. Gloucestershire, UK: Sutton Publishing, 1999.

Hemingway, Ernest. *Death in the Afternoon*. 1932. Reprint. New York: Scribner, 2003.

———. *The Old Man and the Sea*. New York: Charles Scribner's Sons, 1952.

Herndon, Venable. *James Dean: A Short Life*. Garden City, NY: Doubleday and Company, Inc., 1974.

Hinton, S. E. *The Outsiders*. 1967. Reprint, New York: Dell Publishing, 1989.

Hirsch, Foster. *A Method to Their Madness: A History of the Actors Studio*. New York: W. W. Norton, 1984.

Hofstede, David. *James Dean: A Bio-Bibliography*. Westport, CT: Greenwood Press, 1996.

Holley, Val. *James Dean: The Biography*. 1995. Reprint, London: Robson Books, 1999.

Howlett, John. *James Dean: A Biography*. 1975. Reprint, London: Plexus, 1997.

Humphreys, Joseph (consultant). *Jimmy Dean on Jimmy Dean*. London: Plexus, 1990.

Hyams, Joe (with Jay Hyams). *James Dean: Little Boy Lost*. New York: Warner Books, 1992.

Kael, Pauline. *I Lost It at the Movies*. Boston: Little, Brown and Company, 1965.

Kazan, Elia. *Elia Kazan: A Life*. New York: Alfred A. Knopf, 1988.

Kearns, Doris. "Angles of Vision." Marc Pachter, ed., *Telling Lives: The Biographer's Art*, 1979. Reprint, Philadelphia: University of Pennsylvania Press, 1985.

Kitt, Eartha. *Confessions of a Sex Kitten*. New York: Barricade Books, 1989.

Knipfel, Jim. *Slackjaw*. 1999. Reprint, New York: Berkley Books, 2000.

Kreidl, John Francis. *Nicholas Ray*. Boston: Twayne Publishers, 1977.

Larsen, Don (with Mark Shaw). *The Perfect Yankee: The Incredible Story of the Greatest Miracle in Baseball History*. Champaign, IL: Sagamore Publishing, 2001.

Levant, Oscar. *Oscar Levant: The Memoirs of an Amnesiac*. 1965. Reprint, New York: Bantam, 1966.

———. *The Unimportance of Being Oscar*. 1968. Reprint, New York: Pocket Books, 1969.

Select Bibliography

McCambridge, Mercedes. *The Quality of Mercy: An Autobiography*. New York: Times Books, 1981.

McGilligan, Patrick. *Film Crazy: Interviews with Hollywood Legends*. New York: St. Martin's Press, 2000.

McLeish, Kenneth. *Arts in the Twentieth Century*. 1985. Reprint, Middlesex, UK: Penguin Books, 1986.

Martinetti, Ronald. *The James Dean Story*. 1975. Reprint, London: Michael O'Mara Books, 1996.

Massey, Raymond. *A Hundred Different Lives: An Autobiography*. Boston: Little, Brown and Company, 1979.

Mellow, James R. *Hemingway: A Life without Consequences*. New York: Addison-Wesley Publishing Company, 1992.

Morley, Sheridan. *Elizabeth Taylor*. London: Pavilion Books, 1989.

Oumano, Elena. *Paul Newman*. New York: St. Martin's Press, 1989.

Richie, Donald. *George Stevens: An American Romantic*. 1970. Reprint, New York: Garland Publishing, 1985.

Riese, Randall. *The Unabridged James Dean: His Life and Legacy from A to Z*. Chicago: Contemporary Books, 1991.

Rubin, Gretchen. *Forty Ways to Look at Winston Churchill: A Brief Account of a Long Life*. New York: Random House, 2004.

Russo, William. *The Next James Dean*. New York: Xlibris Corporation, 2003.

Salinger, J. D. *The Catcher in the Rye*. Boston: Little, Brown and Company, 1951.

Sarris, Andrew. *The American Cinema: Directors and Directions, 1929–1968*. New York: E. P. Dutton and Company, 1968.

———. *Confessions of a Cultist: On the Cinema, 1955–1969*. 1970. Reprint, New York: Simon and Schuster, 1971.

Schatt, Roy. *James Dean: A Portrait*. 1982. Reprint, New York: Ruggles de Latour, 1990.

Schickel, Richard. *Brando: A Life in Our Times*. New York: St. Martin's, 1991.

Sheridan, Liz. *Dizzy & Jimmy: My Life with James Dean*. New York: Regan Books, 2000.

Spoto, Donald. *Rebel: The Life and Legend of James Dean*. 1996. Reprint, New York: Cooper Square Press, 2000.

Steinbeck, John. *East of Eden*. 1952. Reprint, New York: Penguin Books, 2002.

Steinberg, Cobbett. *Reel Facts: The Movie Book of Records*. New York: Vintage Books, 1978.

Strasberg, Lee. *A Dream of Passion: The Development of the Method*. Boston: Little, Brown and Company, 1987.

Tosches, Nick. *Dino: Living High in the Dirty Business of Dreams*. New York: Dell, 1992.

Truffaut, Francois. *The Films in My Life*. 1975. Reprint, New York: Da Capo Press, 1994.

Tuska, Jon. *Billy the Kid: His Life and Legend*. Westport, CT: Greenwood Press, 1994.

Walker, Alexander. *Elizabeth*. 1990. Reprint, New York: Grove Press, 1997.

Wiley, Mason, and Damien Bona. *Inside Oscar: The Unofficial History of the Academy Awards*. New York: Ballantine Books, 1993.

Young, Jeff. *Kazan: The Master Director Discusses His Films: Interviews with Elia Kazan*. New York: Newmarket Press, 1999.

Zinsser, William, ed. *Extraordinary Lives: The Art and Craft of American Biography*. Boston: Hougton Mifflin Company, 1986.

Shorter Works and Interviews

Adams, Nick. "Jimmy Dean—Why We Loved Him." *Movie Life*, September 1956.

———. "What Dean Told His Best Friends." *Movie Life*, October 1956.

Breen, Ed. "James Dean's Indiana: The Stage along Sand Pike." *Traces of Indiana and Midwestern History*, Fall 1989.

Cash, Rosanna. "Janis Joplin." *Rolling Stone*, April 15, 2004.

Cawelti, John G. "The Question of Popular Genres." *Journal of Popular Film and Television*, Summer 1985.

"Clyde McCullough." In *Total Baseball*, eds. John Thorn and Pete Palmer with David Reuther. New York: Warner Books, 1989.

Conn, Earl L. "At Guard for Fairmount—James Dean" (unpublished, 1957–58). Author's files.

Dean, Emma Woolen. "James Dean—The Boy I Loved." *Photoplay*, March 1956.

"Demon Dean." *Photoplay*, July 1955.

Dickens, Charles. "A Madman's Manuscript [Chapter XI]." In *Pickwick Papers: Part One*. New York: P. F. Collier and Son, 1837.

"Does the Legend Betray the Man." *Movieland*, 1957 Annual.

Elkin, Frederick. "The Psychological Appeal for Children of the Hollywood B Western." In *Focus on the Western*, ed. Jack Nachbar. Englewood Cliffs, NJ: Prentice Hall, 1974.

"Footsteps on the Sands of Time." In *Black and Gold '49*. Fairmount, IN: Fairmount Journalism Department, 1949.

Friedrichsen, Frank. "James Dean—Hates to Be Loved?" *Movie Stars Parade*, July 1955.

———. "The Short Tragic Life of Jimmy Dean." *Movie Stars Parade*, December 1955.

Gapnik, Adam. "A Critic at Large: The Big One." *New Yorker*, August 23, 2004.

Gehring, Wes D. "Hollywood's Dilemma about Posthumous Release." *USA Today Magazine*, May 2003.

———. Interviews with Conrad Lane, July and August, 2004.

———. Interview with Earl L. Conn, April 2003.

———. Interview with Marcus Winslow Jr., July 23, 2004.

———. Interview with Ray White, May 6, 2004.

———. Interview with Roger Smith, June 17, 2004.

———. "Reel World: James Dean: Comedian and Impersonator." *USA Today Magazine*, September 2004.

"Giant: 1952 [Notes]." In *Giant*, Edna Ferber. Reprint, New York: Perennial Classics, 2000.

Harris, Julie. "How I Remember James Dean." *Picturegoer*, June 16, 1956.

Harvey, James. "Irene Dunne Interviewed by James Harvey." *Film Comment*, January–February 1980.

Hatch, Robert. "Theater and Films." *Nation*, December 3, 1955.

Hopper, Hedda. "Keep Your Eyes on James Dean." *Chicago Tribune Magazine*, March 27, 1955.

Hyams, Joe. "James Dean." *Redbook*, September 1956.

"Jimmy Dean: The Star Who Never Died." *Movieland*, October 1956.

Korman, Seymour. "The Last Hours of James Dean." *Chicago Tribune Magazine*, February 5, 1956.

"Lee Strasberg." In *Current Biography Yearbook: 1960*, ed. Charles Moritz. New York: H. W. Wilson Company, 1960.

Limet, Beverly. "The Secret Happiness of Jimmy Dean." *Movie Life*, August 1956.

Louis, Merry. "Jimmy Dean: The Boy Who'd Like to Be Brando." *Movie Play*, January 1956.

McCarten, John. "The Current Cinema." *New Yorker*, November 5, 1955.

———. "The Current Cinema: Southwestern Primitives." *New Yorker*, October 20, 1956.

Marlowe, Derek. "Soliloquy on JD's Forty-Fifth Birthday." *New York Magazine*, November 8, 1976.

Meltsir, Aljean. "James Dean: His Life and Loves." *Motion Picture*, September 1956.

"Moody New Star: Hoosier James Dean Excites Hollywood." *Life*, March 7, 1955.

Nall, Adeline (as told to Val Holley). "Grant County's Own." *Traces of Indiana and Midwestern History*, Fall 1989.

"New Pictures: 'East of Eden.'" *Time*, March 21, 1955.

"New Pictures: The Giant." *Time*, October 22, 1956.

Nielsen, Evelyn Washburn. "Secrets from Jimmy Dean's Past." *Movie Stars Parade*, July 1956.

———. "The Truth about James Dean." *Chicago Tribune Magazine*, September 9, 1956.

———. "What Jimmy Dean's Home Town Can Now Reveal." *Movie Stars Parade*, August 1956.

"Old at all . . . for a legend." *Chicago Sun-Times Midwest Magazine*, January 24, 1971.

Packard, Alice. "The Real Jimmy Dean." *Movie Stars Parade*, May 1956.

Rebel Without a Cause review. *Saturday Review*, October 1955.

"Salvador Dali." In *Dictionary of the Arts*, ed. Charles Murray. London: Brockhampton Press, 1997.

Scullin, George. "James Dean: The Legend and the Facts." *Look*, October 16, 1956.

See the Jaguar review. *Cue*, December 13, 1952.

"Senior Class." In *Black & Gold '49*. Fairmount, IN: Fairmount Journalism Department, 1949.

Sterritt, David. "TV's Biographer with a Golden Pen." *Christian Science Monitor*, September 22, 1975.

Thomson, David. "George Stevens." In *The New Biographical Dictionary of Film*, ed. David Thomson. New York: Alfred A. Knopf, 2003.

Williams, John. "The Strange Love-Making of James Dean." *Movie Stars Parade*, October 1955.

Wood, Natalie. "I Can't Forget Jimmy." *Movie Life*, December 1956.

———. "You Haven't Heard the Half about Jimmy!" *Photoplay*, November 1955).

"Young Dean's Legacy." *Newsweek*, October 22, 1956.

Newspapers (see individual citations in Notes).

Chicago Tribune, 1955, 1956.

Des Moines Register, 2004.

Fairmount News, 1949, 1955.

Hollywood Reporter, 1955, 1956, 1968.

Indianapolis Star, 1955, 1985.

London Observer, 1957.

Los Angeles Times, 1954, 1973, 1977, 2000.

Louisville Courier, 1976.

Marion Chronicle, 1956.

Muncie Star, 1975, 1996.

New York Daily News, 1952, 1980.

New York Journal-American, 1952, 1955.

New York Herald Tribune, 1952, 1954, 1955.

New York Post, 1954, 1955, 1956.

New York Times, 1954, 1955, 1956, 1984, 2004.

New York World Telegram and Sun, 1954.

New York World Telegram, 1955, 1956.

Philadelphia Inquirer, 1973.

Variety, 1955, 1956, 1974.